Study Commentary on Haggai, Zechariah
and Malachi

A Study Commentary
on
Haggai, Zechariah and Malachi

Iain M. Duguid

 Books

EP Books
Faverdale North, Darlington, DL3 0PH, England
e-mail: sales@epbooks.org
web: www.epbooks.org

EP Books USA
P. O. Box 614, Carlisle, PA 17013, USA
e-mail: usasales@epbooks.org
web: www.epbooks.us

First published 2010

British Library Cataloguing in Publication Data available

ISBN-13 978 0 85234 712 6   ISBN 0 85234 712 X

Printed and bound in the UK by the MPG Books Group

To Wayne Houk,
brother in Christ and inspiration in loving, sharing
and applying the gospel to the heart

Contents

	Page
Acknowledgements	9

Introductory matters 11
A neglected trio of books 11
Historical background 13
The structure of the books 16
Theological themes 18

Haggai

Consider your ways! (1:1-15) 27
The best is yet to come (2:1-9) 37
A new holiness, a new blessing (2:10-19) 47
Just rewards (2:20-23) 56

Zechariah

Keep the faith! (1:1-6) 67
All quiet on the eastern front? (1:7-17) 75
Be still before the Lord! (1:18 – 2:13) 85
Reclothed and restored (3:1-10) 96
Hope for a day of small things (4:1-14) 105
How shall we then live? (5:1-11) 114
The kingdoms of this world belong to our God
    and to his Christ (6:1-15) 121
Ritual or reality? (7:1-14) 130

Are we there yet? (8:1-23)   137
Prisoners of hope (9:1-17)   146
The true source of blessing (10:1-12)   154
No compassion (11:1-17)   161
The final frontier (12:1-9)   169
Repentance and cleansing (12:10 – 13:9)   173
Through trials to glory (14:1-21)   179

Malachi

'I have loved you' (1:1-5)   189
Defiled worship (1:6-14)   199
Give God the glory! (2:1-9)   208
Our faithlessness to the faithful God (2:10-16)   214
Do you really want justice? (2:17 – 3:5)   222
Giving God his due (3:6-12)   228
Hard words for God (3:13 – 4:6)   234

List of abbreviations   243
Notes   245

Acknowledgements

A long time has passed since David Clark first invited me to work on this volume. I would like to thank the EP board, and in particular the series editor, John Currid, for their patience and long-suffering with my slow progress. I would also like to thank Anne Williamson for her careful editing work that uncovered and corrected many of my mistakes, inconsistencies and grammatical infelicities. Those that remain are, of course, all my own work.

Over the past several years, I have had the opportunity to preach and teach this material at various locations in different contexts and am grateful for the feedback from students, pastors and laypeople in several countries. In particular, it has been a privilege to use Haggai and the early chapters of Zechariah to teach students how to preach Christ from the Old Testament prophets every year at the Sovereign Grace Ministries Pastors' College in Gaithersburg, MD. Every time I go there, I am encouraged and strengthened by their kindness and enthusiasm for the gospel. I would like to thank Jeff Purswell for continuing to invite me regularly for a week that is refreshing to my soul.

My family deserves the highest thanks. It is a joy to see my children walking with the Lord and growing in their knowledge of their own hearts. Jamie, Sam, Hannah, Rob and Rosie, you have no idea how proud I am of you, and how much I delight in you. Barb, you have faithfully put up with my sins and deficiencies for over twenty-five years as my wife: thank you for your insight, wisdom, love and joy in the gospel.

Thank you to Wayne, Josh and Megan, the newest members of our household and ministry team. I couldn't begin to do the work of ministry without your love and faithful service: your gifts and heart for ministry are an enormous blessing from God to me, and I pray that he will richly bless you during your time in Grove City.

Introductory matters

A neglected trio of books

The last three books of the Old Testament have not always received the attention they deserve from the church. This is in some ways surprising, since the Gospel writers quote Zechariah 9 – 14 more often than any other biblical source in explaining Christ's sufferings and death. Yet in other ways, it is not so surprising that these books have been neglected. Part of the reason lies in the difficulty of the material: the visions that are shown to us in these books are complex, and the oracles often seem obscure. However, if we pay careful attention to the context of the passages and listen to the interpretation of the visions given by the accompanying angel, many of the obscurities can be clarified.

Another 'problem' with these books, however, lies in the fact that they come from the time after the exile, when all that was left of God's people was a small remnant living in poverty in Judah. They address a community who were living in a day of small things (Zech. 4), with little glory and no great triumphs to show off to a watching world. In a day like ours, which puts such a premium on charismatic leaders whose ministries exude glory and success, these books may be seen as something of an embarrassment. But if, like the apostle Paul, we are content to be broken vessels without glory in ourselves so that the glory of Christ crucified may be all the more plainly displayed

(2 Cor. 4), then we shall find much blessing in these books. In them, we shall read of the comfort and challenge that come from the presence of the living God in our midst, even when his glory is not on public display. In them, we shall also read of the anticipation of the day when the glory of God would come to earth in the person of Christ and bring about the long-promised salvation of his people. Our goal in the application sections of this commentary will be to follow the lead of the Gospel writers, and see how Christ's person and work are anticipated and fore-shadowed in the words of these ancient prophets.

Historical background

Prophecy always has a historical context, and knowing that context helps us to avoid reading the prophets' words as disembodied timeless truths. In the case of these books, the crucial historical fact that casts its shadow over every verse is the destruction of Jerusalem, which began the exile of the southern kingdom of Judah, and the return from Babylon a generation later. This holocaust had a profound impact on the prophets' understanding of God's character and of his purposes for his people, revealing his holiness in judgement and his longsuffering grace and mercy in forgiveness and restoration.

In some ways, the story of Israel should have ended with the exile. According to the covenant God made with his people at Mount Sinai, their obedience would lead to blessing and living for a long time in the land their God had given them, while their unfaithfulness would lead to economic and political disaster, culminating in exile from the land (Deut. 28). That terrible prediction came true in two stages. The northern kingdom of Israel was overrun by the Assyrians in 722 BC. Their capital, Samaria, was destroyed and her people were scattered throughout the Assyrian empire, never to return. The southern kingdom of Judah persisted until 586 BC, when they too were defeated by Babylon and the city of Jerusalem was razed to the ground. However, the Babylonians had a different policy of exile from the Assyrians: instead of dispersing conquered peoples in small groups throughout the empire, they resettled them in communities in the

Babylonian homeland. Thus, in the providence of God, the Judean exiles retained their identity.

When the Persians took over the Babylonian empire under Cyrus in 539 BC, they adopted yet another policy towards the captive peoples. They encouraged many of them to go home, and they funded the reconstruction of national sanctuaries to the deities of these lands.[1] This was a shrewd piece of religious politics on the part of Cyrus, yet it also fulfilled the Lord's promise to bring his people back to their land and provided the financial resources for rebuilding their sanctuary in Jerusalem. Some Jews returned home immediately, with the temple vessels that Nebuchadnezzar had taken from Jerusalem, and the foundations of the house of God were soon repaired (Ezra 1; 5:15-16). Yet there was also considerable opposition to this rebuilding work from some of the surrounding authorities, and work on the temple quickly ground to a halt (Ezra 4).

Meanwhile, the Persian empire was experiencing a significant amount of political turmoil. Cyrus was killed in 530 BC, during a military operation on the eastern frontier, and was succeeded by his son Cambyses. While Cambyses was engaged in an attempt to invade Egypt in 522 BC, there was a coup at home in Mesopotamia led by a man named Gaumata, who claimed to be Cambyses' brother. Cambyses died while returning home from Egypt to engage the rebellion, and his place was taken by Darius, one of his generals. Darius successfully eliminated Gaumata and gained control of the empire.

The events described in Haggai and the early chapters of Zechariah take place between 520 and 515 BC, as Darius was consolidating his power. It was during this time that the Jews completed the construction of the temple, under the leadership of the governor Zerubbabel and the high priest Joshua, and urged on by the prophecies of Haggai and Zechariah. There is a general consensus that the book of Haggai and at least the first eight chapters of Zechariah were recorded shortly after this. There is much less agreement in scholarly circles about the date of Zechariah 9 –14, which deal with a diverse variety of different topics. There are, however, good reasons for believing that these chapters too belong to this period of history.[2] Certainly there was a great deal of internal conflict within the community during the early Persian period (from 515 to 475 BC), of the kind which these chapters seem to presuppose. Moreover, there are a number of strong thematic links between Zechariah 9 – 14 and 1 – 8 which seem to bind them together as a structural unity.

The book of Malachi contains none of the date markers that are contained in Haggai and Zechariah, so identifying its historical context is a little harder. The Second Temple had clearly been rebuilt and had been in operation for some time (Mal. 3:1-8), while the Edomites had experienced a loss of the territory they gained during the sixth century BC (Mal. 1:2-5). These features, along with the fact that the prophet seems to address the same kinds of issues that troubled God's people during the time of Ezra and Nehemiah in the 450s and 440s BC, suggest a date for the book somewhere in the middle of the fifth century BC. During this period, the small province of Judah was poor and underpopulated, with strong enemies on all sides and a great deal of pressure to assimilate to the surrounding culture through intermarriage. The agricultural economy was weak, in part because of drought and crop diseases and in part because of the pressures of heavy taxation, and they were subject to the whims and demands of distant overlords. This was also apparently a time of spiritual weakness, with a corrupt priesthood and lax observance of God's law among the lay population as well.

The structure of the books

Haggai

1. The need to rebuild the temple (1:1-15)
2. The need to look forward to the Lord's return (2:1-9)
3. The need to pursue holiness (2:10-19)
4. The reward for faithful obedience (2:20-23)

Zechariah

Part I (Zechariah 1 – 8)
1. Introduction and call to repentance (1:1-6)
2. A cycle of seven night visions, and an additional vision* (1:7 – 6:8)
   a. the four horsemen (1:7-17)
   b. the four horns and craftsmen (1:18-21)
   c. the man with a measuring line (2:1-13)
      *the cleansing of Joshua the high priest (3:1-10)[3]
   d. the lampstand and two olive trees (4:1-14)
   e. the flying scroll (5:1-4)
   f. the woman in the ephah (5:5-11)
   g. the four chariots (6:1-8)
3. The crown for the high priest (6:9-15)
4. Oracles in response to the question of fasting (7:1 – 8:23)

Part II (Zechariah 9 – 14)
1. First oracle (9 –11)
    a. judgement upon the nations (9:1-8)
    b. peace for God's people (9:9-17)
    c. return from the nations and restoration (10:1-12)
    d. the foolish shepherd (11:1-17)
2. Second oracle (12 –14)
    a. first assault upon Jerusalem, leading to judgement upon the nations (12:1-9)
    b. transformation of God's people (12:10 – 13:9)
    c. second assault upon Jerusalem, leading to judgement upon the nations (14:1-9)
    d. transformation of the entire world (14:10-21)

Malachi

1. First dispute: the Lord's love for Israel (1:1-5)
2. Second dispute: the importance of true worship (1:6 – 2:9)
    a. The people's defiled offerings (1:6-14)
    b. The defiled priests (2:1-9)
3. Third dispute: the significance of covenantal unfaithfulness (2:10-16)
4. Fourth dispute: the inevitable coming of justice (2:17 – 3:5)
5. Fifth dispute: the proper response to the Lord's faithfulness (3:6-12)
6. Sixth dispute: the reward for faithful service (3:13 – 4:6)

Theological themes

The fundamental theological context of these books is the return from the exile, which represents a state of partial restoration for God's people. The exile was the result of the sinful disobedience of their forefathers (Zech. 1:2-6). But now, through repentance and return, a new beginning was possible (Zech. 1:6), a new beginning with the Lord present in their midst to bless them (Hag. 1:13; 2:4). Those who had returned from the exile were part of God's plan of cosmic transformation, in which he would shake the heavens and the earth and accomplish his original purpose in calling his people out of Egypt (Hag. 2:5-9). Yet the realities of everyday life in the ravaged land to which they returned seemed depressingly mundane and difficult, causing the people to be caught up in their own affairs (Hag. 1:1-11) and to doubt God's love for them (Mal. 1:2). The exiles found themselves caught between two worlds, between the promises of heaven and the realities of earth. They were living in the 'now', but longing for the 'not yet'.

God's presence

In the aftermath of the exile, when God abandoned his people and his temple because of their sin (Ezek. 8 – 11), the question of the possibility of God's presence with the remnant who had returned was pressing. Ezekiel himself had prophesied that the Lord would return to dwell among them (Ezek. 37:27) and that the glory would return to a renewed temple (Ezek. 43:1-5). But was that promise part of the 'now' or of the 'not yet'? The message of Haggai and Zechariah was that now was the time for rebuilding, for the Lord had already returned to his repentant people (Hag. 1). The Lord's scouts had traversed the earth and found everything 'at rest', the necessary prerequisite for temple building (Zech. 1:10-11; cf. Deut. 12:10; 2 Sam. 7:1). The Lord had promised that he would return to Jerusalem and that his house would be rebuilt (Zech. 1:16). The glory would once more reside within Jerusalem (Zech. 2:5), which would again be the city of God's choosing (Zech. 2:11-12). This return and the rebuilding of Jerusalem were in themselves evidence of the Lord's unfailing love for Israel, in contrast to the fate of nations such as Edom, who experienced complete destruction (Mal. 1:2-5)

Yet the Lord's presence could not be taken for granted. The two central visions in Zechariah concern the cleansing of the temple and its functionaries. In the first, Joshua the high priest is cleansed from his defilement by an act of the divine council, enabling him to fulfil his duties and supervise the temple ministry (Zech. 3:1-7). In the second, the lampstand, one of the central symbols of God's presence in the temple, was fully functioning once more, fed with an inexhaustible supply of oil from two olive trees (Zech. 4:1-14). The consequence of this restoration of the worship in the temple would be a cleansing of the land from its iniquity (Zech. 5:1-11) and the final defeat of all of God's enemies (Zech. 6:1-8). Yet in the book of Malachi, the Lord had to rebuke his priests for failing to keep the temple undefiled, accepting second-rate offerings from the people (Mal. 1:6-9). It would be better that the temple doors should be shut than that such offerings should be made (Mal. 1:10), a devastating charge when you consider the joy that accompanied the restoration of the temple in Haggai and

Zechariah. In the face of such disobedience, the Lord's presence in the midst of his people now becomes a threat rather than a promise (Mal. 3:1-3).

The Messiah

In the midst of an uncertain world and a disappointing present, these books point our eyes forwards to things yet to come. The vital event which will initiate the blessings of the 'not yet' is the coming of the Messiah. This epoch-transforming figure appears under a number of designations. He is 'my servant, the Branch' (Zech. 3:8), who will bring about the cleansing of the land in a single day and will usher in the conditions of final blessing (Zech. 3:9-10). He is the one who will ultimately build the temple of the Lord (Zech. 6:12-13). He is Jerusalem's king (Zech. 9:9), 'my shepherd' (Zech. 13:7) and 'the one they have pierced' (Zech. 12:10). These images are familiar from earlier Old Testament prophecies of a future king. For example, 'the Branch' (*zemah*) refers to the future righteous scion of the line of David in Jeremiah 23:5 and 33:15 (compare the similar imagery in Isa. 11:1 and Ezek. 17:22). The promise of a new good shepherd to replace the former bad shepherds is found in Jeremiah 23:4 and Ezekiel 34:23, while the mourning over the pierced one most closely resembles Isaiah 53, where the affliction is described of 'my servant' (Isa. 52:13) who grew up like a tender shoot (Isa. 53:2).

The cleansing of the land and the Lord's final victory (Zech. 5:1 – 6:8) may be *assured* realities, but they are not yet *present* realities in the days of Haggai and Zechariah. First the Lord must appear to shake the heavens and the earth (Hag. 2:6-7). Likewise in Malachi it is only when the Lord himself appears in his temple that pure and acceptable offerings will be made once more (Mal. 3:4) and the hearts of fathers and children will be turned to one another in new relationships of peace and faithfulness (Mal. 4:6).

The final victory of God

Yet there were important signs of hope even in those days. The importance of men like Zerubbabel (Hag. 2:20-23) and Joshua the high priest (Zech. 3:8) is that they are tokens of the Lord's favour in the present and signs that the outcome of the conflict is assured. The reality of that conflict is everywhere present in these books, both on the angelic level, where the adversary (*haśśāṭān*) stands ready to accuse Joshua (Zech. 3:1), and on a human level, where the foes include the 'four horns' (Zech. 1:18) and the 'mighty mountain' which faces Zerubbabel (Zech. 4:7). Nor will the future be free from struggle. Enemies still remain, both outside (Zech. 12:2-3) and within (Zech. 11:4-16), and there will continue to be wars and rumours of wars until the final cataclysmic assault on Jerusalem by the nations (Zech. 12:2-6; 14:2-5; cf. Ezek. 38 – 39), a day of the Lord's fiery wrath (Mal. 4:1).

But the struggle, though real and intense, is not God's final word. The enemies are merely the foils who serve to demonstrate clearly God's unshakable commitment to his people and his city. The Lord is going to give peace in this place (Hag. 2:9). The adversary stands rebuked by the Lord himself (Zech. 3:2); the mountain of opposition and difficulty becomes level ground before him (Zech. 4:7), and those who assault God's people touch the apple of his eye (Zech. 2:8). God himself will be a wall of fire around Jerusalem in the present (Zech. 2:5), and will intervene to give them victory over the nations that come against them (Zech. 9:8; 12:2-4; 14:3-5). The day of fiery wrath for God's enemies will be a day of sunny favour for those who fear his name (Mal. 4:2). Because the Lord is on Israel's side, final victory is secure.

This final victory will bring about a transformation in the inhabitants of God's land. Joshua's transformation from defilement to purity is itself symbolic of a similar work which God is doing all around him. The people will be purified (Zech. 5:1-4); their iniquity will be taken away (Zech. 5:5-11); a spirit of grace and supplication will be poured out upon them (Zech. 12:10); a fountain of cleansing will be opened for them (Zech. 13:1); and false prophets will be banished (Zech. 13:2-6). Then, finally, they will enter their rest, seated under vine and fig tree, enjoying length of days and bountiful harvests and an endless supply of living water (Zech. 3:10; 8:3-13; 10:6-12; 14:8-9,20-21). This change will have implications not only for the promised land, but for the entire world. The nations appear in these books not just as God's enemies, but as a future part of God's people, joining wholeheartedly in his worship (Zech. 2:11; 8:20-23; 14:16-19; Mal. 1:5,14).

Connections to the New Testament

The conviction of the New Testament writers is that the 'not yet' of the prophets has now arrived. With the coming of Christ, the 'last days' have broken into history (Acts 2:16-17). This means that God's presence is now experienced among men in a new way, in Jesus the Messiah. Thus, two separate themes in Haggai, Zechariah and Malachi coalesce into a single theme in the New Testament. John the Baptist was the Elijah who foreshadowed the Lord's coming to his temple (Matt. 11:14), while Jesus is himself the new temple (John 2:19-21). He is both the manifestation of the glory of God in the midst of his people (John 1:14), and that new temple's Lord. He is the 'Root of David'

(Rev. 5:5) and the one whose arrival brings 'rest' to his followers (Matt. 11:28; Heb. 4:1-11). He is the one who reclothes his people in clean garments of fine linen (Rev. 19:8).

But he does so at great personal cost to himself. In order to clothe his church with priestly garments, our great High Priest must himself be stripped naked and hung on a cross, where he bore the sins of his people on their behalf. Indeed, the majority of the direct citations of these books in the New Testament appear in the Passion narratives. Matthew and John both quote Zechariah 9:9-10 in their accounts of Jesus' triumphal entry into Jerusalem on a donkey (Matt. 21:4-5; John: 12:14-15). Jerusalem's king has finally come. Matthew further cites Zechariah 13:7 as a prediction of Jesus' abandonment by the disciples (Matt. 26:31; cf. Matt. 9:36 and the theme of Jesus the Good Shepherd in John 10:11); John also points to Zechariah 12:10 as a prophecy of the soldier's piercing of Jesus' side (John 19:37; cf. Rev. 1:7). Matthew relates the fulfilment of Zechariah 11:12 in Judas' betrayal of Jesus for thirty pieces of silver and its subsequent use to buy a potter's field (Matt. 27:9-10). The New Testament thus repeatedly depicts Jesus as being the Messiah of whom these authors spoke.

Even while the end of the ages has broken into history in Christ, yet history continues. There also is a 'now' and a 'not yet' in the New Testament. The 'now' continues to be a time of trials and tribulation (Acts 14:22). Not until the 'not yet' will we see the final victory of God, with all things placed under the feet of Christ (1 Cor. 15:24,25). Then at last we shall see the rising of the sun of righteousness and be in the place where there is no more suffering or sorrow, only the unhindered presence of God in the midst of his people (Rev. 21:3-4). In the meantime, the onslaught of Satan and his forces against God's flock continues with ever greater ferocity (Rev. 20:7-8). But with the coming of Christ the key event of history that assures the final victory of God has already happened. God will not stand by and watch his people devastated; instead, he will intervene and fight for them, destroying the forces of the Evil One and bringing about a re-creation on a global scale as the nations flock to the heavenly Jerusalem. The vision that the whole promised land will be holy to the Lord (Zech. 14:20-21) finds its fulfilment in the heavenly new Jerusalem, which is depicted as a gigantic Most Holy Place, with cubic shape and ubiquitous pure gold (Rev. 21:16,18). On that day, everything impure and unclean will be banished for ever, while those who have washed their robes in the blood of the Lamb will have free access to the throne of grace (Rev. 21:27; 22:14).

Haggai

Consider your ways!
(Haggai 1:1-15)

The year was 520 BC. Peace had returned to the Persian empire after a period of political instability. The newspapers of the day would have celebrated the fact that Darius was now firmly in control. Meanwhile, in a backwater of the empire, Judah, nothing much was happening. Most of the people had long since ceased to expect any dramatic intervention on God's part. Eighteen years had passed since the decree of the Persian emperor Cyrus had allowed them to return to Judah and had given them permission to rebuild their temple. But now they had settled into an uncomfortable status quo, grinding out their meagre daily existence, coming to terms with a difficult and ordinary life. Why struggle to accomplish great things for the Lord when the days in which you lived were self-evidently the days of small things? Was this the way the promises of God would end — not with a bang but with a tremulous whimper? By no means. They had reckoned without the God of the promises. Into that situation of quiet despair, God called and sent his prophet with a message of new hope for his people.

1:1. In the second year of Darius the king, in the sixth month, on the first day of the month, the word of the LORD came by means of[1] Haggai the prophet to Zerubbabel son of Shealtiel, governor of Judah, and to Joshua son of Jehozadak, the high priest...

The book of Haggai is obsessed by exact dates, with six precise chronological markers, giving day and month as well as year, in the space of two chapters. This precision in chronological matters is unique to Haggai and Zechariah among the biblical prophets,[2] and serves a number of purposes.

In the first place, it locates the events against the backdrop of wider world history. The prophetic call to the people to rebuild the temple took place in **'the second year of Darius the king'** (1:1) — that is, 520 BC. This was a time when stability was returning to the Persian empire after a period of unrest. In 522 BC, a man named Gaumata led a successful revolt against the Persian emperor Cambyses, who was absent on a campaign in Egypt. Cambyses died while returning from Egypt and though Darius, a military officer of noble birth, was able to assassinate Gaumata and take over the throne, there were still a number of rebellions in different parts of the Persian empire that needed to be crushed.[3] It was not until the early months of 520 BC that Darius had a firm grip on the empire.

More pressingly, though, the date reminds us that from the perspective of the faithful among the Judean returnees, the clock was ticking on the seventy-year period Jeremiah had prophesied for the exile (Jer. 25:11-12).[4] Starting with the fall of Jerusalem in 587 BC, sixty-seven years had now passed. At least some amongst the returnees were probably counting down the days, watching for the restoration of Jerusalem.

This proclamation of Haggai took place **'in the sixth month, on the first day of the month'** (1:1). The sixth month covered late August and early September, the harvest time for the fruit trees, such as grapes, figs and pomegranates. It is three months on from the harvest of grain and corn, which took place at the end of June and early July, and thus a natural time to assess the success (or otherwise) of the agricultural year. The first day of the month, the 'new moon', was a festival occasion, a day of rest and celebration before the Lord (see Num. 10:10; 28:11-15). Thus crowds may have been expected to gather for the sacrifices at the altar of the temple, which had been rededicated shortly after the edict of Cyrus permitting the exiles to return home (see Ezra 3). In all likelihood, this festival, supervised by the civil and religious leaders, Zerubbabel and Joshua, provided the context in which Haggai's proclamation took place.

'Zerubbabel', as the civil governor, was a Persian appointee. Yet, although doubtless chosen because of his loyalty to his Persian masters, at the same time he was also a descendant of David and therefore an almost inevitable focal point for hopes for the future. The similarities between Zerubbabel and Sheshbazzar, the prince who led the initial return from exile in Ezra 1:8, has led some authors, both ancient and modern, to identify the two men. However, this is improbable. While it is certainly true that some other biblical figures bear two names, this usually occurs where one name is Hebrew and the other the name given to him by pagans; here, however, both names are clearly Babylonian.[5]

'Joshua ... the high priest' was another returnee from among the exiles. He too may have been appointed by the Persian authorities, who at this time were interested, for their own reasons, in strengthening the central institutions of Judean culture.[6] None the less, whatever human political reasonings were the superficial cause of these appointments, the Lord's messenger brought word to Zerubbabel and Joshua and to all the people that there was a deeper cause behind the scenes.

1:2. Thus says the Lord of hosts: 'This people says, "The time has not come, the time for the house of the Lord to be rebuilt."'

Haggai's proclamation took the form of a prophetic disputation: the citation of a current piece of 'conventional wisdom' which is then challenged by a word from the Lord (cf. Ezek. 11:2-12; 37:11-14 for similar examples of the form). In this case the saying was: **'The time has not come, the time for the house of the LORD to be rebuilt'** (1:2). Nobody was disputing the necessity of rebuilding the temple at some point; they were simply stating what seemed to them to be self-evident — that now was not the time. Their reasons for that conclusion are not stated, but it is not hard to guess what they would have included. In the short term, it was harvest time and everyone was busy. More broadly, these were difficult economic times all round; there was a general lack of funds for such an ambitious project. The Persian army was in the process of making preparations for a massive campaign in Egypt and may well have made extensive demands on the resources of their vassal states along the invasion route. In addition to these specific factors, though, there seems also to have been a general sense of discouragement, and even despair, about the future, born of long experience of difficult times.

1:3-4. The word of the LORD came by means of Haggai: 'Is it time for you yourselves to dwell in your wood-panelled houses, while this house is desolate?'

The Lord's response to their 'conventional wisdom' was to show their inconsistency in following through their own presuppositions and to reveal the lack of true, biblical wisdom in their thinking. If now was such a bad time to build God's house, why was it time for them **'to dwell in [their] wood-panelled houses'**? (1:4). There has been debate as to whether *s^epûnîm* means buildings that are panelled or roofed with wood; both interpretations are possible. More important to note, however, is the connection with Solomon's

Temple: in three of the four other uses of this verb in the Old Testament to describe a building it has reference to Solomon's Temple (1 Kings 6:9; 7:3,7). The point is that they have been quite happy to put precisely the kind of time and resources into building their own houses that they have been claiming are not there to restore God's house.

1:5-6. Now thus says the LORD of hosts: 'Give thought to your ways. You have sown abundantly, bringing in little. There is eating, but no fulness; drinking, but not to satisfaction; being clothed, but not enough to bring warmth. The hired labourer hires himself out for a purse with holes.'

For all their busyness in pursuit of their own ends, they have not been achieving the goals they had hoped for. Though they had sown abundantly, they had not reaped accordingly. Instead, **'There is eating, but no fulness; drinking, but not to satisfaction; being clothed, but not enough to bring warmth'** (1:6). It was as though they were earning wages, and then putting those wages in a bag with holes in it (1:6), so that what they got out of life was not what they had put into it. They were not experiencing the fulness of God's blessing, but rather an inadequate, unfulfilling life in which every pleasure proved disappointingly incomplete.

Why was life this way? The problem was certainly not with God's lack of power to bless. Their God was **'the LORD of hosts'**, a title that focuses on his power.[7] The problem lay rather in their own actions, which is why the Lord tells them repeatedly to **'Give thought to your ways'** (1:5,7). They were not acting in faithfulness to their covenant obligations as God's people, which is why he addresses them as 'this people', not 'my people' (1:2). They have put their own interests before God's interest and have reaped the consequences of that set of priorities — a life of futility.

Futility curses were a standard part of many ancient Near-Eastern covenants;[8] here, those curses had become a reality in the lives of the Israelites because of their unfaithfulness.

1:7-11. Thus says the LORD of hosts: 'Give thought to your ways. Go up to the hill country, fetch wood and build my house, so that I may delight in it and be glorified,' says the LORD. 'You sought abundance, but look, poverty! You brought it home and I blew it away. For what reason? This is a declaration of the LORD of hosts: it is because of my house, which is desolate while you are each running about on behalf of your own house. Therefore, because of you the heavens have withheld their dew and the earth has withheld its produce. I have summoned drought upon the land and upon the mountains, upon the grain, upon the new wine, the oil and upon that which the soil brings forth, upon mankind and domesticated animals and upon all the labour of your hands.'

The solution was straightforward: to abandon their excuses and reorder their priorities. In place of the wood they had eagerly gathered to panel their own houses, now they should go out to the hill country and gather wood for God's house (1:8). The prophet underlines his point with a pun: in place of running about (*rāṣîm*) on behalf of their own houses (1:9), they should instead turn God's house from a useless and desolate ruin into a place in which God may delight (*rāṣâ*, 1:8) and may be glorified. Their present distress was, in fact, the logical consequence of their own priorities: because God's house was **'desolate'** (*ḥārēb*, 1:9), therefore he had summoned **'drought'** (*ḥōreb*, 1:11) upon the fruits of the soil and the efforts of their hands. Until their priorities were reordered, they could hardly expect to see greater fruitfulness in their land.

1:12. Zerubbabel son of Shealtiel and Joshua son of Jehozadak, the high priest, and all the remnant of the people
listened to the voice of the LORD their God and to the words
of Haggai the prophet as [one] whom the LORD their God had
sent. The people were afraid before the LORD.

The result of Haggai's preaching was immediate.
Zerubbabel, Joshua and all the remnant of the people
recognized the voice of the Lord as it came to them
through Haggai, his prophet (1:12). Calling them **'the
remnant of the people'** focuses attention on the
judgement for unfaithfulness that God's people have
already experienced, but at the same time also on
God's promises that his judgements upon their sin
would not completely obliterate them (e.g. Isa. 10:21).
Now those who had returned were convicted anew of
their sin of unfaithfulness to the Lord with respect to
the temple, and in consequence they became **'afraid
before the LORD'** (1:12). This attitude is not merely
one of reverence before the Lord (so NASB); rather, it
is the appropriate holy dread that falls on those who
recognize God's commandments and the ways in
which they have fallen short of meeting their demands.[9] They recognized God's justice in judging
them.

1:13-15. Then Haggai, the messenger of the LORD, spoke
the LORD's message to the people: 'I am with you, declares
the LORD.'
    Then the LORD roused the spirit of Zerubbabel son of
Shealtiel, governor of Judah, and the spirit of Joshua son of
Jehozadak, the high priest, and the spirit of all the remnant of
the people, and they went in and worked on the house of the
LORD of hosts, their God. It was the twenty-fourth day of the
sixth month in the second year of King Darius.[10]

As they turned their hearts towards the Lord, they
found the Lord turning towards them, announcing

through Haggai the comforting good news: **'I am with you'** (1:13). After repentance and restoration came prompt action: **'the LORD roused the spirit of Zerubbabel ... of Joshua ... and ... of all the remnant of the people, and they went in and worked on the house of the LORD of hosts'** (1:14). Godly sorrow is never an end in itself; it always issues in an appropriate response of renewed obedience. It was now **'the twenty-fourth day of the sixth month in the second year of King Darius'**. A mere twenty-three days had passed since the first word of the Lord to his people through Haggai.

Application

It is not hard to preach a guilt-inducing sermon from Haggai 1. You simply give your message the title, 'God loves a cheerful builder', and harangue your congregation for living with all modern comforts while the current building campaign is still far short of its target. If you are inclined towards the health-and-wealth gospel, the passage is even more attractive, with its implication that the reason why you are not experiencing prosperity (interpreted as a new car and a home beside the golf course) is because you are not giving enough to God's work. The problem with such an approach to this passage is that we end up preaching not Christ, but a more effective materialism. We treat seeking God as a means to building our own kingdom, whether the form of that kingdom for us is a bigger local church or personal prosperity and fulfilling relationships.

To be sure, Haggai tells the people that they may expect God's blessing from now on, a blessing that under the Mosaic covenant was demonstrated in physical prosperity (2:19; cf. Lev. 26:3-12). But material blessing was not God's primary response to their obedience. Rather, it was an assurance of God's presence with them in their current circumstances (1:13; 2:4) and of his future activity on their behalf, shaking the heavens and the earth and bringing the long-desired Messiah (2:6-7,21-23).

We too need to repent of the ways in which we have focused on building our own houses, not the Lord's. The result of this wrong focus in our lives has also been frustration. This is the fundamental problem of materialism: it is an unreliable and inevitably unfulfilling master. The pleasures it promises often prove elusive, and even those it brings to us turn out in the end to be temporary and unsubstantial. Haggai declares to the people of his day a different vision for which to live. Repent and humble yourself before God and pour your energies into building God's house, the visible symbol of his enduring presence in the midst of his people. In the language of Jesus, 'Seek first God's kingdom, and all these things will be given to you as well' (Matt. 6:33).

The visible symbol of God's presence in the midst of his people is no longer the temple, though, as it was in Haggai's time. Nor is it the church building. Rather, according to the New Testament, it is Jesus Christ himself. Thus, in John 2, when Jesus had ejected the moneychangers from the temple, he said, 'Destroy this temple and in three days I will raise it up again' (John 2:19). He did not have in mind redoing Haggai's task in three days. Rather, he meant that his body would be raised up on the third day. As Immanuel ('God with us'), he physically represented God's presence in the midst of his people. Now that Jesus has ascended to heaven and poured out his Spirit upon the church, God's presence is represented in the world by us, his people. As the body of Christ, the church is the new temple, made up of Jews and Gentiles being built together as a holy dwelling place for God (Eph. 2:16-22; see also 2 Cor. 6:16 – 7:1).

If this is what building God's house means, it is a task far beyond our capabilities. It is not simply a matter of collecting wood and stone, but of collecting and shaping living stones. Thankfully, building God's house is not ultimately our task but Christ's. He is the one who bore the cost of building it. It was relatively easy for Jesus to come in judgement and make a whip to drive the sinners out of God's physical house in Jerusalem. It was a far more painful task for him to come as a Saviour and make sinners fit to live in God's house. To do that would require God the Father to turn the whip upon his own Son, so that he might take upon himself the punishment that our sins deserved. Both aspects of Christ's ministry are crucially important. On the one hand, he has taken upon himself the punishment that we deserved for our self-centred failure to seek God's kingdom and to build his house. On the other, in cleansing the temple he has himself shown the zeal for God's house and kingdom that we lacked. That righteousness of his has now been credited to us, as if it were our own, just as our sin of being perpetually interested only in our own houses has been placed to his account.

God's work of building his new temple, the church, by means of his Spirit is the foundation and encouragement for our work. It was because God roused their spirits that Haggai's hearers set to work with enthusiasm (1:14). It is because God is at work in our earthly bodies by his Spirit that we are called and empowered to glorify God with our bodies (1 Cor. 6:19-20). It is because God is committed to establishing his kingdom in and through us that we are called to seek that kingdom first, above all other things.

The result of seeking first God's kingdom will not necessarily be earthly prosperity, or even large, 'successful' churches. Jesus' earthly ministry was characterized by neither of those things. But God does promise his repentant people his presence with us now, and the fulfilment of his own kingdom goals in the longer term. He has blessed us with every spiritual blessing in the heavenly places in Christ (Eph. 1:3). What else do we need or desire? In place of our preoccupation with food that does not fill, with drink that does not satisfy and with clothing that cannot warm our souls, God promises us the bread of life, a fountain of living water and clothing to cover our spiritual nakedness.

The best is yet to come
(Haggai 2:1-9)

We live in an 'instant' world. We have grown used to instant communication, instant coffee and instant credit. We don't even have to wait for the television to warm up any more. As a result, we are very impatient with processes that take time. We want ourselves and our churches to be instantly sanctified, and we quickly grow discouraged when there seems to be little perceptible progress. Yet God's ways are not our ways. To reverse the poetic line, though the mills of God may grind exceeding small, they also often appear to us to be grinding exceedingly slowly. This was the fundamental issue with which the prophet was dealing in his second prophetic oracle. The people had started the rebuilding process, but the progress seemed agonizingly slow and the end result destined to be disappointingly inferior to the original. God, however, had a word for them through his prophet.

2:1. [In the second year of King Darius][11] in the seventh [month] on the twenty-first day, the word of the LORD came by means of Haggai the prophet…

As with the other oracles in this prophetic book, this section begins with a date formula: the **'twenty-first day'** of **'the seventh [month]'**. The year is not expressed, so presumably the reference to 'the second year of King Darius' at the end of the previous chapter is expected to do double duty. In any event, it is clear that we are still in the same year as the events of the previous chapter, some six weeks after the initial oracle and four weeks after the beginning of the rebuilding work (see 1:1,15).

The date itself is of significance. The twenty-first day of the seventh month was near the end of the Feast of Tabernacles, the last and greatest of the three annual feasts. This would have been the occasion for a major congregational gathering, at which Zerubbabel and Joshua would naturally have been present. This religious convocation provided Haggai with a platform from which to address them both, and the nation at large. The Feast of Tabernacles was a particularly apt setting for his message. It served as a time for remembering the great deeds of God in the past, and an important aspect of the celebration was the fact that the people were required to live outside in shelters for seven days, recalling the wilderness wanderings of Israel before they entered the land (Lev. 23:33-43). These shelters were to be made from interwoven tree branches, and it appears that during the festival tree branches and fruit were carried in joyful procession (Neh. 8:14-15; cf. Lev. 23:40). It would also have been a natural occasion to remember the dedication of Solomon's Temple, which had taken place at this same feast (1 Kings 8:1-3).[12]

The celebration of the Festival of Tabernacles, with its wilderness overtones, would have been particularly poignant and meaningful for 'the remnant of the people' (2:2) because those taking part had themselves only recently experienced a kind of second exodus in their return from Babylon. The returnees saw themselves as a community re-creating the days of Joshua.[13] For them, the experience of dwelling as strangers and aliens in an unwelcoming world and being granted a fresh start in the land promised to Abraham was not simply something to be recalled from the dim and dusty pages of history, but was fresh in their minds.

2:2-3. 'Say to Zerubbabel the son of Shealtiel and to Joshua the son of Jehozadak, the high priest, and to the remnant of the people: "Who of you who remain saw this house in its former glory? How do you see it now? Is it not like nothing in your eyes?"'

As they looked back to the dedication of the first temple in the time of Solomon, and to the entry into the land under Joshua, they could hardly fail to be aware of the differences, as well as the similarities, between their own time and the experience of those who had gone before them. The present realities seemed depressingly mundane, hardly able to match up to the celebrated mighty acts of God in the past. Where was the **'former glory'**? The new temple seemed an empty symbol, lacking the splendour of the former days. Although its physical dimensions were approximately the same as those of the former temple, it was no longer the central symbol of kingdom and (in the glory days of the past) of empire. Now it was a small cog in the plans of someone else's empire, apparently irrelevant to the flow of world events.[14] Its treasuries were empty. Was Cyrus' permission to rebuild the temple really anything more than tokenism?

But the glory that was missing from the temple was not merely external and financial. Those who heard Haggai's words could hardly have failed to see the reference to Ezekiel's visions, in which the glory (*kābôd*) of the Sovereign Lord departed from the Jerusalem temple before it was destroyed by the Babylonians (Ezek. 10). During the exile they had experienced profoundly the real absence of God from their midst, an absence that had been caused by the sins of God's people. It was all very well to rebuild the structure, but without the return of God's presence it would remain a worthless, empty shell. Yet the Lord's words encouraged them to see that he really had returned to their midst, even though the fruits of that return were not yet visible.

2:4-5. 'But now be strong, Zerubbabel; be strong, Joshua son of Jehozadak, the high priest; be strong, all the people of the land,' declares the LORD. 'Work, for I am with you,' declares the LORD of hosts. '[This is] the matter that I covenanted with you when I brought you out of the land of Egypt: my Spirit will abide in your midst. Do not be afraid.'

God's response to the people's discouragement is not to challenge the reality of the problems. He doesn't disagree with their assessment that the present state of affairs is 'as nothing in your eyes' (2:3). However, he proceeds to encourage the rebuilding by underlining what this generation has in common with the past.

First, there is the common command to the leaders and to all the people to **'be strong'** (2:4), a command that echoes the similar commands to be strong issued by David to his son Solomon (1 Kings 2:2) and to Joshua and all the Israelites (Josh. 1:6; Deut. 31:6,7). No matter what the obstacles may be, the obligation on God's people is clear: **'Work.'** They are to do what they can in obedience to God's command, not to wring their hands over what they cannot do.

But even more encouragingly, there is a promise for this generation that underlines their links with the past. They are to be strong and work not simply because God has commanded them to do so, but also because he has committed himself to be with them. They are to trust that, as they do what they can do, God will do what he has committed himself to do.

The Lord's promise that **'I am with you'** was already given to the remnant in Haggai 1:13, but even there it was not a new promise. Its roots lie deep in the soil of Israelite history. Indeed, God's presence in the midst of his covenant people was essentially the heart of the covenant relationship that he established with the Israelites at Mount Sinai in the time of Moses. The Lord would be their God and they would be his people, a kingdom of priests and a holy nation (Exod. 19:6). Moses went so far as to declare that if God were not to be present with them, then nothing significant would mark Israel out from the other nations of the earth (Exod. 33:15-16).

This lasting relationship was sealed in the physical sign of the tabernacle, a movable tent for God's presence to dwell in the midst of the mobile camp of Israel. There the glory that had appeared to Moses and the elders on Mount Sinai (Exod. 24:16) appeared to the people (e.g. Lev. 9:23; Num. 16:42). In the book of Chronicles, this visible presence of the glory of God in the midst of his people was also associated with the dedication of Solomon's Temple (2 Chr. 7:1-3).

In the context of this history, God's promise to do what he had covenanted when he brought the Israelites out of Egypt is a commitment for his presence to be in the midst of his people once again in a lasting way. In other words, **'My Spirit will abide in your midst.'** Not even the nation's lengthy history of sin could ultimately destroy the Lord's covenant commitment to Israel. The rebuilt temple would not be a hollow shell or empty icon, but would in the future symbolize again the reality of God's lasting presence with his people for blessing. Indeed, it is the presence of God's Spirit that provides the assurance of ultimate success for their labours. As Zechariah 4:6 puts it, '"It is not by might, nor by power, but by my Spirit," says the LORD of hosts.' With the promise of God's Spirit, there is no need for them to fear that their labour will be in vain.

2:6. For thus says the LORD of hosts: 'Yet a little [while] and I will shake the heavens and the earth, the sea and the dry land.'

The Lord's answer to the discouragement of his people with the present is not merely to point their eyes backward to the past. He also invites them to look forward to the future. This again fits naturally with the context of the Feast of Tabernacles. This festival was not invented for the wilderness period, a time when they would have little fruit to rejoice over and little need to recall the pilgrim state. Rather, it was intended for after they had entered into the promised land and had settled there. It was a festival designed to recall to their minds the sense of longing for the promised land and thereby to remind them that, even in the best of times, this world was not their home. Even after they possessed the earthly land of Canaan, they were not to settle down completely, but were to look for a better, heavenly land which they could never possess in this life — only in the life to come.

If the festival had that forward-looking note of longing even in the best of times, how much more would that character have needed to be felt during the worst of times! God's word of encouragement in the midst of their difficulties was that after only a little more waiting he would once again intervene deci-sively. God promised to **'shake the heavens and the earth, the sea and the dry land'** (2:6). The language of the earth shaking is typical of theophanies — appearances of God. Thus, when God appeared at Sinai the mountain shook (Exod. 19:18; see also Ps. 68:8). This image became standard as part of the poetic description of God's appearing as a warrior to deliver his people (Ps. 18:7-15). Here, however, the all-encompassing merisms ('heavens / earth'; 'sea / dry land') envisage the ultimate theophany, whereby God would appear to transform the present world order into the final eschatological state. The present visible world order, in which the nations were triumphing and the Lord's people were in subjection and poverty, is not the way the world will end. There is a new world order coming, which will arrive through the appearing of the Lord himself.

2:7-9. 'I will shake all nations and the treasures of all nations will come. I will fill this house with glory.' The LORD of hosts has said it. 'Mine is the silver and the gold,' declares the LORD of hosts. 'The latter glory of this house will be greater than the former.' The LORD of hosts has said it. 'In this place I will establish peace,' declares the LORD of hosts.'

This transformation of the world will not simply affect the natural world order. The Lord will also **'shake all nations'**. This worldwide transformation should probably not be thought of in positive terms for the nations here, as a universal turning to the Lord in the last days. That thought is present elsewhere in the Old Testament, for example in Isaiah 2:2-4, and was apparently in the minds of the translators of the Authorized (King James) Version, when they rendered **'the treasures** [*ḥemdat*] **of all nations will come'** as 'the Desire of all nations shall come', following the Vulgate.[15] This translation is grammatically impossible, however, since the verb is plural.[16] Here the idea is simply that in this worldwide shaking the ill-gotten gains of the nations will be shaken loose and brought to their rightful home in Jerusalem, adding physical glory to the restored temple. The Lord lays claim to them all: **'Mine is the silver and the gold.'** The end result will be a greater glory for the temple than that which it had earlier.

Nor will this glory simply be external and financial. Just as the absence of glory was more than these, so also the return of the glory will be more than these: **'"In this place[17] I will establish peace," declares**

the LORD of hosts.' Peace (*šālôm*) involves an all-encompassing state of harmony and fruitfulness. It certainly includes prosperity, but is far more than mere prosperity. It is nothing less than a total restoration of all relationships, including those between man and God, between man and his fellow man, and between man and the created order. When the glory returns to the new temple, and God once again dwells in the midst of his people, the result will be nothing short of full salvation.

Application

How does your life look, when measured against God's standard? For many of us, if we are honest, our progress towards holiness is less than we had expected and hoped. Can our lives be transformed? Can our churches become living and vibrant centres of holy living? The word of the Lord through the prophet Haggai provides a resounding 'Yes' to those questions, along with the pointers to God's profound programme of complete transformation for us as individuals and as his church.

First, this passage points us to *a wonderful plan*: the perfect balance of dependence and activity. In answering the question, 'How can our lives be changed?', our culture offers only half an answer: 'Be strong and work hard, and everything will turn out right in the end.' That is an important part of the answer; the Lord also tells his people, 'Be strong ... and work' (2:4). Transformation of a life or a church is not simply a matter of sitting back and waiting for divine intervention. However, the admonition to work hard is not enough by itself; when we find ourselves faced with an overwhelming mound of rubble, for most of us the temptation to despair will prove too strong. The call to work flows out of, and is built upon, the prior assurance of God's work. God has promised not to abandon the good work he has begun in each of his saints; rather, he will bring it to completion on the day of Christ Jesus (Phil. 1:6); therein is the basis for us to tackle once again the stubborn indwelling sins that have defeated us so often before.

God has committed himself to build his church in such a way that even the gates of hell will not prevail against it (Matt. 16:18); therein lies our confidence to tackle the abounding rubble in our local manifestation of the church. This balance of hard work and confident dependence upon God is his plan for powerful and thoroughgoing change. As Paul puts it in Philippians 2:12-13, 'Work out your salvation with fear and trembling, for it is God who works in you to will and to act according to his good purpose' (NIV).

Secondly, this passage points us to *a wonderful goal*: being filled with God's glory. Some of the discouragement of Haggai's contemporaries was good. They realized that it was not enough just to rebuild the temple building. Without what the temple symbolized, God's presence in their midst, the whole effort would be meaningless. Similarly, God's wonderful goal for you and me is not simply to transform our marriages, change our lives and fill our churches, great though that would be. He wants our lives and our churches to act as display cabinets of his glory and his grace. As Paul puts it, God predestined us to be adopted as his sons through Jesus Christ so that we might be to the praise of his glorious grace (Eph. 1:5-6).

This truth cuts against the grain for us, because we want God's wonderful plan for our lives to result in at least a little glory for us. We want his grace to be shown through us to others, yet want ourselves not to be too evidently in need of that same grace. We have not yet learned, with Paul, to delight in weaknesses, in insults, in hardships, in persecutions and in difficulties (2 Cor. 12:10). Yet it is precisely in our weakness that his glory is made most evident.

Thirdly, this passage points us to *a wonderful Saviour*. What Haggai's contemporaries longed to see was the glory of God once again filling his house, transforming the present world order and flowing out from there in peace (2:7-9). The fulfilment of this promise awaited the coming of Jesus. At his birth, the angels sang to the terrified shepherds of God's glory and of peace on earth (Luke 2:13-14). They went, not to the temple but to a manger, and returned glorifying God. A few days later, the infant Jesus made his first trip to the temple, where the aged Simeon described him as 'a light for revelation to the Gentiles and for glory to your people Israel' (Luke 2:32). The glory of God had returned to the temple, and those whose eyes God had opened beheld that glory and glorified God.

This incarnation, and the perfect life and sacrificial death that followed it, is the basis of the gospel of peace that is now preached not simply to Israel but to the nations also. Just as Haggai's contemporaries could look back to God's mighty work at the Exodus and conquest and draw hope for the present, so too we can look back to the coming of Christ as the foundation of our hope. Yet, even though the Old Testament manifestations of God were accompanied with glory such that no one could look on the face of Moses when he came down from Mount Sinai after receiving the law, nor could the priests minister in the first temple when it was filled with God's glory, how much greater is the glory of the new covenant! (2 Cor. 3:7-11). What is more, it is our beholding God's glory in the gospel that increasingly transforms us into the likeness of God, as we come to reflect his glory more fully (2 Cor. 3:18).

Fourthly, this passage points us to *a wonderful hope*. Just as the Feast of Tabernacles was a time to look forward as well as look back, so we too as Christians are called to look in two directions. We look back to the cross and God's mighty work in accomplishing our salvation and establishing our peace. In Christ, God has already shaken the entire world order. Yet we also look forward to the world-shaking that is still to come, when God will bring all of history to its consummation in Christ. God has already established his kingdom, manifested his glory and given us peace. But there is a day coming when God's kingdom will be fully and finally established, when his glory will fill the world and his peace will reign for evermore. This too is an antidote to our temptation to despair. The rubble that surrounds us in our lives and in our churches is not the end of the story. There is more to come, a cosmically happy ending in which all of Christ's people will be transformed by him into his likeness.

A new holiness, a new blessing (Haggai 2:10-19)

Have you ever thought about the contagious power of dirt? Why is it that it only takes one drop of motor oil to pollute a gallon of water, while innumerable gallons of water will not turn motor oil into something drinkable? Why is it that when your kids touch the wall with their grubby hands they leave a dirty mark, while when you touch the same wall with your clean hands you don't leave a clean mark?[18] The answer is that dirt is far more contagious than cleanliness. The same inequality is as true in the moral realm as it is in the world of house-cleaning; it this inequality — and God's answer to it — that the prophet is addressing in this section of his book.

2:10-11. On the twenty-fourth day of the ninth month in the second year of Darius, the word of the LORD came to Haggai the prophet: 'Thus says the LORD of hosts: "Ask the priests for a legal opinion."'

Once again the oracle begins with a date, **'the twenty-fourth day of the ninth month in the second year of Darius'** (2:10). In this case, it is not a date which had a natural significance of its own, as part of the festival calendar. However, it is none the less the most prominent date in the whole book, being repeated three times (2:10,18,20). The significance that the prophet laid on this date most probably came from the event mentioned in verse 18: it was the date of the formal (re)founding of the temple (see the exposition below).[19] It was also exactly three months since the people began the rebuilding work on the temple in response to Haggai's first prophecy, and his contemporary Zechariah had now been prophesying for about a month as well (Zech. 1:1).

In Old Testament Israel, the **'priests'** served many functions. In addition to their well-known role as those who offered sacrifices to God, they were also the guardians, exponents and interpreters of the law (*tôrâ*, Deut. 33:10). In the absence of widespread general access to the written law, it was the priests' job to know what that law said, and its wider implications for cases that were not explicitly addressed in the written code. The response to this kind of enquiry was itself called a *tôrâ*, and it was this type of authoritative **'legal opinion'** that Haggai sought from the priests of his day.

This legal function of the priests was as central to their role in Israelite society as the task of delivering the Word was for the prophet and good counsel was to the elders (Jer. 18:18). It was also crucial to the moral health of God's people that the priests should be faithful in this task, or in many cases the people would not know which way was right and would stumble into sin. Indeed, this was Ezekiel's central indictment of the priesthood of his day — that, instead of teaching God's law faithfully, they 'do violence to my law and profane my holy things; they do not distinguish between the holy and the common; they teach that there is no difference between the unclean and the clean' (Ezek. 22:26, NIV).

2:12-14. 'Suppose a man should carry consecrated meat in a corner of his garment, and with that corner he touches bread or stew or wine or oil or any food, will it transmit holiness [to them]?'

The priests answered and said, 'No.'

Then Haggai said, 'If a defiled person touches any of these, will it defile [them]?'

The priests answered and said, 'It will defile [them].'

Then Haggai answered and said, 'So is this people and this nation before me,' declares the LORD. 'So is every work of their hands that they offer there: it is defiled.'

The case which Haggai posed to the priests for their determination was straightforward enough. It involved someone carrying **'consecrated meat in a corner of his garment'** (2:12). The meat would have become consecrated through being part of an animal offered on the altar in a sacrificial ritual. Depending on the ritual, the whole of the animal was not necessarily offered as a sacrifice. For some sacrifices, such as the whole burnt offering (the *'ōlâ*), every part of the animal had to be offered up on the altar (see Lev. 1:3-9). With other sacrifices, such as the sin offering (the *ḥaṭṭā't*) and the guilt offering (the *'āšām*), part of the sacrifice was given to the priest as his perquisite (Lev. 7:7). He or other members of his family could eat it, but only in the holy place (Lev. 7:6). Neither of these cases would quite fit Haggai's description because there would be no meat being carried elsewhere.

However, the situation in the case of a fellowship offering (the *šelāmîm*) was different. In this case, in addition to the meat given to the priest, some was returned to the offerer for a celebratory meal (Lev. 7:12-15). Moreover, if this fellowship offering was the result of a vow or was a freewill offering, the meat did not even have to be eaten the same day, provided that it was all consumed by the end of the next day (Lev. 7:16-17). The scenario envisaged by Haggai is a person carrying home the leftovers of his fellowship offering in a corner of his garment, since clothes had no pockets in those days.

The question Haggai asked concerned what happens if the fold with that consecrated meat in it touched other neutral objects, such as other food items. Would they thereby also become holy? That question was not directly addressed in the written law, although the matter of consecrated meat touching unclean items was (Lev. 7:19), and the answer Haggai received from the priests was probably based on the implicit logic of that text. In certain contexts in the Old Testament holiness is potentially contagious by touch (Exod. 29:37; 30:29; Ezek. 44:19),[20] but it is not necessarily transmitted indiscriminately to everything. In a direct contact between the holy and the unclean, however, the unclean pollutes the holy, rather than the holy purifying the unclean.[21] Thus, although a consecrated object will not necessarily transfer holiness to a neutral item, something that is unclean will necessarily infect whatever it touches (Lev. 7:19). Moreover, the one who has become unclean must not be permitted to have any contact with the consecrated food, or it too would become defiled (Lev. 7:21).

But Haggai's interest in this question-and-answer session was not academic. His goal was not simply to establish the exact details of arcane theological case studies as an end in themselves. He was not interested in determining how many angels could dance on the head of this particular theological pin. Rather, his goal was to use this relatively self-evident ruling to address the very practical issues that faced his own contemporaries, **'this people and this nation'** (2:14). They had become defiled, and in consequence everything they touched became similarly defiled. **'Every work of their hands'** in this context refers specifically to agricultural produce, as it did in Haggai 1:11.[22] They had been bringing the animals which they reared to offer in the sacrificial rituals of the temple altar, but it had all been worthless. Because they themselves were unclean, their offerings were defiled by contact with them and were therefore unacceptable in God's sight. They must themselves first be changed before their offerings could be accepted by God.

2:15-17. 'But now, give thought from this day onward: before stone was placed upon stone in the temple of the LORD, how did you do?[23] One went to a heap of twenty [measures] and there were ten; one went to a wine vat to scoop fifty measures and there were twenty. I struck you with the scorching wind and grain mildew, and all the work of your hands with hail, yet you did not [turn] to me,' declares the LORD.

The events of this day would mark a significant change in their standing before God, however. They were to watch the change in their circumstances unfold and reflect on the key turning point: the day when **'stone was placed upon stone in the temple of the LORD'** (2:15). As Haggai 2:18 makes clear, this dated turning point is not the beginning of the rebuilding work in an absolute sense, but the formal ceremonial laying of the foundation stone. The rebuilding work had begun back in 538 BC under Cyrus, as Ezra 3:10 records, but was soon discontinued because of opposition from those around Judah. But now at Haggai's urging a new start had been made on the project under Zerubbabel, a new start marked by a formal foundation-laying ceremony (see Zech. 4:9).[24]

In the past, before this crucial day of formally restarting the construction programme, the people had been experiencing the full weight of the covenant curses. The fields which promised so much returned little at harvest time; the winepresses that seemed so full actually delivered precious little. Nor was this just a random fluctuation in the vagaries of wind and weather. It was the direct result of the judgement of God upon them. **'Scorching wind'** and **'grain mildew'** (2:17) were two of the covenant curses threatened by God in Deuteronomy 28:22. The same pair are part of the judgement enacted by God against his unfaithful people in Amos 4:9. **'Hail'** (2:17) likewise frequently appears in the Old Testament as a mark of divine judgement (Exod. 9:25; Ps. 78:47,48; 105:32).[25] They had been experiencing the disciplinary hand of God. But, as in the time of Amos, the imposition of these covenant curses by God had not borne fruit in bringing the people to repentance. On the contrary, in spite of all of this, **'you did not [turn] to me'** (2:17).

2:18-19. 'Give thought from this day onward, from the twenty-fourth day of the ninth [month], from the day when the foundation of the temple of the LORD was laid, give thought. Is there still seed in the grain pit? Until [now] the vine, the fig, the pomegranate and the olive tree have not borne [fruit]; from this day I will bless.'

From this point on — the point where the rebuilding work was formally restarted — things would change, however. The **'grain pit'** was the place where grain was stored both for food and for sowing for the next crop. The answer to Haggai's question, **'Is there still seed in the grain pit?'** (2:19), is 'No'. The seed for next year has by this time already been sown, though it is far too soon to predict by normal means the outcome of that labour.[26] The prophet is encouraging the people during the anxious period of waiting to see whether there would be a better harvest this year, unlike the past. There will be a dramatic transformation in their fortunes from curse to blessing now that the rebuilding work on the house of the Lord has recommenced. Whereas in the past **'the vine, the fig, the pomegranate and the olive tree'**, the four key fruit-bearing trees, have not returned a good harvest, from now on the Lord's blessing will be evident in their fruitfulness. All of this blessing will flow out from the re-established temple. In fact, it is simply the working out of God's declaration through Haggai back in verse 9: 'In this place I will establish peace.'

Application

The Old Testament categories of ceremonial cleanliness and holiness are not primarily indicators of moral achievement, but of status. That which was ceremonially clean, and especially that which was holy, was fit to be in the presence of God. That which was unclean could not approach a holy God without the danger of instant incineration. Morality can certainly have an impact on status, but only in one direction. That which is holy can easily be profaned through contact with that which is defiled. Yet morality can never make the defiled holy.

In Haggai's day, people continued to bring offerings, in the shape of various types of agricultural produce, to the ruins of the temple, hoping to influence God to bless them (2:14). Yet according to Haggai, such religious exercises — even those prescribed by God in his Word — were actually totally worthless because the offering of defiled hands is itself defiled and therefore cannot be accepted by a holy God. A 'good work' can never make a sinner right with God; on the contrary, a sinner will necessarily corrupt any 'good work' he turns his hand to. Even when he prays to the true God, he sins because the motives of his heart are corrupt and the corrupt motivation trumps the otherwise good act (James 4:3).

This truth faces us with a dilemma, just as it did Haggai's first hearers. The basic problem which they and we both have is that we are defiled by our sin. Every one of us has been affected by Adam's first sin. As soon as we are born, sin comes naturally to us, not just through bad peer influences or hereditary family patterns. Our problem lies with the fact that we are born with hearts that are corrupted to the core of our beings (Jer. 17:9). We need to be made right with God if we are to experience his blessings and not sink for ever under his curse. Yet religion, even the true religion, cannot bridge the gap. God cannot simply come alongside us and help us as we help ourselves, because we are defiled and he is holy. Our salvation must necessarily come to us from outside us, from an act of God.

It is this radical plan of salvation that Haggai announces to his hearers. Their circumstances will not be transformed by a slow process of moral improvement, but rather through God's decision to act to give peace to his people through dwelling with them, symbolized by the rebuilding of the temple (2:9). This work was now begun, and the result would be new life, *shalom* in all its fullness, from then on. A radical change from curse to blessing had taken place on that day, as God once again dwelt in their midst (2:19).

Although the effects of this change would be visible for Haggai's hearers in agricultural fruitfulness, there was a lot more at stake here than having enough to eat. The material blessings of the old covenant were always symbolic of the deeper spiritual blessings that flow from a relationship with God. These too come to us not through a slow process of moral improvement, whereby I try my best to make myself fit to live with God, but rather through the dramatic and decisive work of God. Just as the re-establishment of the temple was the critical turning point for the people of Haggai's day, so the coming of Christ — the definitive temple of God, as we have seen in our previous expositions — is the radical turning point from curse to blessing for the world. Joy to the world! God is with us! With the coming of Christ into the world, now there is peace on earth among those on whom God's favour rests, as the angels sang (Luke 2:14).

Sadly, though, many of those to whom Christ came would not receive the peace he offered them. When Jesus had entered the city of Jerusalem in triumph, he wept over it and cried out in sorrow, 'If you, even you, had only known on this day what would bring you peace — but now it is hidden from your eyes' (Luke 19:41-42, NIV). Their inability to recognize the one to whom the temple pointed, the one in whom peace with God was truly to be found, would indeed cost them dearly. They would experience a return to the dark days of Jerusalem's destruction. The 'stone upon stone' of the temple rebuilt in Haggai 2 would become 'no stone upon stone' of the temple destroyed in Luke 19:44.[27] Jesus came to that which was his own, and his own did not receive him (John 1:11).

Yet some did receive him, and along with him the blessings that flow from relationship with God. They discovered that to receive Christ was to be reborn as a child of God (John 1:12). Just as the coming *of* Christ to the world is a radical turning point in redemptive history, so also coming *to* Christ is a radical turning point in the life of the believer. From the moment that a person is in Christ, everything has changed. The one who believes in Christ is nothing less than a new creation; the old has gone and the new has come (2 Cor. 5:17). Believers are no longer children of God's wrath, as we all once were. Now we are raised with Christ and seated with him in the heavenly realms (Eph. 2:3,6). Before we came to Christ everything we did was defiled in God's sight. Even our righteous acts were like filthy rags, unable to be admitted into God's presence because of their defiling power (Isa. 64:6).[28] But now we have become God's workmanship, created in Christ Jesus for good works (Eph. 2:10). By grace, we have been saved and enabled for the first time to do works that are genuinely good in God's sight! Everything we have — even our sanctification — comes from God's free gift of salvation in Christ, not from our hard work. It is fitting, then, that he should receive all the praise and glory for it.

Just rewards
(Haggai 2:20-23)

The temple and the king were two of the most foundational elements in God's choice of his people. Thus in Psalm 78:68-72 the psalmist gives as the dual evidence of God's election of Judah the temple built on Mount Zion and the call of David as the shepherd-king of Israel. It is no surprise, therefore, to see Haggai's thought move from the restoration of the temple in Jerusalem to the question of the future of the Davidic line. With the rebuilding work begun, the next natural question was: 'Lord, will you at this time restore the kingdom to Israel?' (Acts 1:6, ESV).

2:20. The word of the LORD came a second time to Haggai on the twenty-fourth of the month...

The fourth and last oracle of the prophet Haggai came on the same day as the third oracle, the **'twenty-fourth'** day of the ninth month (2:10). This was the date of the refounding of the temple in Jerusalem, the official beginning to the reconstruction work. In the previous oracle, he had spoken of the present covenant blessings that would flow from that rebuilding work, and the reality behind it of God's presence in the midst of his people for blessing. Now he looked forward to the eschatological significance of the work begun there.

2:21-23. 'Say to Zerubbabel, governor of Judah, "I am about to shake the heavens and the earth, I will overturn the throne of the kingdoms and I will destroy the strength of the king-doms of the nations. I will overturn the chariot and her drivers; the horses and their riders will go down, each by the sword of his brother. In that day," declares the LORD of hosts, "I will take you, Zerubbabel son of Shealtiel, my servant," declares the LORD, "and I will make you like a seal, for I have chosen you." This is a declaration of the LORD of hosts.'

The oracle was addressed to a single individual, **'Zerubbabel, governor of Judah'**. Yet it was not a word for him alone; otherwise there would have been no need to add it to this collection of oracles. It is a word addressed to Zerubbabel that also speaks to a wider audience, just as the initial oracle addressed to Zerubbabel and Joshua the high priest required a re-sponse of action on the part of the whole community.

The word addressed to Zerubbabel is, in essence, a reassurance that God's long-term plans for his people have not changed. This would have been a natural question in the minds of those who had experienced the exile and return: 'Yes, we have come back to the promised land, but is it possible for us still to have the same relationship, given what has happened? Will God still care about us in the present? Does he still have a plan for us in the future?' The first of those questions, about God's care for them in the present, had been the focus of Haggai's earlier oracles. The future had been mentioned in passing in Haggai 2:6-9, in terms of the future of the temple. But now in this last oracle, Haggai takes up the broader question of what the future would hold in terms of the outlook for the nations and for God's people.

The future for the nations is expressed in general terms and traditional language. The Lord is **'about to shake the heavens and the earth'**, just as he de-clared back in Haggai 2:6. As we noted earlier, this picks up on the traditional terminology for a theophany, or appearance by God. Now, however, the shaking is not simply the response of the natural elements to the awesome majesty of God; it is something that God actually does to them. God will shake the heavens and the earth as we might shake a child's toy snow-globe, sending everything topsy-turvy within the world.

More precisely, though, God's shaking will result not in the disordering of the world, but rather in the proper ordering of a presently disordered world. Haggai's contemporaries knew all about the world the psalmist described in the first part of Psalm 2, with the kings of the earth and the powers-that-be taking their stand against the Lord and his anointed. They had seen the Lord's anointed rejected and cast off, and the thrones and dominions of this world apparently triumphing over him and over God's people. Haggai's prophecy declares that the second half of Psalm 2 still has a future: the nations will be shattered and God's chosen one will be restored to favour.

Haggai 2:22 carries the first half of that message: God promises to **'overturn the throne of the kingdoms'** and **'destroy the strength of the kingdoms of the nations'**. The language is deliberately unspecific about which particular world power is in view, as it is in Psalm 2. It is not just the present form of world domination of Haggai's day, in the (relatively) benevolent form of Persian overlordship, that will be brought down. Every authority, principality, or power that sets itself up against the Lord and his anointed will ultimately come to nothing.

To make that point powerfully, Haggai uses language saturated with traditional themes. The verb **'overturn'** (*hāpak*) would remind his hearers of the fall of Sodom and Gomorrah in Genesis 19:25,29 (see also Isa. 13:19; Amos 4:11);[29] **'destroy'**, on the other hand, would remind them of God's action in rooting the

Canaanites out of the land, which was a repeated theme in Deuteronomy (e.g. Deut. 7:23-24; 31:3-4). The image of overturned chariots, with horses and riders going down, could hardly fail to evoke a picture of the Exodus, when Egypt's elite soldiers (who might have coined a slogan similar to that of the U.S. Marines: 'the few, the proud, the chariot-drivers') went down into the Red Sea (Exod. 15:4-5). The image of military confusion and anarchy, **'each** [falling] **by the sword of his brother'**, is also drawn from Israel's traditions of holy war, in which a key element was the Lord throwing their enemies into confusion (Judg. 7:22; 1 Sam. 14:20; 2 Chr. 20:23).[30] All the evidence of God's faithfulness to his people in the past is marshalled by the prophet to reinforce his message for the future. The warning of Psalm 2 to the nations of the consequences of rebellion against God remains in full force, and the day is coming when it will be seen as an earthly reality.

Psalm 2 speaks not merely of the fate of the rebellious nations, however; it also addresses God's choice of his anointed to rule in Zion. Is there still any future for that promise, in the light of the continued failures of the line of the house of David? The exile was not just a judgement on Israel and Judah; it was also a rejection of the line of David. That is the point made by Psalm 89, where, after rehearsing the promises made to the Davidic line, the psalmist cries out in anguish:

But you have rejected, you have spurned,
    you have been very angry with your anointed
      one.
You have renounced the covenant with your
      servant
    and have defiled his crown in the dust
                       (Ps. 89:38-39, NIV).

It looked as though the eternal covenant made with David and his descendants had been broken and trampled underfoot. David's descendants appeared to be cast off for ever. This idea was perhaps most graphically expressed in the image of Jeremiah 22:24-26. There the Lord declared to King Coniah (Jehoiachin) that, even if he were a seal on the Lord's right hand, he would tear him off and give him over to those who seek his life. In the ancient world, a seal (*ḥôtām*) was either worn on a ring or on a chain, so that it could be kept close to its owner at all times. It was the means by which he would seal documents and attest to their authenticity. Like modern-day credit cards, it was a prized possession because of the consequences of its loss. Yet the Lord says through Jeremiah that this status of being treasured is no longer operative in Jehoiachin's case. The protection that the Lord's anointed might expect from his Overlord had been withdrawn. The declaration of Psalm 2:6, 'I have set my king on Zion, my holy hill', was effectively rendered null and void.

The image used by Haggai deliberately reverses that previous image of rejection and announces the restoration of the Lord's protection. **'In that day'** — that is, in the day of the shaking of the earth previously announced — Zerubbabel need not fear. The Lord would **'take'** him and **'make'** him **'like a seal'**, for he had **'chosen'** him. The language used reinforces the point that Zerubbabel, as a descendant of the Davidic line (1 Chr. 3:19), represents the renewal of that ancient commitment on God's part. The concepts of 'taking' and 'choosing' belong together as the language of election, especially the initial election of David (see Ps. 78:70). Obviously, a dynastic succession precludes by definition the choice of ruler by God in each generation. However, the break in dynastic succession allows the possibility of a new choice, just as the cutting down of the tree of Jesse allows the possibility for a new shoot to grow from its stump (Isa. 11:1). What the Lord is declaring in this oracle is that the presence of Zerubbabel is evidence that the stump is not dead; he is, as it were, a green shoot coming forth from the old line (an image that will be developed further by Zechariah), a sign of life.

What has Zerubbabel done to deserve this accolade? He has simply done what the kings of Judah ought to have done, but often failed to do, namely listen to God's Word through the prophet and obey it. The civil leader of God's people was never a free agent, the captain of his own ship. He was a vassal under the lordship of the Great King, God himself. It is this role that Zerubbabel has played in the refounding of the temple, thereby earning the title **'my servant'**, an appellation that was used particularly of David and of the expectation of an ideal successor in his line (see 2 Sam. 3:18; Psalm 78:70).[31] He has not built his own house, but has laboured to rebuild God's house, precisely the calling he received in Haggai 1.

Does that mean that Haggai viewed Zerubbabel as the rightful Davidic king and thought that the people should rebel against Persia and enthrone him? Not at all. The language used by Haggai to describe Zerubbabel, although honorific and optimistic with regard to the future, carefully avoids any call to present action. He gives no command to the community to crown Zerubbabel, along the lines of his command to restart work on the temple.[32] No action is demanded on the part of Zerubbabel or of the community. On the contrary, they are to wait in expectation for the day when *God* will act to bring about this state of affairs. But they are not to wait for a future without hope, a future in which God had cast off his people and his anointed. They are to wait with hope and anticipation because God has already begun to act to restore his people and to fulfil his ancient promises. That is the significance of the fact that the text mentions Zerubbabel by name. In Zerubbabel, God had already reinstated his interest in the Davidic line. The future had already begun.

The future was not yet consummated, to be sure; they still awaited the indeterminate time in the future, **'that day'** when God would intervene to crush those opposed to him and exalt his anointed to reign. They were still to look for the day when the Lord would give the nations to his anointed as his inheritance and the ends of the earth to him as his possession (Ps. 2:8). But they could wait with confidence because the decree of the Lord's purpose to install and maintain his king on Zion, his holy mountain, was once again in force (Ps. 2:6). The presence of Zerubbabel in their midst was the evidence of that, evidence now stamped as authentic through the word of the Lord's prophet.

Application

As Christians, what we see is not all that there is. In the midst of this present chaos we await a future of hope, a future that God has already begun to unfold for us in Christ. As we wait for that future, this passage points us to three sources of confidence in the midst of the difficulties of life.

First, Haggai reminds us of *God's past action to judge the wicked and deliver his people*. By the use of traditional language and imagery, Haggai turns the minds of his hearers back to the times when God overturned the cities of Sodom and Gomorrah, destroyed the Canaanites in front of Joshua and overthrew the chariots and horsemen of Egypt. In all of these events, God had established his power to judge the wicked and save his people.

Yet *the Lord had also committed himself to future action on behalf of his people*, and this is the second source of their confidence. That future action would be a world-shaking event, a total reordering of the powers-that-be into a wholly new constitution for reality. By picking up on the language of the past to describe the events of the future, the prophet is declaring that God will do it again. The past is not simply old history; it is the paradigm for a bright future.

Thirdly, though, *this future intervention casts its shadow forward into the present.* Haggai allowed those who might be tempted to despair and to give up, on the grounds that obedience was of no value in the present, to overhear God's Word to Zerubbabel. In the world's eyes, Zerubbabel's life had little significance. He was a minor government official in a backwater province, the inheritor of a cast-off royal line. Yet, in spite of his lack of outward majesty, God had chosen Zerubbabel and given him a significant task to undertake, that of rebuilding his house. Zerubbabel had heeded the call of the prophet and led the people in the rebuilding programme. His reward was to hear God say to him, in effect, 'Well done, good and faithful servant. You have been faithful over a little; I will set you over much' (Matt. 25:21, ESV). Even in the day of small things, obedience is not useless or unobserved. It may not yet be the day for shaking the world, but present small faithfulnesses will receive their reward.

Yet Zerubbabel was not simply a personal model of obedience for the returned communities to take as a pattern for their own lives. His existence, as a son of David who had been faithful and who heard the words of the curse on his forefather Jehoiachin reversed, was a sign of hope for the whole community. God's choice of David and his offspring as the hope of the world was not at an end. We look to the greater son of Zerubbabel as the one in whom our hope is found, Jesus Christ (Matt. 1:13). He too had no form or majesty to attract people to him. He had no position that would grant him respect in the world. He humbled himself and took on the form of a servant, then stooped even lower, to the point of death on a cross, a form of death that was reserved for those who were accursed by God (Phil. 2:5-8). Was this the Lord's anointed? On the cross, he looked more like a new Jehoiachin, utterly cast off by God, than a new Zerubbabel, God's chosen servant. Passers-by cried out, 'Let him save himself, if he is the Christ of God, his Chosen One!' (Luke 23:35, ESV). He seemed self-evidently under God's curse, rejected by the Father.

Nor was that perception entirely wrong. He was under God's curse and abandoned by him for our sin. But underneath that temporary rejection by God was an eternal promise that could not be broken. God had chosen this son of David to be a light to the Gentiles and to bring salvation to his own people. God would establish his anointed as the name above every name precisely through this act of self-sacrifice on behalf of his people. Just as the sins of the Davidic kings once brought exile and destruction upon their subjects, so now the righteous death of this Davidic king brings life to all who trust in him.

In the meantime, though, as we wait for the final shaking of heaven and earth, our calling is to be faithful. Like Zerubbabel, we are to be faithful in the little things, the daily grind of chores and studies, of work and witnessing, of labouring for God and for our daily bread. Sometimes our task may seem to us like that given to Sisyphus in Greek mythology, who daily rolled a stone up the hill, only for it to be returned to the bottom every night. Christian ministry, in particular, often looks like the ministry of stone-rolling. But none of our labours will be wasted in the purposes of God. So we trudge on, hoping that we too may simply hear the words of our God: 'Well done, good and faithful servant! You have been faithful over a little; I will set you over much.'

Zechariah

Keep the faith!
(Zechariah 1:1-6)

I love long-distance running. Of all sports, it is perhaps the most simple, at least at the level at which I
practise it. There are only two things to remember:
you have to start, and then you have to keep on going
until you finish. No complicated rules; you don't even
have to remember the score. Just begin and keep on
running until the finish line comes into view. Those
who returned from exile and reoccupied the promised
land in response to the decree of Cyrus in 538 BC had
been stirred to begin the work of rebuilding the temple
under the preaching of Haggai. Two months after
Haggai's first oracle, which was given in the sixth
month of Darius' second year (520 BC), God added the
voice of another prophet, Zechariah, to cheer, cajole
and encourage his people onward in the race. The
visionary form of the prophecy is often complex to
interpret in its details, yet its essential message is a
call to persevere over the full distance of the race.

1:1. In the eighth month of the second year of Darius, the
word of the LORD came to Zechariah son of Berekiah, son of
Iddo, the prophet...

'The eighth month of the second year of Darius'
(1:1) is November/December 520 BC, two months after
Haggai's first oracle and overlapping the short span of
his prophetic ministry. This is the first of three date
formulas that serve as major structuring devices in

Zechariah 1 – 8 (the others are in 1:7 and 7:1). Thus, we may divide Zechariah 1 – 8 into three major sections: 1:1-6; 1:7 – 6:15 and 7:1 – 8:23, with the first and third sections bracketing and highlighting the visions.

The prophets Haggai and Zechariah were not merely contemporaries. Zechariah 8:9 explicitly refers to Haggai's work, though not his name, and there are a number of literary features that serve to link Haggai and Zechariah 1 – 8 strongly together.[1] It is striking, for example, that in Haggai 1:1 – Zechariah 8, there are now a total of seven dated revelations (Hag. 1:1; 2:1; 2:10; 2:20; Zech. 1:1; 1:7; 7:1). Only in the first and the last of these date formulas do we begin with reference to the regnal year of 'Darius the king', followed by the calendar date.[2] This is just one of the devices used to link these books, and especially Haggai with Zechariah 7 – 8.[3] We shall look at those correspondences more closely when we get to chapters 7 and 8, but for now it is enough to notice that in terms of structure Haggai 1 – 2 and Zechariah 7 – 8 form bookends around the visions of Zechariah 1 – 6. These structural elements once again direct our gaze towards what is central, namely the vision of Zechariah 3.

'Zechariah' means, 'The LORD remembered.' It is a common biblical name, which espouses an appeal to the Lord to remember his promises, but it was perhaps particularly fitting for the ministry of this prophet. Zechariah's message brought God's faithfulness to the fore, and urged the people to faithfulness in return.

Unlike Haggai, Zechariah has an extensive genealogy. This may be due to the frequent occurrences of his name in the biblical record, just as in our culture we might feel the need to identify which particular Bob or Jim we were talking about, while a friend named Toby (or Zechariah!) would need no further qualification. More likely, though, his genealogy might have merited mention because of the significance of his particular ancestors. Whereas Haggai was perhaps descended from a long line of nobodies, Zechariah was a descendant of **'Iddo'** — one of the priests who headed families at the return from exile with Zerub-babel (Neh. 12:4). That would account for the fact that when these two prophets appear together in the book of Ezra, they are always referred to as 'Haggai' and 'Zechariah ben-Iddo' (Ezra 5:1; 6:14). The genealogy also underlines the fact that Zechariah comes from a priestly heritage (as did some other prophets, notably Ezekiel), a detail worth remembering in what follows. Although the Hebrew is grammatically ambiguous, it seems evident that **'the prophet'** here refers to Zechariah, not Iddo.

1:2-3. 'The LORD was very angry with your fathers. But you shall say to them, "Thus says the LORD of hosts: 'Turn to me,' declares the LORD of hosts, 'and I will turn to you,' says the LORD of hosts."'

The opening oracle that came to Zechariah was an exhortation to turn to the Lord. It starts out by re-hearsing the past: **'The LORD was very angry with your fathers.'** **'Your fathers'** in this context are the generations that lived prior to the exile, and especially the generation upon whom the exile came, whose sins were the cause of God's wrath and its consequences. The exile was not a random disaster, an 'act of God' in the insurance-industry jargon — an unpredictable, freak event that no one could have anticipated. Rather, it was an act of God in the strict sense — an outpouring of the curses threatened in Deuteronomy on covenant-breakers (see Deut. 28:36-37).

God's wrath against covenant-breakers as the cause of exile is a central theme in the so-called Deuteronomic History, the account of Israel's past that runs in connected fashion from Joshua to

2 Kings and is informed by the world view of the book of Deuteronomy.[4] This message of God's wrath is both bad news and good news for the prophet's hearers. On the one hand, it forces them to face up to the bad news: the Lord is a God who acts in anger against sin and covenant-breaking. But, paradoxically, concealed within the bad news are also the seeds of the good news: 'Though the Lord was very angry with our fathers, he is not (necessarily) angry with us!' There may be a future beyond the judgement.

That observation brings us to the central thrust of this oracle: **'"Turn to me," declares the LORD of hosts, "and I will turn to you"'** (1:3). Both the word *šûb* (**'turn'**) and the phrase **'the LORD of hosts'** occur four times in four short verses. Though the people have been brought back physically from exile, they have not yet been radically changed by their experience. Their commitment to the Lord falls far short of the new-covenant obedience anticipated in Ezekiel and Jeremiah, and is resulting in a failure to experience the blessings of the covenant (see Hag. 2:17). But the past is not determinative of the future. Repentance can bring about a new beginning.

1:4. 'Do not be like your fathers to whom the former prophets called, "Thus says the LORD of hosts: 'Turn from your evil ways and your evil deeds.'" But they did not listen, nor did they pay attention to me,' declares the LORD.

Here the prophet continues his appeal to the present generation to be different from those who lived before the exile. In the past, God spoke to his people through **'the former prophets'** (another common theme in Joshua – 2 Kings). The content of that message could be summed up as: **'Turn from your evil ways and your evil deeds.'** This is not just a good summary of the gist of the message of all the prophets (see, e.g., Ezek. 33:11); it is an almost exact citation of Jeremiah

25:4-5. All along, the prophets had insisted on righteous living among the people of God. The implication
of this for the post-exilic generation was straightforward: it was not enough for them to rebuild the
temple. If God was going to dwell once more in their
midst, they must likewise be transformed into a holy
people. Turning to God cannot be accomplished in a
vacuum; it cannot occur without a commensurate
turning from evil. As the earlier prophets had repeatedly declared, the unclean cannot dwell in the presence of God (Isa. 6:5; Ezek. 18:1-32). Or, as the writer
of Hebrews put it, 'Without holiness, no one will see
the Lord' (Heb. 12:14). The former generation did not
heed that message, and so reaped the consequences
of God's wrath.

1:5. 'As for your fathers, where are they? And do the prophets live for ever?'

The reality that unrepented sin had awful consequences should have been self-evident to Zechariah's
audience. Their **'fathers'**, the generations leading up
to the exile, were obviously buried under the judgement of God: the ruins of that holocaust were everywhere in front of their eyes. But even **'the prophets'**
did not **'live for ever'**. Good and bad alike have
perished under the judgement of God. All flesh has
been utterly destroyed like grass before the all-
consuming fire of God's wrath. The reason for highlighting the transitory nature of even the prophets, the
best and most faithful of the previous generations, is
to set up a contrast with the following verse, in which
we learn what alone does endure.

1:6. 'Did my words and my statutes, which I commanded my
servants the prophets, not surely overtake your fathers?'

Then they turned and they said, 'Just as the LORD of hosts planned to do to us, according to our words and our acts, he has indeed done to us.'

'Surely' (*'ak*) begins the sentence in Hebrew and highlights the contrast between what precedes and what follows. Though neither good nor bad among God's people live for ever, three things do endure: God's word (or more precisely, his **'words'**), his **'statutes'** and his plan to punish those who are covenant-breakers. Even though the prophets may come and go, their word endures for ever, because it is God's word; the grass withers, the flower fades, but the word of our God endures for ever (Isa. 40:8).

The word **'overtake'** (*nāśag*) is a hunting and military term that points the prophet's hearers back to the covenantal curses in Deuteronomy (Deut. 28:15,45).[5] This outcome is exactly what God had warned ahead of time: if the people would not obey the Lord's voice, the curses would overtake (*nāśag*) them until they were destroyed. The prophet is thus not merely declaring that sin has certain consequences; rather, he is underlining the fact that sin has *covenant* consequences.

Zechariah's words were not without effect: **'Then they** [that is, Zechariah's audience] **turned.'** Unlike their fathers, who were not changed even by the experience of exile (see Ezek. 33:30-32), the new generation were not inattentive to the Lord's voice through his prophet. Zechariah's hearers recognized the validity of God's judgement upon them (whether in the shape of the exile itself, or the straitened financial circumstances that followed it). Presumably, this initial turning to God also took the form of enthusiastic participation in the building work on the temple. Now, therefore, they might expect to see God's response, as promised (1:3), in what follows. Since Haggai and Zechariah's generation have proved themselves different from their forefathers and have turned to the Lord, now the stage is set for the Lord to turn to them and return to their midst. This theme dominates the subsequent night visions. Whether this initial turning of the people to the Lord is enough by itself is an issue that will emerge later. For now, however, it is significant that they have begun well.

Application

This prophetic oracle describes two groups of people who respond to God's word in different ways. The 'fathers', the generations prior to the exile, heard God's word repeatedly, yet did not respond to it; in consequence, they were buried by the wrath of God. The present generation, however, responded positively to the call to turn to God and therefore may anticipate a different future.

The average congregation is likely to include men and women whose situation reflects that of both groups. Everyone present is a sinner, who has heard the Word of God, either directly or through general revelation (Ps. 19:1-4; Rom. 1:18-25). Every one of us experiences in some measure the effects of sin in the brokenness of our lives. This passage addresses very directly those who are living carelessly sinful lives, whose position is analogous to that of the previous generations, and also believers who are tempted to despair by the consequences of sin (their own or that of others) in their lives.

This passage teaches us that sin has two basic dimensions.

First, it involves *the failure to listen and to respond to God's word* delivered through his messengers. If that was true in Zechariah's day, when God's word was delivered through the prophets, how much more is it sinful for us to fail to hear the climactic Word of God, now delivered to us through the Son? (Heb. 1:1-2). How shall we escape if we neglect such a great salvation? (Heb. 2:3).

The second dimension of sin is that *this neglect of God's word flows out into all manner of evil habits and actions*. Sinful acts flow out of a sinful attitude of turning away from God. None of us can escape the conviction of such sweeping categories. All have sinned and fallen short of the glory of God (Rom. 3:23). Just as the

ancient Israelites broke the covenant God made with them at
Mount Sinai, so all of us have failed to keep God's moral law. On a
fundamental level, we are all covenant-breakers.

If it is true that we are all covenant-breakers, then the passage
sets before us a fearful reality. God's judgement upon covenant-
breakers is sure. The exile had demonstrated that once and for all.
Sin has covenant consequences: its wages are death (Rom. 6:23),
and those wages must ultimately be collected. This remains as
true today, in the new-covenant era, as it was then. This is the bad
news of the gospel. However, Zechariah reminded his hearers that
the past does not need to dictate the future. Restoration to God's
favour is possible. If the present generation were to return to the
Lord, they would find him returning to them.

Repentance starts with a recognition of God's justice. The
people of Zechariah's day needed to see that the Lord was
justified in his anger that brought on the exile. What is more,
repentance itself is multidimensional: it begins with listening to the
words of the one whom God has sent, and flows out into a new life
of obedience to God. Repentance includes both turning *to* God
and turning *from* wickedness (2 Tim. 2:19). The encouraging truth
is that, just as sin has sure consequences, so too does repentance. Those who turn to God may be confident that he will not turn
them away.

How, though, can God be both the sure judge of sinners and
the sure receiver of the repentant? God forgives our sins because
they have already been paid for at the cross. Our covenant Head,
Jesus Christ, has already paid the price for all of his covenant-
breaking children. He was made holocaust for our transgressions.
Thus, by strict justice, God cannot demand payment for them from
us. As we turn to God and place our faith in Jesus Christ, the
ultimate Prophet through whom God has spoken to his people, we
may be sure of being received by the Father, for Christ's sake. We
need not despair, even though our lives are at present still deeply
marked by the effects of sin. But if we turn away from the Son and
do not listen to his invitation to come, how shall we escape from
the burning wrath of God against covenant-breakers?

All quiet on the eastern front?
(Zechariah 1:7-17)

Things are not always what they appear to be on the surface. In L. Frank Baum's novel, *The Wizard of Oz*, the wizard manifests himself in terrifying splendour before Dorothy and her three friends in the city of Oz. To behold him is a fear-inducing sight, for he appears in the shape of an enormous head that speaks and breathes smoke. Yet at the end of the story, Dorothy's dog Toto knocks over a screen and unveils a rather less fearsome reality. The wizard turns out to be a second-rate fairground illusionist, who has been hiding his own weakness behind a dramatic persona. The superficial show conceals a deeper emptiness.

What we see in the visions of Zechariah 1 – 6 is a similar removal of the screen. Once again, the ultimate realities are revealed not to be what appears on the surface. In this case, it is the surface that is peaceful and calm, even banal, the apparent triumph of the forces of evil over the people of God. In Zechariah's day, history appeared to be following a smooth course towards the triumph of the wicked. The visions of Zechariah unveiled a deeper reality, however — a reality far more fearsome than even the pretence of the Wizard of Oz. God Almighty is neither dead nor sleeping, nor is he a second-rate illusionist. On the contrary, he sees all, controls all and is in the process of bringing about all of his perfect plans for his people.

1:7. On the twenty-fourth day of the eleventh month (the month of Shebat) in the second year of Darius, the word of the LORD came to Zechariah the prophet, son of Berekiah, son of Iddo...

As in the book of Haggai, the main sections of Zechariah 1 – 8 are marked off by date formulae. The date here, **'the twenty-fourth day of the eleventh month ... in the second year of Darius'**, is three months after the opening oracle, on or around 15 February 519 BC. There is no obvious importance associated with this date in the Bible; however, it was not long before the new year, a time often associated in the ancient Near East with the building of temples. The identification of the month by its Babylonian name here and in 7:1 (unlike in the other date formulae thus far in Haggai and Zechariah) serves at least two functions.

First, the use of the Babylonian name underlines the foreignness of the surroundings of the people of God after the exile,[6] where even the passage of time is now defined with reference to the gods of other nations.

Secondly, its use here may suggest a word-play: although spelled differently, **'Shebat'** sounds like *šabbāt* (Sabbath). It thus poses the question: 'Is this pagan month of Shebat really going to be the month of true "rest" for God's people?' As we shall see, the issue of rest for them is very much in view in this vision.

1:8-9. At night, I saw a man mounted on a dark brown horse. He was standing among the myrtle trees in the depths. Behind him were dark brown, light brown and white horses.

Then I said, 'What are these, sir?'

The angel who was speaking with me said to me, 'I myself will show you what these are.'

The opening words, **'at night'**, form the introduction not only to this vision, but to the entire sequence of visions that follow. It is not clear whether the visions were all received in the course of a single night, but at the very least they form a coherent and structured whole, a sequence of seven visions, plus the episode that depicts the reclothing of Joshua.[7] The outer visions of the sequence are balanced in a way that centres our attention on the message of chapters 3 and 4. Essentially, the visions move from the universal to the particular (from the Lord's universal reign over the whole world to his redeeming purposes in Jerusalem and Judah), focusing our gaze on the renewed temple in Jerusalem as the heart of God's transforming plan for his people and the world.

It is perhaps significant also that the visions are received at night. The night is the time when it is dark and hard to see anything, and yet the prophet sees clearly God's revelation. In the world in which the exiles lived, it was hard to see God at work with their eyes. The prophet, however, assures them that there is more happening behind the scenes than they can see. As Hamlet famously put it, 'There are more things in heaven and earth, Horatio, than are dreamt of in your philosophy.'

What the prophet saw was **'a man mounted[8] on a dark brown horse'**, accompanied by others on horses of assorted colours, located **'among the myrtle trees in the depths'** (1:8). The prophet's natural response to this puzzling sight is to say to the interpreter who accompanied him, **'What are these, sir?'** This vision, like those that follow it, is far from self-evident in its meaning. The obscurities of this mode of revelation are many, and it would be easy to focus a large amount of attention on them. However, such an approach, which easily slides into allegory, seems to miss the fact that the prophet's question is not left unanswered. Zechariah receives a response to his query from the angel, who promises, **'I myself will show you what these are'** (1:9). Yet the conversation that follows, which must be understood as giving Zechariah the essential message of the vision, sheds no light at all on the significance of the various colours of horse or the particular variety of tree, and that suggests that these details are not important. The approach of this commentary to interpreting and applying the visions takes its cue from that observation. We shall stand back and enquire after the clear import of each vision as a whole, especially in the light of the interpretative comments and oracles that are interspersed among the visions, rather than seeking significance in every minor detail.

What we see when we step back and view the vision as a whole is a group of horsemen concealed in shadows and thick vegetation. The horses on which they are mounted are within the range of normal colours for horses,[9] **'dark brown'** (*'ādōm* is often rendered 'red', but that is not how we typically describe that colour of horse in English), **'light brown'** (or possibly 'dappled')[10] and **'white'**. **'Myrtle trees'** are evergreens, and so would have thick foliage to enable easy concealment of the horsemen, even in the middle of winter when many trees lose their leaves. The location of the myrtles **'in the depths'** (or shadows) is difficult, since the word only occurs here. However, whatever its precise nuance, it seems to add to the note of secrecy and hiddenness that is a prominent feature of this vision.[11]

1:10-11. Then the man who was standing among the myrtles answered and said, 'These are the ones whom the Lord sent to patrol the earth.'

Then they answered the angel of the Lord who was standing among the myrtle trees and they said, 'We have patrolled the earth. Look! The whole earth is peaceful and quiet.'

The interpreting angel has the ability to enter the vision and converse with the characters in it. In response to the promise to enable Zechariah to under-stand the significance of the vision, the chief of the horsemen responds by identifying his companions as **'the ones whom the LORD sent to patrol the earth'** (1:10). The significance of this observation would not have been lost on anyone living in the Persian empire. As the Greek historian Herodotus tells us, the Per-sians were famous for their intelligence-gathering and communications networks. They had their informants and moles throughout their empire and an efficient system of mounted couriers to collect and distribute information from the far-flung corners of their realm, just as the Neo-Babylonians had before them.[12] The horsemen of Zechariah's vision are the divine counter-part of the Persian secret service. These are the Lord's spies, or special operations forces, whose task is secretly to observe what is going on in the world, providing accurate and up-to-date information, upon which the Lord may act. The Lord had sent them out on a data-gathering expedition, and now Zechariah sees them reporting back to their secret headquarters.

The content of their report is not secret, however. The horsemen have patrolled the whole earth and found it **'peaceful and quiet'** (1:11). This is an accu-rate description of the political state of affairs at this time, but it is far more than a merely historical note. Such 'peace and quiet' or, to use the biblical phrase, 'rest from your enemies all around' was a prerequisite for temple building (see Deut. 12:10; 2 Sam. 7:1). Yet in this case, it was the nations of the world that were experiencing this state of blessing, not Jerusalem and Judah. From the perspective of God's repentant people (1:6), something is self-evidently wrong with this picture.

1:12-15. Then the angel of the LORD answered and said, 'O LORD of hosts, how long will you withhold compassion from Jerusalem and the cities of Judah, which you have afflicted these seventy years?'

The LORD answered the angel who was speaking with me comforting words, words of consolation.

Then the angel who was speaking with me said, 'Cry out, saying, "Thus says the LORD of hosts: 'I am zealous for Jerusalem and I have a great zealousness towards Zion. I am very angry with the nations that are untroubled. I was angry for a little while, but they assisted with the harm.'"'

This incongruity between the comfort of the nations and the difficult state of God's own people is not simply felt on earth. It elicits a cry of intercession from the leader of the horsemen, now identified as **'the angel of the LORD'**. He addresses God as **'LORD of hosts'**, God's military title, and asks, **'How long will you withhold compassion from Jerusalem and the cities of Judah, which you have afflicted these seventy years?'** (1:12).

'Seventy years' refers to Jeremiah's prophecy of the length of the exile in Jeremiah 25:11-12; it is also, in round terms, the period that has passed between the fall of Jerusalem in 586 BC and Zechariah's day. The assumption of the angel's intercession is that the judgement of the exile was always intended to be limited and that its full extent will soon be exhausted.

Nor is the angelic intercession disappointed. The Lord responds to his cry of 'How long?' with comforting **'words of consolation'** (1:13). The prophet is then commissioned to spread this good news of the restoration of divine favour. In contrast to the secrecy of the mission of the angelic horsemen, Zechariah is to **'cry out'** the good news. God is no longer angry with his people and refusing to show them favour. He was angry with them for their covenant-breaking, an anger that led to the seventy-year affliction of the exile. But now his zealous passion for his city and his temple, for **'Jerusalem'** and for **'Zion'**, has been restored.

The change in the fortunes of God's people also means a change in fortunes for the nations, those who at present are **'untroubled'** (1:15). Now his anger will be redirected away from Judah to those who took advantage of her unprotected state. The exile was a consequence of the fact that the Lord was 'very angry' with his people (1:2), just as Deuteronomy 29:28 had threatened. But though God's anger against them for their sin was great, it was only for a little while.[13] Now it is turned outward towards Judah's enemies who gleefully **'assisted'** in the destruction of Judah. They were tools in God's hand to bring about his judgement, but that does not provide them with immunity from facing God's judgement themselves for their acts of malice.

1:16-17. Therefore, thus says the LORD: 'I will turn to Jerusalem with compassion. My house will be rebuilt within her,' declares the LORD of hosts. 'A measuring line will be stretched out over Jerusalem.' Cry out again, saying, 'Thus says the LORD of hosts: "My cities will again overflow with good things. The LORD will show compassion again upon Zion and will again choose Jerusalem."'

The prophet's focus is only briefly diverted onto the fate of the nations. The heart of his message is the good news that he has for his own people. In response to Judah's repentance and turning to God (1:6), they will see him **'turn to Jerusalem with compassion'** (1:16). The angel of the Lord's intercessory question (1:12) will be answered in the affirmative. God's **'house will be rebuilt'** in their midst, the goal towards which Haggai's prophecies had been directed. The result would be a new era of blessing. The **'measuring line'**, the first stage of any building project, would once again be **'stretched out over Jerusalem'** as the old ruins were brought back to new life.

Nor is this a completely new beginning, a new start with no continuity with what has gone before. Four times in Zechariah 1:17, we hear the word **'again'** (*'ôd*), highlighting the fact that what is in view is the fulfilment of all the old covenant promises.[14] In place of the present curse, God's people will experience the blessings of the former covenants, because of God's sovereign will to bless his people. In strongly covenantal language, God announces that he will again **'choose'** (*bāḥar*) Jerusalem (1:17). The covenant with David is thus declared by no means null and void, in spite of the sins of the Davidic line. God will achieve the goals and purposes of blessing intrinsic to it, one way or another.

Application

The fundamental issue that faced Zechariah's first hearers was unrealized eschatology. They had suffered the consequences of the covenant-breaking of their parents in the shape of the exile. Now they had returned to the land and repented. Would things get better now? Were the seventy years of which Jeremiah spoke nearly up? More fundamentally still, was the covenant with Abraham, with its promise of blessings on those who blessed him and a curse on those who mistreated him, still in force? If so, why were the nations that had oppressed God's people at rest and at ease, while they themselves were still suffering?

To these questions and concerns, the opening vision of Zechariah gives several answers.

First, in the midst of the darkness and obscurity of life, the Lord is able to unfold the true state of affairs clearly to his servants the prophets, and through them to his beleaguered people. God's revelation allows them a glimpse of the true nature of things.

Secondly, God is not absent, but sees everything that goes on. We may not be aware of their activity, but his heavenly patrols pass back and forth throughout the earth, observing everything that occurs and reporting speedily on what they have seen.

Thirdly, God is not unconcerned with the pain of his chosen ones. Their cry, 'How long?' is already taken up on the lips of the angel of the Lord himself, and his intercession receives an immediate answer from God. The covenants the Lord has made with them have not been cancelled. Blessing shall again flow from Zion to God's people, as the temple is rebuilt and the Lord dwells with them once more. Meanwhile, the nations that are in rebellion against God and are opposed to his people, though currently at ease, will soon experience a terrible outpouring of God's wrath.

Fourthly, the seventy years of wrath poured out on Judah were just 'a little while' in God's plan. He paints on a larger canvas than we conceive, and in the end will be faithful to fulfil everything he has promised. That fulfilment must result in nothing less than the complete salvation of those who are his.

The questions and concerns of Zechariah's readers today are the same as those of his original audience. We too struggle with issues of unrealized eschatology, both individually and corporately as Christ's church. Things around us are not always as they should be, whether for us or for God's opponents. We don't always understand what God is doing, or why he works in the way he does: we see faithful missionaries taken from the field through cancer while partying pagans exhibit the best of health. We see churches that preach a false gospel of health and prosperity filled with worshippers, while faithful ministries often seem to attract few adherents. In situations like these, we too are often tempted to doubt God. Like Zechariah's hearers, we have a light to hold onto in the midst of general darkness, the Word of God. For us this word is made more sure, since it is now written down and attested by the witness of the Spirit. If we abandon that light and trust instead in our feelings, we shall be left floundering in the darkness. It is still true in our day that God sees, God cares and God answers.

This is not good news for all mankind. For the nations of Zechariah's day, it meant that their present state of ease was artificial and temporary, about to give way to the outpouring of the wrath of the God who saw and cared about their sin and would act to judge it. The same is still true for those who are falsely at ease.

Peace and quiet here and now do not mean eternal peace and quiet.

For God's people, on the other hand, this truth is good news. Even when all appearances are to the contrary, God cannot abandon his own. His wrath is only for a moment, but his covenant faithfulness is for ever. His judgement extends to the third and fourth generation, but his covenant love to a thousand generations.

This was Zechariah's good news to his generation: God's wrath had burnt itself out in the seventy years of the exile, but his faithful love endured for ever. How much more may we who are Christians be assured of that truth! God's wrath has been satisfied once and for all by its outpouring on Christ in our place on the cross; his blessing flows to us now from the one to whom the temple on Mount Zion pointed forward, Jesus Christ. It is in him that we are chosen, in him that we receive God's compassion, in him that we are blessed with every spiritual blessing. God's sovereign choice of Christ and all who are in him for eternal life is the foundation for our certain hope in a tragically disordered world.

However, the definitive answer to unrealized eschatology awaits the return of Christ, when God will ultimately set all things to rights. To those whose lives are easy now, there is the stern word of final judgement: 'Depart from me ... to the eternal fire prepared for the devil and his angels' (Matt. 25:41). Yet those whose eyes are aching with longing for God will be satisfied. The rebuilt Jerusalem of 515 BC was a mere shadow of the good things that are as yet still to come. God is building a new Jerusalem, a place of fulness of blessing, where every tear will be wiped away, every pain eased and every sorrow comforted.

Be still before the Lord!
(Zechariah 1:18 – 2:13)

War encompasses a strange mixture of elements. There is silence, but also noise, intense activity and periods of boredom, exhilaration and despair — often encompassed in a very short span of time. The first of Zechariah's night visions was a static tableau. There were horsemen who had been active enough, to be sure, but at the moment the prophet saw them they were simply reporting in, half-hidden among the greenery. But now that the special forces have completed their secret and silent reconnaissance, it is time for action and noise, themes that fill the second vision. There is movement and sound on all sides of the prophet as the divine war machine swings into action. The end result is exhilarating victory for God's children, the despair of defeat for his enemies and a different kind of silence.

*1:18-19.*15 Then I lifted up my eyes and I looked and I saw four horns. I said to the angel who was speaking with me, 'What are these?'

He said to me, 'These are the horns that scattered Judah, Israel and Jerusalem.'

The prophet moves straight from one vision into the next, in this case, a vision of **'four horns'**. The reference to four horns has led some interpreters to think that an idolatrous four-horned altar is in view, but it is simpler to regard the horns simply as symbols of military strength, as in Jeremiah 48:25, and the number **'four'** as indicative of totality. The number 'four' seems to have a similar function elsewhere in Zechariah: there are (correspondingly) four craftsmen in Zechariah 1:20, four winds in 2:6 and 6:5, four chariots in 6:1 and perhaps also four horsemen in 1:8, though the number is not made explicit there.[16]

Once again the prophet responds to the vision with a question: **'What are these?'** In this case, it is not that the objects themselves are obscure. However, Zechariah needs help in deciphering the significance of these horns. What do they represent? The angel responds that **'These are the horns that scattered Judah, Israel and Jerusalem.'** That is, the horns represent all of the world powers that have raised themselves up against the Lord's people at whatever period of history — hence the inclusion of the scattering of **'Israel'** in 722 BC together with the historically distinct scattering of **'Judah … and Jerusalem'** in 586 BC. In line with Psalm 2, the vision depicts the nations as raging against the Lord's people. However, unlike in Psalm 2, their assault has been successful: Judah, Israel and Jerusalem were **'scattered'** (*zārâ*) by them. Implicit in the use of this word is not only the effect of the nations' assault on God's people, but also the reason for it. In Leviticus 26:33, God threatened to **'scatter'** (*zārâ*) the Israelites among the nations as a punishment for breaking the covenant. The horns are thus depicted as God's covenant agents of judgement who have devastated his people on his instructions.

1:20-21. Then the LORD showed me four craftsmen. I said, 'What are these coming to do?'

He said, 'These are the horns that scattered Judah so much that no man could raise his head. These [craftsmen] have come to terrify them, to throw down the horns of the nations that lifted horns against the land of Judah to scatter them.'

The horns are not alone, however. They are now faced with opposition in the form of **'four craftsmen'**. The word *ḥārāšîm* covers those who work with different kinds of materials and is thus better translated by the English word **'craftsmen'** (NIV, NKJV, ESV) than by a more specific word, such as 'smiths' (those who work with metal, NEB, NLT) or 'carpenters' (those who work with wood, KJV). There are **'four'** of them, forming an equal and opposing force to the horns. The angel responds to the prophet's question, **'What are these coming to do?'**, by first underlining what the horns have been doing. They had **'scattered Judah so much that no man could raise his head'**. In the ancient Near East, defeated captives were made to lie down with their heads under the foot of the conquering king. **'No man could raise his head'** is thus another way of asserting that their victory over Judah was absolute.

But when it comes to the enemies of God, the bigger they come, the harder they fall. The horns which wreaked terrifying destruction on Judah will be terrified by the coming craftsmen. Those who **'lifted horns'** against the land of Judah will themselves have their horns thrown down. Not only does the number of the craftsmen match the number of the horns, the punishment matches the crime. Those who lifted themselves up against the Lord's people will find themselves put in their place.

The identity of the coming craftsmen is left deliberately vague. The key point is not who they are, but what they are coming to do. The nations who assaulted Judah and who are now at rest (1:11,15) will be judged for their attack on God's people. Even though they came as God's agents of judgement to scatter the Israelites, they are not thereby exempt from the provisions of the covenant with Abraham. Those who assault God's people will find themselves under assault by God.

2:1-2. Then I lifted up my eyes and looked: there was a man with a measuring cord in his hand. So I said, 'Where are you going?'

He said to me, 'To measure Jerusalem, to see how wide and long it is.'

The declaration of judgement upon God's enemies itself foreshadows the restoration of God's people. After the destruction of the horns, Zechariah sees another man in motion, going **'with a measuring cord in his hand'**. The word for measuring cord (*ḥebel middâ*) is different from that used in Zechariah 1:16. The term found there, *qav*, is more generic, describing a line employed for a variety of construction and demolition tasks, whereas here it indicates specifically a cord used for measurement. This time the prophet directs his question to the man himself, rather than to the interpreting angel. He asks where the man is going and is told that he is going **'to measure Jerusalem'**. Its overall dimensions must be determined to ensure that it is of sufficient size for the future population; here, however, it is not the dimensions that are of significance so much as the act of measuring itself. This preliminary survey is a sign of the building work to come, in the same way that the sighting of the first swallow is a sign of the coming of spring.

2:3-5. Then the angel who was speaking with me went out and another angel came out to meet him. He said to him, 'Run, speak to that youth: "Jerusalem will be inhabited like an unwalled village because of the number of people and animals within her. I myself will be a wall of fire all around her," declares the LORD; "I will be the glory within her."'

The youth has no sooner set out on his mission than another divine emissary is sent in haste after him. The building survey would prove to be an impossible task because the boundaries of the new Jerusalem will be undefined. In place of the large, but still measurable, city of Ezekiel's vision (Ezek. 45:6), Zechariah's new Jerusalem will become **'like an unwalled village'**, infinitely expandable to meet the needs of the population. This will be necessary because of the vast number of **'people and animals within her'**. No definable space, however large, could be sufficient for such a crowd.

Yet at the same time, the obvious drawback of unwalled villages, the lack of protection for the inhabitants, will no longer be an issue.[17] On the contrary, the Lord himself will be **'a wall of fire all around her'**. This description not only evokes the image of divine protection found in Psalm 125:2:

> As the mountains surround Jerusalem,
>   so the LORD surrounds his people
>   both now and for evermore (NIV);

it also calls to mind the Garden of Eden, protected by a flaming sword. Yet in this case, the purpose of the fiery barrier is not to keep Adam out, but to protect an abundance of humanity (*'ādām*) on the inside! Not only will humans and animals find a home inside the new Jerusalem, the **'glory'** of God itself **'will be ... within her'**. As Ezekiel 43 anticipated, the presence of God in the midst of his people, represented by the glory of God in the temple, would again become a reality.

2:6-7. 'Come on! Come on! Flee from the land of the north,' declares the LORD. 'Indeed, I dispersed you like the four winds of heaven,' declares the LORD. 'Come on, Zion! Escape, you who inhabit Daughter Babylon.'

In view of this forthcoming reality, those who had yet to join the returnees in Judah should hesitate no longer. The word *hôy* is often translated in other contexts as 'Woe!' or 'Alas!', but it is an exclamation

that can cover a range of emotions, including lamen-
tation, doom or exhortation — hence the translation
adopted here: **'Come on!'** The summons is addressed
to those still in **'the land of the north'** — that is,
Babylon. Strictly speaking, Babylon is more to the
east than north of Judah, but the journey to or from
Babylon always passed through the lands north of
Judah, since a more direct path is blocked by the
desert. Though they had been comprehensively **'dispersed'** by the Lord, as if blown all over the place by
'the four winds of heaven', or, as we would put it, to
the four points of the compass, now the Lord was
summoning them to escape and return home.

Those who are God's people still in exile are personified as **'Zion'**,[18] even though they are far away
from their true home. They are urged to escape from
'Daughter Babylon', the personification of their true
home's arch-rival.[19] What has Zion to do with Babylon
any longer, now that the Lord has returned in glory to
Jerusalem?

*2:8-9. For thus says the LORD of hosts: 'After glory, he sent
me to the nations that plundered you. For the one who
touches you touches the pupil of my eye. For look, I am
about to wield my arm against them and they will become
plunder for their servants. Then you will know that the LORD
of hosts has sent me.'*

The opening part of this verse, rendered here as **'After
glory, he sent me to the nations'**, is the most difficult passage to translate in the whole book of Zechariah. Each word is open to more than one interpretation. The main interpretative questions are as
follows: Is **'after glory'** part of the description of the
circumstances in which this message came to Zechariah, or part of the message? Is **'after'** a temporal
preposition here, or does it express purpose? Is **'glory'**
a name for God, the manner in which the message

came ('with insistence'), or the goal of the sending? Who is the one sent — a manifestation of the Lord himself, or the prophet? In what sense is he sent **'to'** the nations?

Given these uncertainties, any interpretation must necessarily remain tentative, and the best approach is to choose the reading that adds least to what could be discerned from the surrounding context and from similar passages elsewhere in the prophets.

We may start by observing that elsewhere in Zechariah the messenger formula, **'Thus says the LORD of hosts'**, always introduces direct speech, so the most natural reading will take **'after glory'** as part of what the Lord says. Moreover, the pursuit of God's own reputation as a motive for the restoration of Judah and Jerusalem is a prominent theme in the book of Ezekiel (see Ezek. 36:22-38; 39:21-29), so reading 'after' in the sense of 'in pursuit of' would fit well here.[20]

In terms of the identity of the person sent, the next verse seems to alternate between first-person references to the Lord (**'I am about to wield my arm'**) and to the prophet (**'Then you will know that the LORD of hosts has sent me'**; cf. 4:9; 6:15), as does Zechariah 2:11. Since the prophet was identified as the very mouthpiece of God, his words could easily switch from the 'I' of the king to the 'I' of the herald. It is simplest, therefore, to regard the one sent to the nations as Zechariah himself. To be sure, Zechariah had no personal ministry to the nations in the sense of preaching among them; however, like many of the prophets, his words declared the coming fate of the nations and counselled them to adopt an appropriate posture before the Lord in his appearing (2:13).

To sum up, then, the best understanding of this difficult passage is as follows: 'In pursuit of [his own] glory, [the LORD of hosts] sent me [Zechariah, with a message] concerning the nations that plundered you.'

The content of that message to the nations is as clear as the previous phrase is obscure: 'Don't touch!' The one who touches Judah or Jerusalem now touches the **'pupil'** of God's **'eye'**.²¹ In English the phrase 'apple of my eye' means the object of special affection; here, however, the idea is more that of the special protection that is afforded to a sensitive part of the anatomy — hence the translation **'pupil of my eye'**. It is no longer 'open season' for attacking God's people. Even though in the past God had brought the four horns to scatter them because of their covenant-breaking, so that **'the nations plundered'** them, now God would reverse the situation. Instead of the nations coming to plunder, the Lord would **'wield [his] arm against them'**, making them **'plunder for their servants'**. In the language of the vision, the mighty horns would be thrown down (1:21). The end result of this action will be the glorification of God and the authentication of his prophet: **'Then you will know that the LORD of hosts has sent me.'**

2:10-13. 'Shout and rejoice, O Daughter Zion, for, look, I am coming and I will dwell in your midst,' declares the LORD. 'Many nations will join themselves to the LORD in that day. They will be my people and I will dwell in your midst. Then you will know that the LORD of hosts sent me to you. The LORD will take possession of Judah as his portion upon the holy land and he will again choose Jerusalem. Be quiet, all flesh, before the LORD, for he has roused himself from his holy habitation.'

The two verbs in **'Shout and rejoice'** indicate simultaneous action: 'Shout joyfully.' This is the language of the enthronement psalms and other passages that look forward to the arrival of the divine King, such as Zephaniah 3. There is ample reason to rejoice: the King is coming to **'dwell'** in the **'midst'** of his people. No longer will they be despised by the nations and their God be regarded as of no account. On the contrary, **'Many nations will join themselves to the LORD in that day.'** There will be a widespread conversion of the Gentiles: they too (the Gentiles!) **'will be my people'**. This envisages a covenant relationship between God and the nations, so that they are joined to the Lord and he makes them his people (cf. Isa. 56:3-5). Nor are these separate covenants, with a 'Plan A' for Israel and a 'Plan B' for the Gentiles. The end result will be one nation, **'my people'**, with God dwelling in their (**'your'**) midst.

This single plan for world redemption is centred on God's covenantal commitment to make his people a holy nation. Just as he did under Joshua, God will again **'take possession of Judah as his portion'**. The goal of the exodus from Egypt was that the Lord would bring his people in and plant them on the mountain of his inheritance, the place he had made for his dwelling, the sanctuary that his hands would establish (Exod. 15:17). That goal, reiterated in the covenant with David in 2 Samuel 7, will reach its fruition as the Lord '[takes] possession of Judah as his portion' and **'again choose[s] Jerusalem'**. Not only will the sanctuary be rebuilt, it will also accomplish its task of sanctifying the land, for this new Judah will be **'the holy land'** (cf. Ezek. 37:27-28). The phrase 'the holy land' (*'admat haqqōdeš*) occurs only here in the Old Testament. However, a similar expression is used in Exodus 3:5 to designate the ground where Moses encounters God at the burning bush. God will accomplish his sanctifying plan to make his people fit for him to dwell among.

Since God is on the move and active, it is time for the created order to fall silent. **'All flesh'** must hold its peace since God has **'roused himself from his holy habitation'**. God, the divine Warrior, has swung into action from his heavenly dwelling place. That action cannot be thwarted by human opposition; indeed,

Psalm 2 informs us that the Lord laughs at any attempt to form an alliance against him (Ps. 2:4). All that is left for the enemies (and the friends!) of God to do is to close their mouths and wait for the Lord to make the final moves before the curtain comes down. Just as schoolboys who have been chattering confidently in the absence of the teacher are silenced by word of his return, so the nations who have been confidently posturing and boasting of their strength are summoned to be silent before the All-Powerful One.

Application

There are two essential points to be made from this passage, with application to three classes of hearers.

First, *judgement will come on those who elevate themselves against the Lord and his people*. In the past, the nations came at God's bidding to bring judgement upon Israel and Judah. They broke the conditions of the Mosaic covenant and received the penalty they deserved. But if judgement began with the house of God, what will it mean for the nations? (1 Peter 4:17-18). The nations will be held accountable for indulging their appetite for ferocity at the expense of God's people. Their present state of rest (1:11) can only be temporary. As God promised in Psalm 75:10, 'The horns of all the wicked I will cut off, but I will lift up the horns of the righteous.' God can summon up skilled destroyers to take down the wicked whenever he wishes, just as the police can call on SWAT (Special Weapons and Tactics) teams when an emergency arises.

Secondly, after the judgement upon the nations comes *the final establishment of rest for God's chosen ones*, in which the goal of all of the covenants finds its fulfilment. God's purpose is not simply to punish the nations, but to restore the world, to re-establish the Edenic state of God dwelling in the midst of his people on holy ground. God will return in glory to dwell in the midst of his city with an unnumbered quantity of Adam's descendants. The wall of fire will protect them, rather than keeping them at a safe distance. How will all of this happen? In the song of Zechariah, the father of John the Baptist, we see that Christ is the one who comes not only to destroy the wicked but to raise a horn of salvation for his people (Luke 1:69-75).

There are also three key imperatives in this passage that show us the three groups called upon to respond to this message.

The first is directed to *the unreturned exiles* in 2:6-7. This addresses those who are God's people but are still scattered. The challenge to this group is to get in step with God's programme. Return to Zion, the place of God's presence, and join in whole-heartedly with what God is doing.

The second imperative, in Zechariah 2:10-11, addresses *those already in Zion*. These faithful ones are exhorted to sing and rejoice, to celebrate what God has done and is about to do. Rejoice as you contemplate the glorious future that awaits us, a future that extends beyond ethnic Israel to bring the nations too into God's covenant people.

The third imperative is addressed to *the nations who are still rebellious*. This speaks to the unbelievers who hear this passage. Be still, be silent in the face of this awesome coming. In the language of Psalm 2, bow down now while there is still time to receive his mercy, or you will certainly be destroyed by his wrath. Kiss the Son now, lest his anger be kindled against you!

Reclothed and restored
(Zechariah 3:1-10)

For the first time in the book of Zechariah, this vision introduces us to a historical person, Joshua the high priest. In fact, both of the central visions of the sequence, Zechariah 3 and 4, concern the two individuals who are central to the life of the restored community, Joshua and Zerubbabel, and their significance as signs of God's future purposes for his people. Joshua and Zerubbabel had already become active participants in the rebuilding work on the temple initiated by Haggai (Hag. 1:14), but Zechariah shows us the broader significance of their existence as signs of the greater things yet to come.

3:1. Then he showed me Joshua, the high priest, standing before the angel of the LORD, with the Accuser standing at his right hand to accuse him.

Zechariah's visions now take him to the heavenly court, where the interpreting angel shows him a trial in progress. The defendant, **'Joshua, the high priest'**, is **'standing before'** the judge, language which fits both a legal and royal setting, as does the English word 'court'. The judge is **'the angel of the LORD'**, who himself represents the Lord, the Judge of all the earth. 'The angel of the LORD' is very closely associated with the Lord, so that he can sit in jurisdiction over such an important case, and the words attributed directly to the Lord in the next verse are apparently spoken by the angel of the Lord as his representative.[22] None the less, he is at the same time distinct from the Lord, so that a dialogue between the two of them is possible (see 1:12). This therefore seems best explained as a Christophany, a visible manifestation of the Second Person of the Trinity prior to the incarnation.[23]

Also present at the trial is **'the Accuser'** (*haśśāṭān*). Although this enemy of God's people has been active from earliest times in the Garden of Eden, his identity as 'the Accuser' — which is literally what 'Satan' means — became more prominent as history unfolded. In the Old Testament he appears under this title seeking to lead God's people astray and then making charges against them in the context of the heavenly court (Job 1 – 2; 1 Chr. 21:1). This depiction may have received added weight after the exile from the well-developed spying system employed by the Mesopotamian authorities in the Neo-Babylonian period.[24] Unseen informers reported regularly to the king on various activities of his subjects, leading to punishment for the alleged transgressions. Satan's very name indicates his activity here: he is present to **'accuse'** (*śāṭan*) Joshua — that is, to present evidence before the heavenly court which he thinks should lead to Joshua's condemnation.

3:2. The LORD said to the Accuser, 'May the LORD rebuke you, Accuser! May the LORD who has chosen Jerusalem rebuke you! Is not this a log that has been rescued from the fire?'

The Accuser has potentially a very strong case, as is apparent from Joshua's defiled state in verse 3. However, before he is even allowed to present his evidence, it is immediately ruled out of order. It is important to note the significance of this ruling. Far from Satan being permitted to bring charges, the presiding authority responds: **'May the LORD rebuke you, Accuser!'**

The Lord does not merely examine the Accuser's case and find it wanting. Rather, he rules that any possible evidence that might be brought is inadmissible. No charge whatever can be brought before the court against Joshua, because the Lord himself is the one **'who has chosen Jerusalem'**. The Lord's election of Jerusalem and Joshua's position as one who has been **'rescued from the fire'** — that is, one brought safely from the holocaust of the exile — mean that he is free from any possible condemnation. He is not merely found 'not guilty'; he is judicially declared immune from prosecution.

3:3-5. Now Joshua was clothed in excrement-soiled clothes and he was standing before the angel. Then he answered and said to those who were standing before him, 'Take away the excrement-soiled clothes from him,' and he said to him, 'See, I have removed your iniquity from you and am dressing you in festival clothes.'

Then I said, 'Place a clean turban on his head,' and they placed a clean turban on his head and they dressed him in [fresh] clothes while the angel of the LORD was standing there.

This ruling is crucial because Joshua is, in fact, guilty as charged — or as he would have been charged had the Accuser been given the chance to do so. He is **'clothed in excrement-soiled clothes'** (3:3). This is attire that is not simply dirty, or even disgusting, as the common translation 'filthy' would suggest, but intrinsically defiling. He is self-evidently ceremonially unclean, yet he finds himself **'before the angel'** of the Lord, and therefore in the presence of the God whose eyes are too pure to look upon sin (Hab. 1:13). The fires of judgement in the exile have not purified him at all, but have left him in his iniquity. Nor is this simply Joshua's personal problem. As high priest, it is his task to act as the intermediary for the people on the

Day of Atonement (Lev. 16), removing their impurity. If the high priest is unfit to be in the presence of God, then the whole sacrificial system is compromised and all hope for the people is gone.

But God does not simply judicially rule any condemnation for Joshua out of order. He also subsequently acts to cleanse Joshua from his **'iniquity'** (3:4). What the fire of God's wrath could not accomplish, God achieves by his grace. Negatively, he commands his servants, **'Take away the excrement-soiled clothes,'** which removes Joshua's sin and shame. Positively, he commands that Joshua be clothed in **'festival clothes'**, garments suitable to stand in the presence of the King of kings. In a context where filthy garments represent iniquity, these 'festival clothes' can only represent an altogether new righteousness that accompanies Joshua's new status, which is imputed to him by grace.

Finally, the prophet himself breaks in and requests the completion of this act of reclothing with the placing of a **'clean turban'** (*ṣānîp*) on Joshua's head (3:5). This turban is not distinctively priestly clothing; rather, it has overtones of glory and even royalty (Isa. 3:23; 62:3). This is literally the 'crowning' moment of the whole ceremony: Joshua is reclothed in ceremonially pure, festival garments in the presence of **'the angel of the LORD'** as a sign of God's acceptance of him and, in him, of the people he represented.

3:6-7. Then the angel of the LORD charged Joshua: 'Thus says the LORD of hosts: "If you walk in my ways and if you keep my charge, and if[25] you also judge my house and guard my courts, then I will grant to you access [or 'men who go'][26] among these who stand [before me]."'

Joshua's new clothes are not a signal to sit back and bask in his new-found glory. Like the cleansed prophet in Isaiah 6, Joshua is immediately **'charged'** with a task and granted a promise. His task is to **'walk in my ways'**, **'keep my charge'**, **'judge my house and guard my courts'** (3:7). The first two of these requirements are very general ways of describing faithful behaviour within a covenant context,[27] while the second pair identifies what that behaviour requires of a faithful priest. Joshua is to judge God's house and guard his courts — that is, to ensure that the worship in the temple is pure and undefiled by idolatry (compare Ezek. 44:23-24). This is not a new obligation in the post-exilic setting; it is simply a recommissioning to the tasks that would have been his responsibility prior to the exile, albeit now without the oversight of a king.

The promised reward for Joshua if he obeys these stipulations is some form of **'access among these who stand'** before the Lord. The exact meaning of the word 'access' is uncertain: it may be that the access is mediated by angelic messengers (see note 26), but however the word is translated, Joshua is promised unusually direct communication with the divine council. He is not in this on his own: he can take his concerns to the Lord and expect to be heard, and he can also expect to receive guidance and direction from the throne room. The Lord will not be silent or distant any longer. The staircase to heaven is once again open for traffic (see Gen. 28:12).

3:8-10. 'Listen, Joshua — you and your associates who sit before you. They are indeed men of portent, for I am about to bring my servant, the Branch. For look, the stone which I have set before you: upon one stone there are seven eyes [or facets]. Look, I am engraving its inscription upon it,' declares the LORD of hosts. 'Thus I will remove the iniquity of this land in one day. In that day,' declares the LORD of hosts, 'each man will invite his neighbour under his vine and under his fig tree.'

Even this remarkable promise of divine attentiveness is merely a shadow of things to come. For **'Joshua'** and his **'associates'**, the whole priestly class, were **'men of portent'**: their very existence after the holocaust of the exile was a sign of God's blessing, a blessing that had far more to give than the people had yet experienced. They had already experienced the first fruits of that favour in the return from exile and the reversal of the curse that had rested upon the people because of their covenant-breaking, but the future held even more. Specifically, the future blessing involved the coming of **'my servant, the Branch,'** and the complete and instantaneous removal of **'the iniquity of this land'**. When that happened, the complete blessing of the restored covenant relationship would be experienced: **'... each man will invite his neighbour under his vine and under his fig tree.'** The fertility and peace of the land would be fully restored, just as at the height of the empire under Solomon (1 Kings 4:25; see also Micah 4:4).

The name of this coming future figure is **'my servant, the Branch'**.[28] There is a reference here to Jeremiah 23:5, which itself promises a reversal of the rejection of Jehoiachin by the Lord in Jeremiah 22:30. Through the prophet Jeremiah, the Lord declared that none of Jehoiachin's seed will sit on his throne. None the less, God will again raise up a righteous descendant for David who will reign with justice and will establish salvation for his people. Only the intervention of God could accomplish such a thing, an intervention on a par with the exodus from Egypt (Jer. 23:7-8). This promise is now reiterated by Zechariah and linked to the sign of the existence of Joshua and his fellow priests.

Joshua's attention is directed to an engraved **'stone'**. This stone is most probably part of the high priest's clothing, a gemstone with seven facets[29] associated with the turban and inscribed with an

'inscription'. Aaron's turban had just such an orna-
ment, engraved with the words 'Holy to the LORD',
which enabled him to bear the iniquity of the people
before the Lord (Exod. 28:36-38).[30] This stone has
been prepared by God and engraved by him, for he is
the one who will act to remove the 'iniquity of [the]
land' definitively.

Application

The issue in this chapter is the cleansing required by God's people
if they are to stand in his presence. Is Joshua the high priest fit to
stand before God and carry out his calling of removing their
iniquity through the various sacrificial rituals laid down by God?
How can Joshua be fit for such a task, having been born in exile
and brought up in a defiled land? The accusation itself has
apparent merit: Joshua *is* unfit to appear and serve before the
Lord, and God doesn't pretend that a little touch-up is all that is
required. Joshua needs nothing less than stripping and complete
reclothing before he can carry out his task. Satan is eager for the
opportunity to press the charges. Yet his case is immediately ruled
out of order. Joshua will serve as an accepted intermediary before
the Lord because of God's sovereign choice of Jerusalem and of
Judah.

Like Joshua the high priest, we too are unfit to appear before
God. We have all gone astray and deserve nothing other than the
wages of our sin. We need nothing less than total cleansing if we
are to live, a cleansing that is far more than us trying to turn over a
new leaf. Yet because of God's sovereign choice to save for
himself a people, burning sticks like us will not be consumed by
the fire. By his grace, God takes us and justifies us, reclothing us
in borrowed robes of righteousness that enable us to approach the
throne of grace. Since our justification is all of grace, through the
merit of Christ, there can be no condemnation for those who are in
Christ Jesus (Rom. 8:1). Satan's charges against God's saints are
all ruled out of order, inadmissible in the divine courtroom.

God doesn't simply justify sinners, however; he also sanctifies them, turning them into saints who are fit to serve. It is striking that Paul picks up this same imagery of reclothing in Ephesians 4:24 to describe the work of sanctification: put off the old garments; put on the new robes through the Spirit's work of renewing your minds so that you may be fit to serve God. We are to respond to the grace we have received by living in line with the gospel. This is merely fitting behaviour for those who have become a royal priesthood before God (1 Peter 2:9).

The reclothing of Joshua is not the central focus of the passage. Joshua is present as the representative of his people, and the climactic element of the vision is the turban, with its inscribed plate that enables him, as high priest, to bear their iniquity before the Lord (cf. Exod. 28:36-38). The result of this cleansing of the people's representative is renewed traffic between God and man, angelic messengers going back and forth between them.

Zechariah's vision becomes a reality with the arrival of 'my servant, the Branch', the Messiah. Here, with the rich insight of the New Testament fulfilment, we can see how everything Joshua received was enabled by Jesus making the opposite move.

- Joshua received a clean turban on his head. Jesus was crowned with thorns, which were pressed down onto his forehead until the blood ran down his face.
- Joshua was clothed in festival garments. Jesus had the clothing stripped from his back and divided among those who crucified him.
- Joshua was judged and declared clean on the basis of God's choice of him for salvation, found not guilty of defilement that was really his. Jesus was judged by sinners, found guilty on trumped-up charges, and handed over to be scourged and crucified. Yet this too was God's choice (Acts 4:28).
- Joshua's sin was taken away; he was declared innocent, able to stand before God as high priest for his people, bearing their name before God. Jesus, who committed no sin, was made sin by God (2 Cor. 5:21) and was separated from God the Father by that burden.

Our sign is Jesus on the cross. He is the one through whose death the sins of his people were removed in a single day; he is the one through whose death we are restored to fellowship with God, fellowship with our neighbours and the blessings of a restored creation.

Jesus is no longer on the cross. Now he has been raised up from the dead, clothed in glory, crowned in honour, given the name above every name. Now he is our heavenly High Priest, effectively interceding for us before the very throne of God. Now when Satan accuses us, he responds: 'Objection! This client's sin has been paid for on my back. I was burned for him; I bled for her! God has chosen this person.' God the Father responds in turn: 'Objection sustained! Let this one come in! There is now no condemnation for this brand snatched from the fire, for it has all been nailed to the cross with Christ.'

Hope for a day of small things
(Zechariah 4:1-14)

How do you keep going when there is little to show for your labours? It is easy to preach if thousands flock to hear your every word, easy to counsel people whose lives are healed by your wisdom, easy to lead when others are eager to follow. But how do you cope when the reality is the reverse, and it seems that all of your efforts go for nothing? What if you are called to be part of the church in a day and place of small things? Zechariah 4 has the answer.

4:1-3. Then the angel who had spoken with me returned and he roused me like a man who is roused from his sleep.

He said to me, 'What do you see?', and I said, 'I see [literally. "I looked and behold"] a solid gold lampstand, with a bowl at its top with seven lamps on it and seven spouts to the lamps which were at its top. There were two olive trees above it, one to the right of the bowl and one to its left.'

Once again the interpreting angel came to Zechariah and **'roused'** him. He was not actually asleep (otherwise the phrase **'like a man who is roused from his sleep'** would be totally redundant), but his perception of reality during the visionary experience was as much heightened in comparison with ordinary life as wakefulness is compared with sleep. The angel prompted him to recount his vision, which consisted of a **'solid gold lampstand'** flanked by **'two olive trees'**. A **'lampstand'**, or menorah, is almost always a ritual object, especially one made of **'gold'**: there was a single lampstand of gold in the tabernacle (Exod. 25:31-40) and there were ten in Solomon's temple (2 Chr. 4:7,20). The lampstand supported a **'bowl'**, which acted as a reservoir for the oil. Arranged around the bowl were **'seven lamps'**, each of which had **'seven spouts'**. Individual seven-spouted lamps have been uncovered by archaeologists at Late Bronze Age Dothan;[31] however, the combination of seven of these around a single bowl is unique. The result would be forty-nine wicks to give light, a kind of 'super-menorah'. This lampstand was at the centre of the scene the prophet saw, with an olive tree on either side of it.

4:4-6. Then I answered and said to the angel who was talking with me, 'What are these, sir?'
   The angel who was speaking with me answered and said to me, 'Do you not know what these are?'
   I said, 'No, sir.'
   Then he answered and said to me, 'This is the word of the LORD to Zerubbabel: "Not by excellence and not by strength but by my Spirit"', says the LORD of hosts.'

We are not surprised to discover that the prophet does not find the meaning of the vision self-evident. He is forced to ask the angel, **'What are these, sir?'** However, the angel's response, **'Do you not know what these are?'**, suggests that Zechariah should not have found the meaning so obscure. Nor does the angel immediately explain the significance of the lampstand and the trees. Instead, he launches into an oracle addressed to Zerubbabel. Only later, when the prophet reiterates his question, does the angel explain the elements of the vision. He is not being deliberately evasive. Instead, in the oracle he is explaining in plain speech the message of the vision, perhaps assuming that once you know the meaning, it will be simple to explain the different elements that make up the whole picture.[32]

The oracle is addressed to **'Zerubbabel'**, the governor of the people, who, along with Joshua the high priest, had been charged with the task of rebuilding the temple by the prophet Haggai (Hag. 1:1). As with Zechariah 3, therefore, we have a word concerning a named historical individual. God's Word to him is a reminder that the obstacles that face him in the rebuilding task will not be overcome by conventional resources. It is not a matter of mere **'excellence'** (*ḥayil*)[33] or **'strength'** (*kōaḥ*). The resources will come from an outpouring of God's **'Spirit'**, just as was promised back in Haggai 2:5. With that assurance of divine aid given first, the 'great mountain' (4:7) is already rhetorically cut down to size, just as Goliath is scaled down to his proper proportions as soon as David identifies him as an uncircumcised Philistine who has defied the armies of the living God (1 Sam. 17:26).

4:7-10. Who are you, O great mountain? Before Zerubbabel you shall become level ground. He shall bring out the chief stone to shouts of '[May God show] favour, favour to it.'

Then the word of the LORD came to me saying, 'The hands of Zerubbabel laid the foundation of this house, and his hands shall bring it to an end. Then you will know that the LORD of hosts has sent me to you.' For who has despised the day of little things? They shall rejoice when they see the foundation-deposit stone in the hand of Zerubbabel. These seven are the eyes of the LORD that are roaming around in all the earth.

What (or strictly 'who' — the Hebrew has *mî*) is the **'great mountain'**? Perhaps it is best to leave that answer as open as the text does. The great mountain encompasses both the practical difficulties of rebuilding (such as the mountain of rubble that had to be overcome), the political difficulties of rebuilding (opponents, sceptics and enemies) and the spiritual difficulties of rebuilding (spiritual opposition and warfare, of the kind that is evident in the previous chapter). Any and all of these problems will prove too great for unaided human effort to overcome, no matter how naturally gifted the builders are. Yet all of these challenges added together are not grounds for despair if **'the LORD of hosts'** is active by his Spirit. Because the Lord has purposed it, all of these obstacles will become **'level ground'** in front of Zerubbabel. Just as in Isaiah 40:4, the uneven ground will be levelled out and the rough places become a plain when God begins his work of restoring his people.

The result will be that Zerubbabel will bring out the **'chief stone'** of the temple. This 'chief [or "first"] stone' may be a stone from the former temple marking the continuity of the present building with its predecessor,[34] or it may be the capstone marking the completion of the building.[35] One would mark the formal beginning of the rebuilding, the other the end. In terms of the overall meaning, however, there is not a great distinction between these choices, since there is no question of the programme halting halfway: **'the hands of Zerubbabel'** both **'laid the foundation of this house'** and will **'bring it to an end'** (4:9). The people will respond to Zerubbabel's action by invoking God's blessing upon the building. Their cry of ḥēn, ḥēn ('Favour, favour on it!') is a request for divine acceptance of the completed building, recognizing that without such favour the building will be useless.

The completion of the temple would vindicate the prophet's authenticity: then the people would know that he has indeed been sent by the Lord of hosts. The prophet's words were evidently not convincing to all his hearers at the time. Some looked around them and characterized their times as a **'day of little things'**. Shouldn't the day of the Lord be a day of great things and dramatic interventions? (See Deut. 10:21; Ps. 71:19). In spite of the rebuilding of the temple, nothing seemed to them to have fundamentally changed. These critics were not just doubting the legitimacy of the present work; they were actively rejecting it, scorning it as inappropriate and useless. In a similar way, Haggai had encountered those who thought that it was not yet time to rebuild the temple (Hag. 1:2). But God's work may start in small and unobtrusive ways, unseen to all but the observant eye.

Even the sceptics, though, will be brought to **'rejoice when they see the foundation-deposit stone in the hand of Zerubbabel'** and the results that flow from the completion of the temple. Like the 'first stone' in Zechariah 4:7, the exact meaning of the expression translated **'foundation-deposit stone'** (literally, 'tin stone,' *hā'eben habbᵉdîl*) has attracted a variety of interpretations. Older versions, following the Septuagint and Targum, understood this to be a plumbline.[36] However, more recent archaeological explorations have uncovered the practice of incorporating deposits of a variety of precious or semi-precious materials in the foundations of ancient temples,[37] and this seems best to fit into that category of object. Zerubbabel would begin the task and he would also bring it to completion.

At this point, then, we are ready to ask how the oracle clarifies the vision and answers the prophet's question, 'What are these?' The oracle declares that in spite of obstacles and naysayers, Zerubbabel would finish the work of building the temple, not because of his native abilities and gifts, but as a result of an outpouring of the divine Spirit. If that is what the vision is about, it is not too hard to see that the lampstand represents the temple, which, with its seven times seven lights, is once again restored to its purpose in the world.

There are still a number of details that remain to be clarified, however, and it is to these that the passage turns next. What do the lamps represent? **'These seven'** (i.e. the seven lamps on top of the lampstand) **'are the eyes of the LORD that are roaming around in all the earth'** (4:10). **'The eyes of the LORD'** do not merely represent his watchfulness and awareness of everything that is going on. In 2 Chronicles 16:9 exactly the same phrase occurs: 'the eyes of the LORD that are roaming around in all the earth'. The purpose of this watchfulness in Chronicles was to reward King Asa's faithfulness with a victory in war. So also here, God is not merely watching from his temple; he is watching over his people for their good in response to their faithfulness.[38] The temple that was being rebuilt would serve as the foundation for a new relationship of blessing for God's people.

4:11-14. I answered and I said to him, 'What are these two olive trees that are on the right of the lampstand and on its left?'
    I answered a second time and said to him, 'What are the two olive twigs that are beside the two golden pipes which are pouring gold out of them?'
    He said to me, 'Do you not know what these are?' and I said, 'No sir.'
    He said, 'These two are the sons of olive oil who stand beside the Lord of all the earth.'

One part of the vision remains to be clarified, so the prophet asks further questions. What are the two olive trees on either side of the lampstand, and how are they connected to the lampstand? Once again, some of the details are obscure. The **'two olive twigs'** and the **'two golden pipes'** were not mentioned in the original description of the vision. The word translated **'twigs'** (*šibbōlet*) refers more commonly to spikes of grain than to parts of a tree, and the word for **'pipes'** (*ṣanterôt*) occurs only here. However, whatever the nature of these objects, their function is clear: to transmit olive oil directly from the inexhaustible source of the two olive trees to the bowl of the lampstand, thus ensuring that the lamps will never go out. This flowing oil is literally designated **'gold'**, which not only fits the colour of olive oil, but underlines the richness of the provision for this unique golden lampstand.

The source of the oil is the two olive trees which flank the lampstand. The significance of these two trees has been much misunderstood. The angel tells Zechariah that **'These two are the sons of olive oil who stand beside the Lord of all the earth'** (4:14). The phrase **'sons of olive oil'** (*benê hayyiṣhār*) does not mean 'anointed ones'. When anointing is in view, the word for oil is always *šemen*, not *yiṣhār*. *Yiṣhār* indicates 'new oil', which is one of the marks of the fertility that flows from God's blessing (cf. Hag. 1:11).[39] A vineyard that is a 'son of oil' (*ben-šemen*) is a fertile vineyard in Isaiah 5:1. So these trees are the source of endless fertility, and hence unlimited amounts of oil for the lampstand. Moreover, they **'stand beside the Lord of all the earth'** (4:14). They do not stand *before* (*'āmad lipnê*) the Lord to serve him; they stand *beside* (*'āmad 'al*) him as members of his heavenly court.[40] This description does not apply to Zerubbabel and Joshua, who as governor and priest had no direct access to the heavenly court. It could possibly describe Haggai and Zechariah, who as prophets had entrance into the heavenly deliberations. More likely, however, it describes heavenly beings who act as God's agents in supplying unlimited divine assistance to the restored temple.[41]

Application

The key to understanding and applying this vision lies in the oracle, which hints at the problems that the vision addresses. In a 'day of small things', when mighty acts of God seem in short supply, there is a great temptation on the one hand to trust in human wisdom and skill, and on the other hand to despair of ever seeing anything significant happening. The answer to these twin temptations is the prophetic declaration that Zerubbabel will finish what he started, the temple will be rebuilt and the blessing of the omniscient God will be restored to their midst. But this will happen not because of human might or power, but by the work of God's Spirit. If that Spirit is at work in and through us, then no obstacle, whether practical, political or spiritual, can stand in our way. Every mountain, no matter how great, will be made low, every rough place made smooth, for the mouth of the Lord has spoken it (Isa. 40:4-5). Zerubbabel's beginning of the work was a sign of God's purposes, just as the reclothing of Joshua in the previous vision was a sign of God's favour.

The same principles hold true for us in the present-day church. We too may face a 'day of small things', in which there seems little sign of blessing on the church. In that situation, shepherds of God's flock are pulled in two directions. On the one hand, we are tempted to trust in the latest manifestation of the arm of the flesh: we are easily drawn towards modern slick marketing techniques or prompted to change our ministry model to match that of some more 'successful' congregation. If we water down our convictions, we are promised guaranteed results. On the other hand, we may be tempted to despair and to leave the ministry altogether, because there seems to be so little fruit for our labours. What preacher has never faced that temptation on a particularly bleak Monday morning?

The vision of Zechariah 4 does not promise us a technique to fill our churches in a short period of time. Some are called to labour faithfully in places and at times where there is little visible fruit. Just getting the method and the message right is not enough. It is always a work of God's Spirit that builds and establishes his church, not our skill and efficiency. Yet at the same time, we should not lose hope even though the present blessing of God is small. On the last day, God will certainly accomplish his goal of gathering a glorious people for himself, and even our small contribution will play a part in that grand reality.

So where is our Zerubbabel? Where is our guarantee of hope in the midst of sometimes depressing outward realities? Who holds the stone for us? The answer lies in the one to whom Zerubbabel pointed, as descendant of David and governor of God's people — Jesus Christ. Jesus has come and has established the foundation of the new temple in his death and resurrection. It didn't seem much of an edifice that first Easter Saturday. The men walking on the road to Emmaus certainly wouldn't have characterized it as a day of great things. But the seed that was buried in the tomb in dishonour burst forth on the third day in resurrection power! It was impossible for the tomb to hold him! He is the Christ, the Son of God, and on the truth of that statement, he is building his church. Satanic forces continue to strive against it, but even the very gates of hell shall not prevail (Matt. 16:18).

The foundation of God's new house is already laid, not of gold or silver or tin, but the foundation of Jesus Christ (1 Cor. 3:11). We now come along as fellow-builders, carefully seeking to build on that foundation in ways that are faithful to it. Our work will be tested by fire, but what is true will remain, for the reality is that it is God who does the work, not us. The lamp of God cannot go out, for all of God's resources are committed to his presence for blessing in the midst of his people. He has begun a good work in our hearts, and he will certainly bring it to completion in the day of great things when Christ returns (Phil. 1:6).

How shall we then live?
(Zechariah 5:1-11)

It was all very well for the post-exilic community to believe that the temple would be rebuilt. But mere cleansing from past sins and their consequences was not enough. The issue of remaining sin in their midst was also crucial. If the first temple was destroyed because of the people's sins, which brought down God's covenant curse upon their heads, how would this new temple endure, seeing that they were still sinners? The good news of the gospel is that when we become Christians God doesn't just forgive us our past sins, through justification. He has also committed himself to deal with our present and ongoing sins, through sanctification. The challenge of the gospel is summed up in the statement that 'Without holiness, no one will see the Lord' (Heb. 12:14). There is no room for an easy-believism in the presence of a holy God: those who remain unpurified sinners will ultimately be rooted out, for they were never really part of God's flock. The assurance of the gospel, though, is that the end result of the sanctification process for all who are genuinely God's children will be their complete purification, so that they are fit to have God dwell in their midst.

5:1-2. Then I returned and lifted up my eyes and I looked and saw a flying scroll! He said to me, 'What do you see?'
    I said, 'I see a flying scroll twenty cubits long and ten cubits wide.'

The next vision that the prophet encounters is of a gigantic scroll flying in mid-air. Its dimensions (30 feet by 15, or 9 metres by 4.5 metres) are those of a large billboard rather than any conventional writing surface. It has been suggested that the dimensions are significantly the same as those of the forecourt of the temple, the place where judgement would be meted out.[42] However, the measurements may simply serve the purpose of indicating the enormous size of this document: this is a scroll suitable for God himself to write on. They also suggest that the scroll is unrolled so that its fearful contents may be read.[43] Its location between heaven and earth suits a divine decree which has been sent forth and is now in the process of seeking out its target, like a heavenly 'smart bomb' launched from high altitude. You can run from such a mobile missive, but where would you hide?

5:3-4. He said to me, 'This is the curse which is going out over the face of the whole land: for on the one side, according to it, every thief shall be purged out, and on the other, according to it, everyone who swears [falsely][44] shall be purged out. "I am sending it out," declares the LORD of hosts. "It shall come to the house of the thief and to the one who swears falsely in my name. It shall lodge in the midst of his house and it shall destroy it, whether it is wood or stone."'

The purpose of the scroll is clarified by the angel. It is **'a curse ... going out over the face of the whole land'**. The word *'ereṣ* is ambiguous and could theoretically indicate that the whole earth will be purged, but the rest of the oracle indicates that a more restricted focus is in view here.[45] The scroll is a flying covenant document, written on both sides, like the tablets of testimony in Exodus 32:15. Its task is to bring the covenant curses to bear on covenant-breakers, here represented by the **'thief'** and the **'one who swears [falsely]'**. Theft was a sin against one's fellow man, while swearing falsely was an offence against God, since the oath was taken **'in my name'** (5:4; see Lev. 19:11-12, where both of these sins are condemned together). Indeed, the two sins were often connected, since someone accused of theft where there was no hard evidence to corroborate the charge might be brought before the Lord to swear an oath of self-imprecation (Exod. 22:10-11). The temptation to perjury would have been strong and the threat of divine sanction was the only deterrent.

These offences (stealing and false swearing) stand as representatives of all kinds of breaches of the covenant. All covenant-breakers will **'be purged out'**[46] from the covenant community. God himself is **'sending ... out'** the curse, so there can be no escape. The curse will **'lodge in the ... house'** of the covenant-breaker and will **'destroy it'**, no matter what building materials have been used. The threat of destroying the house of a covenant-breaker is attested in both biblical and extra-biblical texts, notably Ezra 6:11.[47] Here, that threat will become a reality as covenant-breakers receive their just deserts.

5:5-8. Then the angel who was speaking with me went out and said to me, 'Lift up your eyes and see this which is going out.'

I said, 'What is this?', and he replied, 'This is a measuring jar[48] which is going out.' And he said, 'This is their iniquity[49] in all the land.'

The lead cover was raised and there was a certain woman sitting inside the jar! He said to me, 'This is wickedness.' He threw her back down into the measuring jar and slammed down the lead stopper into its mouth.

In the second half of Zechariah 5, the prophet receives a second vision that is closely linked to the first. The first vision threatened destruction to the apostates, while the second threatens deportation. Since to be cut off from the covenant community was to be cut off from the source of life, these two punishments are closely related.[50]

What the prophet saw was a **'measuring jar'**, literally, an ephah. Unlike the gigantic scroll, the ephah is a relatively small unit of measure, about a bushel in size. Like the scroll, this measuring jar is also in motion, but in its case the motion is **'going out'**, bearing its contents away. Inside the measuring jar is **'their iniquity in all the land'**, personified as a woman. She is restrained in the jar by a circular **'lead cover'**, literally, a 'lead talent'. A talent was a measure of weight, roughly seventy-five pounds (or 34 kilos). Normally 'talent' was associated with precious metals such as gold or silver, but a base metal like lead was more suitable for this profane task. It is thus an unusual but substantial restraint, which keeps the woman trapped in the jar like a genie in a lamp.[51]

Why is wickedness personified in female form here? Who is the **'woman'**? Most likely it represents an idolatrous image of a female deity.[52] Such cult objects have been routinely uncovered throughout ancient Israel, and the seated position of the woman may represent an enthroned deity, such as Asherah. She represents **'wickedness'** (hāriš'â), which elsewhere is a comprehensive term for all kinds of sin, both religious and social (Deut. 9:4; 2 Chr. 22:2-3). The broad usage to cover sins both against God and against fellow members of the covenant community is perhaps alluded to by the details of the vision. The idolatrous figure, representing sins against God, is contained by an ephah and a talent, the weights and measures that figured prominently whenever the prophets of Israel rebuked the sins of the marketplace (Lev. 19:36; Micah 6:10-11).[53]

It is also possible that the woman to be removed represents the foreign wives that were such a problem in the time of Ezra and Nehemiah (Ezra 9; Neh.

13:23-27). The two issues are not unconnected, since the concern over foreign wives was precisely the potential for the Israelites to be led into idolatry by their spouses (Neh. 13:26). But what is in view in this vision seems rather larger than simply the removal of foreign women, who merely constituted one source of temptation. This vision envisages nothing less than the removal of all iniquity from the land, as promised in Zechariah 3:9.

Having shown the prophet the dangerous contents of the container, the angel is careful that nothing is allowed to escape from this particular Pandora's box. He **'threw her back down'** into the measuring jar and **'slammed down the lead stopper in its**[54] **mouth'**. The language is strong, even violent, showing that there is no danger of the situation getting out of control. Wickedness is not a force equal and opposite to God; it exists under his power and authority.

5:9-11. Then I lifted up my eyes and looked and saw two women going out with the wind in their wings (they had wings like the wings of a stork). They lifted up the jar between earth and heaven.

Then I said to the angel who was talking with me, 'Where are they taking the jar?'

'To build a house for it in the land of Shinar. It will be set up and firmly established there on its stand.'

The wickedness that has been personified in female shape is now removed by two figures of female shape — **'two women'**. They are in motion, with **'the wind** [*rûaḥ*] **in their wings'**. The wind is the divine agency of motion (see Ps. 18:10), indicating that their actions are undertaken at the Lord's bidding. They are also equipped for this task by having **'wings like the wings of a stork'**. The stork was an unclean bird (Lev. 11:19), and it is often suggested that this is why such creatures were appropriate for this particular task.

However, eagles were also unclean birds (Lev. 11:13), yet their wings were a suitable representation of the ever-renewed strength of God's faithful ones (Isa. 40:31). The fact that an animal is unclean for food does not mean that it must always have that figurative significance whenever it appears. Here the choice of stork's wings may simply reflect the fact that storks are large birds who migrate northwards from Palestine each year, travelling in the same direction as the measuring jar, in order to nest and hatch their young.

The women lifted up the jar **'between earth and heaven'** (5:9). Prior to the age of jet transportation, this was the location where divinely initiated journeys took place (see Ezek. 8:3). The **'jar'** of wickedness is not merely being removed *from* the land of God's people; it is being removed *to* a new location, which has been prepared for it (5:11). There, in **'the land of Shinar'** (Babylon), they will build a **'house'**, or temple, for it. There it will stay permanently, **'firmly established ... on its stand'**. The antithesis of a rebuilt house for the Lord in Jerusalem is a rebuilt tower of Babel in Shinar (Gen. 11:2). Similarly, in the New Testament Babylon is depicted as the woman of wickedness who constantly opposes God's people (Rev. 18).

Here in Zechariah, however, there is no sense of threat from a resurgent paganism. Rather, all of the idolaters, along with the object of their idolatry, will have been removed to a safe distance from which they will never again return to trouble God's people by their wickedness. A final separation will take place between believer and unbeliever, with the unbelievers cast out to pursue their empty life in the defiled city of Babylon.

Application

The two visions that make up Zechariah 5 deal with the removal of sins of different kinds in varying ways. What unites them is the comprehensiveness, certainty and finality of God's judgement upon sin. In contrast to the vision of chapter 3, where the sin of Joshua is dealt with redemptively, here sin is dealt with judicially, through the execution and exile of the sinners. Sin cannot be ignored by God; it must be dealt with effectively. If this is not done through the sinner coming to Christ by faith and receiving salvation, then it must be done through the death of the sinner, or his banishment into the uttermost darkness. How shall you escape the coming judgement of God, given its comprehensiveness, certainty and finality, if you neglect the one means of escape he has provided?

But the removal of the impure from the midst of God's people also points to the purification of what remains. If all the sinners are to be destroyed or exiled, then what remains must surely be a purified remnant. It is good news to Israel that the idolater and the thief will no longer be in the land, and that wickedness will feature only in the 'export' line of their balance of payments. It is good news because it points to the certainty of God's sanctifying work. His restored people will at long last become a holy nation, made fit to receive the blessings of the covenant, not its curse. In that pursuit of holiness, Judah is the only place to be. Remaining in Babylon, the natural habitat of idolatry and wickedness, is not a wise choice, no matter how economically attractive it may seem. The Babylonian option is the road to nowhere. The future for God's people lies in the new Jerusalem.

If this is the case, then we should certainly press onward with all of our energy to pursue holiness in the present. 'Sin shall not have dominion over you' (Rom. 6:14) is a promise that should encourage us to live lives of new obedience. It is a promise that God will ultimately cleanse our hearts from all unrighteousness, and that the power of our idols to command our obedience has been broken at the cross. So, therefore, in the meantime, we should no longer surrender our bodies to sin's demands as we used to do, but instead submit them to God as instruments of righteousness (Rom. 6:13).

The kingdoms of this world belong to our God and to his Christ
(Zechariah 6:1-15)

The final image in Zechariah's sequence of night visions brings us full circle. The military and equine imagery invites us to see the invisible army of God on the march, no longer merely observing what is occurring in the world, but actively intervening to transform the world.

6:1-3. Then I returned and I lifted up my eyes and I saw four chariots going out from between two mountains. The mountains were mountains of bronze. The first chariot had dark brown[55] horses, the second had black horses, the third chariot had white horses, while the fourth had speckled horses; [all of them were] strong.

What the prophet saw in this final vision is clearly connected back to the first vision. In place of the four coloured horses that he saw in Zechariah 1:8, he now saw **'four chariots'** with horses of different colours going out from between two **'mountains of bronze'**. The most notable feature associated with **'bronze'** in the Old Testament is its shiny appearance. Thus in Ezekiel 1:7 the fearsome cherubim 'gleam like burnished bronze', while the curse of drought is described vividly by the statement that 'The sky over your head will be bronze' (Deut. 28:23, NIV) — that is, it will gleam with constant, relentless sunshine.[56] The bronze mountains from which the chariots come, therefore, are mountains whose appearance shines with light. This immediately sets up a contrast with the opening vision, where the horses are concealed among the myrtles in the depths. Indeed, whereas the first vision is set in the night, when all around is dark, this one has the appearance of day, or at least of sunrise.[57]

From these mountains come **'four chariots'**. Again, there is a striking difference from the opening vision, with its horsemen. The riders in the dark of the opening vision were the Special Forces' advance teams, carrying out covert operations, surveying the world and reporting back to the heavenly command centre. But chariots were the ancient equivalent of tanks, the key symbol of military power. What is more, these chariots are pulled by no ordinary horses — all of them were **'strong'** — and there are **'four'** of them, the number of completeness. The symbolism is potent. The data gathering is complete and the signal has been given from the divine high command: 'Let's roll!' The heavenly army is on the move; the might of this world's empires is about to be overtaken by the omnipotent power of the Lord of hosts.

6:4-8. Then I answered and said to the angel who was speaking with me, 'What are these, sir?'

The angel answered and said to me, 'These are the four winds of heaven going out from presenting themselves to the Lord of all the earth. The one with the black horses is going to the land of the north, and the white ones will go after them, while the speckled ones will go to the land of the south.'

The strong ones went out and sought to go and patrol the earth. Then he said, 'Go! Patrol the earth,' and they patrolled the earth.

Then he called me and spoke to me: 'See, the ones going out to the land of the north have given rest to my Spirit in the land of the north.'

Once again, the prophet asked the interpreting angel to explain the vision. The angel responded that the chariots represented the **'four winds of heaven'**, who had been **'presenting themselves to the Lord of all the earth'**. The reference to the **'four winds of heaven'** stresses the universality of their range: nowhere in the world is outside their reach (cf. 2:6). But there is also a play on words here: the Hebrew word for 'wind' (*rûaḥ*) is the same as that for 'Spirit' (see 6:8), so these winds also represent the agency of divine power at work in the world. In a similar way in Zechariah 5:9, the wind (*rûaḥ*) in the women's wings was responsible for carrying the ephah of wickedness from Judah to Babylon. The very winds of heaven must do the Lord's bidding: his will is accomplished 'not by [human] excellence, not by [human] strength, but by my Spirit, says the LORD of hosts' (4:6).

The chariots then divide up and go in different directions. We would expect the four different coloured pairs of horses to go to the four points of the compass, especially since they have just been identified with the four winds of heaven. Commentators therefore routinely emend the text to match their expectations. However, the text as it stands mentions only two directions: the **'black'** and the **'white'** horses go to **'the land of the north'**, while the **'speckled'** horses go **'to the land of the south'**. The dark brown horses mentioned earlier are not included in the commission.[58] Perhaps they are being held in reserve, following the analogy of a military campaign. The directions assigned to the divine army may have been influenced by the topography and location of Judah. The major roads head north and south from Judah, since to the west is the Mediterranean Sea and to the east is the desert. Judah's main enemies always came from the north (Babylon, Assyria, Persia) or the south (Egypt), and any military operation beginning in Judah would necessarily proceed outwards on these two fronts.

'The strong ones' — that is the chariots of the Lord of hosts — move out at the divine command and 'patrol the earth', asserting and imposing God's sovereign rule over the whole world. But this assertion of universal sovereignty has a particular focus: not all directions of the compass are equally of interest. The prime target is 'the land of the north' — i.e. Babylon — which is the objective assigned to two of the four chariots. If there is any opposition to the divine invasion force in its assault on Babylon, it is not worth mentioning. Victory is complete: God's 'Spirit' is 'given rest ... in the land of the north', the former home of his enemies. As in Deuteronomy 12:10, 'giving rest' (*Hiphil* of *nûḥ*) implies the full and final defeat of those opposed to God and to his people.

This vision thus answers the question implicit in the previous one, to which it is linked by the repeated use of 'go out' (*yâṣâ'*). In that vision, idolatry was driven (carried) out of God's land to the land of Babel, where a temple was prepared for it (5:5-11). The focus there was on the purification of God's people, with idolatry no longer existing in their midst as a threat to God's presence. Now the focus shifts to answer the question: 'Will these idolaters possess Babylon for ever, in an ongoing enmity to God? Will there always be a threatening location from which to launch regular attacks on God's people from the uttermost north, as Gog does in Ezekiel 38 – 39?' To which Zechariah's vision responds: 'No, God will ultimately send out his power to the uttermost corners of the earth, and his Spirit will reign throughout the world, even in the place where now the seat of idolatry is located.' The nations that at present feel secure in their opposition to God are in for an unpleasant surprise when God rouses himself to action (cf. 1:15,20).

6:9-11. Then the word of the LORD came to me saying, 'Take from the exiles — from Heldai, Tobiah and Jedaiah, who have returned from Babylon; you yourself shall go in on that day; you shall go in to the house of Josiah, the son of Zephaniah. Take silver and gold and make a crown[59] and place it on the head of Joshua, son of Jehozadak, the high priest.'

Having dealt with the final fate of those opposed to God, the prophet turns back to his primary interest — the future of God's people. In Deuteronomy 12:10 rest from enemies all around is the prerequisite for temple-building. Here too, the ideas are linked through a symbolic act of coronation. **'Joshua, son of Jehozadak, the high priest,'** is to be crowned with a **'crown'** of **'silver and gold'**. Such a composite crown is unusual, to say the least, but it reflects the expectation of Haggai 2:8 that both of these precious metals would come to the temple from afar and fill it with glory. This connection highlights an important aspect of the coronation, yet one which is often overlooked. It is not just a matter of who is crowned, but who provides the resources for the sign act, namely a series of designated individuals among the exiles. Identifying these exiles as the ones who provide the resources for this symbolic filling of the temple with glory is not mere fund-raising rhetoric but an important theological statement in its own right. Those **'who have returned from Babylon'** are at the centre of God's plan for the future (see also 6:15).

That plan also involves an honorific place for **'Joshua ... the high priest'**. He is to be crowned, but not in order to convey kingship or power to him personally. As the following oracle makes clear, his crowning is merely symbolic of the reality to come.

6:12-13. You shall say to him, 'Thus says the LORD of hosts: "Look, a man! The Branch is his name; he will branch out from his place and he will build the temple of the LORD. He himself will build the temple of the LORD and he will bear royal majesty; he will sit and rule on his throne. There will be[60] a priest upon his throne and a counsel of peace will be between the two of them."'

This coming reality is still future. This is strikingly made plain by the lack of a personal name for the coming one (and for his priest) in the midst of a narrative filled with personal names. Those who supply the materials and the one to be symbolically crowned all have personal names, but this coming one is as yet merely known by his code name, **'the Branch'**. Once again there is a reference back to the prophecies of Jeremiah, in this case Jeremiah 33:15. There the Lord says, 'I will make a righteous Branch sprout from David's line' (NIV). Zechariah reiterates this promise of a coming king who will flourish and branch out. This coming one will **'build the temple of the LORD'** and **'bear royal majesty'**. The phrase **'royal majesty'** (*hôd*) is used both of God and of earthly rulers, especially kings. It reflects both the authority and the legitimacy of their rule, a contrast to their current situation of subservience to their Persian overlords.

The coming king will sit on his throne, with **'a priest'** seated on a **'throne'** next to him. The continuance of the Davidic monarchy and the Levitical priesthood are intertwined issues in Jeremiah 33. If the king is necessary to rebuild the temple, the Levitical priests are necessary to stand before the Lord in that renewed temple, offering sacrifices (Jer. 33:18). **'Between the two of them'**, the future king and the future priest, there will be **'a counsel of peace'**. This is not simply an assertion that there will be peace and harmony between these two offices, although it certainly includes that. It also implies that the result that flows from this happy state is itself peace (*šālôm*), blessing for all, flowing from this renewed, temple-centred state (see Hag. 2:9).

6:14-15. 'The crown will belong to Helem, Tobiah, Jedaiah and for Hen the son of Zephaniah as a memorial in the temple of the LORD. Those who are far off will come in and will work on the temple of the LORD. Then you shall know that the LORD of hosts has sent me to you. This will happen if you indeed listen to the voice of the LORD your God.'

Just as we began this oracle with named exiles, so we close it in the same way, showing that the prophet's interest is not just in the certainty of future blessing, but in the present responsibilities that need to be observed. Two of the four names are slightly different: Heldai has become **'Helem'** and Josiah has become **'Hen'**. These may perhaps be nicknames. Alternatively, Hen (or more precisely *lḥn*) may be a title for a temple official, whose job it was to care for precious commodities, like this **'crown'**.[61] The crown is to be stored **'as a memorial in the temple of the LORD'**. The purpose of a memorial (*zikkārôn*) is to keep the matter constantly before the Lord, rather than the people, which is why it is located in the temple (cf. Exod. 30:11-16; Num. 10:9-10). Of course, the crown also served secondarily as a reminder to the community of God's plans for their future. After all, the Lord did not commission the crown because he was afraid that otherwise he might forget to do these things, in the way that we might write ourselves a note and stick it onto the refrigerator as an aid to our memory! It serves as an assurance for the people of God's determination to bring these things to pass.

Specifically, this rebuilding is not merely a task for those already in Jerusalem. Those who are at present still afar off will come and assist in the rebuilding task. They too will **'work on** [*bānâ bᵉ*] **the temple of the LORD'**. This unusual idiom indicates that there is both similarity to and difference from the foundational work of the Branch. Their work is secondary, auxiliary to the primary building work of the Branch. They must continue faithfully to **'listen to the voice of the LORD [their] God'**, remaining in the posture adopted in Haggai 1:12. Then they will see their hopes fulfilled.

Application

Taken together, both halves of Zechariah 6 point our attention ahead into the 'not yet'. A memorial crown placed in the temple self-evidently implies that 'These things are not for the present', as does the reference to the promised but unspecified man to come, the Branch. Yet it points our attention to the future as an encouragement to obedience in the present. The concluding exhortation to 'listen to the voice of the LORD your God' is the goal of the whole chapter. We may therefore summarize the message of the chapter under three imperatives.

First, *be hopeful*. God's covenant purposes will be fulfilled. Those purposes include full and final judgement upon his enemies and full and final salvation for his people. Eventually, every knee will be forced to bow, even in the home of idolatry, great Babylon itself (cf. Rev. 18). Eventually, the coming Branch, Jesus Christ, will establish the new temple in his own body. He unites in his person the two offices of king and priest, thereby making his people also kings and priests to God. What the covenant with David and the covenant with Levi pointed forward to is accomplished in his death, resurrection and glorification. The result of his coming is peace even now between us and God (Rom. 5:1). In the future, he will establish his peace throughout the cosmos. All this leaves no room for us to despair, even if our personal corner of time and space seems to be a 'day of small things'.

Secondly, *be thankful*. God's covenant people were once those who were afar off, sent into exile for their sin. They deserved to be permanently cut off, but God's covenant faithfulness transcended their sin and brought them back. Former exiles like these are given a place in God's building programme. Here indeed is grace! Have we not also, as those who once were enemies of God, similar cause to be thankful that we too are saved by his grace and given a place in his building programme, called to build on the foundation of Jesus Christ? (1 Cor. 3:10-11). What a privilege is ours!

Thirdly, *be faithful.* God's people must listen to his voice. That call will often be costly, as it was for Helem and his friends. Building God's house takes our very best, and that for an enterprise that will seem wasteful or speculative to many around us. But faithfulness will not go unrewarded in God's service. The future is certain and it belongs to those who serve God wholeheartedly in the present.

Ritual or reality?
(Zechariah 7:1-14)

Why do we do the various religious acts that the Scriptures call us to? Are these merely an outward conformity on our part to rules and regulations, by which we hope to appease God? Or does our obedience flow out of hearts that delight in the salvation he has given us? The heart is what makes the difference between mere ritual and profound reality.

7:1-3. In the fourth year of Darius the king, the word of the LORD came to Zechariah on the fourth of the ninth month, in Kislev. Bethel-Sarezer,[62] along with Regem-Melek and his men, sent to entreat the face of the LORD, saying to the priests of the house of the LORD of hosts and the prophets, 'Should I weep in the fifth month with abstaining, just as I have done these many years?'

The passage opens with the third and final date formula in the book of Zechariah. The formula separates chapters 7 – 8 off from 1:7 – 6:15 and marks this passage as a new section. This is the seventh date in Haggai / Zechariah 1 – 8, a feature that binds together the two books. Its precise form also creates an *inclusio* with the first date in Haggai 1:1. These two are the only dates in this sequence that begin with reference to the year of **'Darius the king'**, and then are followed by the calendar date.[63] In some ways, therefore, Haggai 1 – 2 and Zechariah 7 – 8 act as bookends around the visions of Zechariah 1 – 6. **'The fourth year of**

Darius' is two years after Zechariah's earlier prophecies; **'the ninth month'** would be December 518 BC. It is thus two years after the ceremony to begin rebuilding the temple, but still two or three years before its completion.

'Bethel-Sarezer' and **'Regem-Melek'** sent an enquiry to the Jerusalem temple addressed to **'the priests'** and **'the prophets'**. It is unusual in the Old Testament to have a query addressed to both priest and prophet. Normally, the priests dealt with issues of interpretation of the Scriptures (see, for example, Hag. 2:11), while the prophets handled questions concerning the will of God (at least after the Urim and Thummim ceased to be viable means of divination; see, for example, 1 Kings 22:6). Here the question dealt with an issue of ritual (hence the involvement of the priests), yet it was a question to which there was no obvious 'Torah-based' answer, a fact which may explain the inclusion of the prophets. Alternatively, the petitioners could simply have been appealing to all of the available authorities.

'Abstaining' (from food and other luxuries) and weeping were ritual acts of mourning aimed at demonstrating repentance and thereby effecting a change of God's disposition towards those who were fasting (see 2 Sam. 12:21-22, where David fasted and wept for his infant son, and Dan. 10:2-3, where Daniel abstained from delicacies while praying for the future of his people). **'The fifth month'** was the time of year when the temple in Jerusalem had been destroyed. For nearly seventy years, they had observed a ritual act commemorating the destruction of the temple. Now that the temple was being rebuilt, it was natural to question whether there was any need to observe the rite any longer. Wasn't the rebuilding itself sufficient evidence that God's disposition towards his people was once again favourable and that fasting could finally be dispensed with?

7:4-7. The word of the LORD of hosts came to me saying, 'Say to all the people of the land and to the priests, "When you fasted and lamented in the fifth and seventh [month] these seventy years, was the fast you observed for me? When you eat and drink, is it not for yourselves you are eating and drinking? Were not these the things that the LORD proclaimed through the former prophets when Jerusalem was inhabited and at peace, with her cities around her and the Negev and the Shephelah were inhabited?"'

The ruling that came to Zechariah in response to this request applied not simply to the petitioners, but more broadly to all the inhabitants of the land, and included the fasts observed in the **'seventh'** month as well as the **'fifth'**. As befits a prophet who was also a priest, the response utilizes more technical terminology to describe how they **'fasted and lamented'**. The fast in the seventh month probably commemorated the assassination of Gedaliah, the governor the Babylonians had installed in Jerusalem, which brought to an end even the semblance of Judean self-rule (Jer. 41:1-3). Both of these fasts persist in the Jewish tradition.[64] The **'Negev'** is the area to the south of Jerusalem, around Beersheba, while the **'Shephelah'** is the lowland region to the west of Jerusalem, the site of many battles between Israel and the Philistines.

How do these three questions from the Lord answer the enquiry of the petitioners? The original enquiry reflected a purely ritual concern: now that the temple is being rebuilt, do we have to keep on ritually humiliating ourselves over its former destruction? The Lord's response through Zechariah pushed the issue deeper, however. The Lord asked, 'When you fasted, was it really out of a genuine concern over the loss of my favour? If you stop fasting and return to normal eating and drinking, does that mean an abandonment of that concern?'

These questions probe the real issue. The Lord was asking, 'Have you learned the lesson that the exile was intended to teach?' The destruction of the temple in 586 BC was not simply the result of the Lord throwing a cosmic temper tantrum, out of which he could be mollified by the right religious rites, without any genuine change of heart on the part of his people. On the contrary, it was the outpouring of the appropriate judgement on Jerusalem and Judea for her sins. If they had learned that lesson, and had truly repented and turned from their sins, then by all means they could stop fasting. The temple was being rebuilt. However, if they had not learned the lesson but had been fasting for themselves all along, then the fasting itself was a waste of time.

7:8-10. The word of the LORD came to Zechariah saying, 'This is what the LORD of hosts said: "Judge justly; let each show covenant faithfulness and mercy to his brother. Do not oppress the widow and the orphan, the stranger and the poor. Do not plot evil against your brother in your hearts."'

How could the people tell whether they were truly sorry for the sin itself, and not simply for the sin's consequences? The answer is that true repentance does not stop with a religious rite of mourning, but presses on into a changed life of obedience to God. Specifically, true repentance will show itself in justice and compassion. The language used here is not a direct quote from any one biblical source, but sounds like numerous passages in the Law and the Prophets. The **'widow and the orphan, the stranger and the poor'** include all of the naturally disadvantaged groups in society, who would be easy targets for the strong. Yet taking advantage of their weakness was forbidden since these people too are **'your brother[s]'**, part of the one family of God.

7:11-14. But they refused to pay attention and they turned their stubborn shoulder and closed their ears from hearing. They made their hearts like flint so as not to hear the law and the words which the LORD of hosts sent by his Spirit through the former prophets. So the LORD of hosts grew extremely angry. 'Just as I[65] called and they would not listen, so also they called and I would not listen,' declares the LORD of hosts. 'I blew them away in a storm to all the nations that they had not known. The land was left too desolate behind them for anyone to pass through or return. They turned the delightful land into a desolate waste.'

This concern for the weaker members of society was precisely what the Lord had required of his people in the former days, before Jerusalem's fall. The **'law'** and the **'words'** of the **'prophets'** were the two parallel means by which God communicated his will to Israel, through the priests and prophets. Yet the former generations **'refused to pay attention'** to God's self-revelation. They turned their backs on the Lord and thus incurred his anger (see 1:2). His judgement came upon them like a mighty storm, which scatters everything in its path (compare the ominous vision of the Lord's coming in the midst of a storm in Ezek. 1:4). They were scattered among **'nations that they had not known'** — that is, nations with whom they had not previously had friendly relationships, which left the exiles as newcomers without any legal standing or recourse, extremely vulnerable. Meanwhile, the **'delightful land'**, which the Lord had promised to give his people, was left **'a desolate waste'**, unfit not merely for habitation, but even for passing through on a journey.

The point being made here is that the judgement that descended on the former generation in the form of the curses of the covenant was inevitable, given their stubborn covenant-breaking. The result of their sin was that any attempt to seek the Lord was fruitless:

since they didn't listen when the Lord called, neither would he heed their calls. This past state of affairs acted both as a warning and as a promise for the future, themes that will be developed further in the following chapter. If the destruction that resulted in the exile was the Lord's work in response to the covenant-breaking of the people, then those who are truly repentant may confidently expect the Lord to bring about complete restoration. If that is their attitude, then the days of fasting may come to an end. But if they are merely going through the ritual motions with their fasting and have no intention of obeying God's Word, then all of their fasting is in vain. Obedience is the necessary prerequisite for blessing, not mere ritual observance.

Application

This chapter begins with a pious enquiry. A reasonable query is sent to the right people in the right tone of voice asking, 'Is God's judgement finally over?' In return, Zechariah asks a probing question: 'What lies at the heart of your religious act? What is your fasting and feasting all about?' The same question could be asked of all of our religious acts: 'Why do you go to church? Why do you read the Bible and pray?' These are all good things to do, but if we are merely doing them for ourselves, then they are a waste of time.

The probing question is followed by a challenging command: 'Keep the law and the prophets; love your neighbour, whom you see on a daily basis, as evidence that you truly love God, whom you do not see' (see 1 John 4:20). Don't rely on religious rituals if there is no matching evidence of a true change of life (see James 1:27). Indeed, this passage proclaims a fearful reality: that judgement comes on all covenant-breakers, even religious ones. The generation that was judged had called out to God, yet they received no response from him because they themselves had not been responsive to his commands. It is not enough to pray, even to the one and only true God. Without obedience, there can be no fellowship with the Lord.

The focus of Zechariah 7 is primarily law rather than gospel. To offer hope, we need to look ahead into chapter 8 (in fact, there might be merit in preaching on the two chapters as a single unit). In Zechariah 8, the challenging command of chapter 7 is placed in the context of a wonderful reality — God's faithfulness to his covenant promise (8:1-3). God's judgement on covenant-breakers is not, and cannot be, his last word to his people. God's final word is redemptive transformation. Fasting will ultimately be transformed into feasting (8:19).

That proclamation of hope in spite of Israel's sin still leaves open the question of how to reconcile the two realities. How can the very angry God (7:12) also be very zealous for his people? (8:2). The same combination of emotions was present back in Zechariah 1:15 -16. The answer is that God's wrath over the sins of his people was satisfied in the destruction and rebuilding of the true temple to which the building in Jerusalem pointed, the body of Jesus Christ (John 2:19). On the cross, Jesus Christ himself was made desolate by the wrath of God as an atoning sacrifice for covenant-breakers.

What is our response? It should be true spiritual fasting and feasting. We should fast as a response to our sin and as a means of seeking the Lord's face in this present barren land. We should also feast as we look forward to the kingdom to come, the marriage supper of the Lamb. This is what we do when we celebrate the Lord's Supper. Both our feasting and our fasting should be carried out in a Christ-centred way, not as a mere ritual, but as an outward expression of genuine inner repentance and faith. When we fast, we do so not to manipulate God, but to recall Christ's sufferings and to testify to the incompleteness of the best that this world has to offer. When we feast, we do so not to feed our flesh, but to feed our hunger for the eternal feast. Finally, our fasting and feasting should never be alone, but should flow out into works of justice and mercy to all, as a sign that in Jesus Christ the kingdom has indeed come.

Are we there yet?
(Zechariah 8:1-23)

At first sight, Zechariah 7 – 8 looks like a miscellaneous collection of oracles.[66] What is it that holds these disparate threads together and gives them the message that they distinctively contribute to biblical revelation? The answer lies in the historical setting of the passage. Times were not simply hard for Zechariah's hearers in the way that they are often hard for God's people, but specifically as a result of God's curse on a nation of covenant-breakers. That was ostensibly why the fasts mourning the events of 586 BC were celebrated. Now, though, the temple was being rebuilt. Was it time yet to stop fasting? (7:3). Had the day of God's favour arrived yet? Was the final state of bliss to be expected any day now?

8:1-3. Then the word of the LORD of hosts came: 'Thus says the LORD of hosts: "I am zealous for Zion with a great zeal; I am zealous for her with a great passion."

'Thus says the LORD: "I will return to Zion; I will dwell in the midst of Jerusalem. Jerusalem will be named 'City of Truth' and the mountain of the LORD of hosts 'the Holy Mountain'."'

The sombre word of judgement in the previous chapter is not the end of the story. Rather, God's commitment to his chosen city is decisive. The seventy years of her judgement are reaching an end, and now there is to be a new beginning, as promised in the similar language of Zechariah 1:14-16. This prospect is so sure that the commitments, **'I will return,'** and **'I will dwell,'** are in the perfect tense, as though they had already happened. In the days ahead, Jerusalem would indeed be the **'City of Truth'** and Zion would be **'the Holy Mountain'**. The dwelling place of the true and holy God would be peopled by truth-telling, holy inhabitants (cf. 2:12). It is not enough for God to return to the land; for his return to be a blessing, the community must also be transformed.

8:4-6. Thus says the LORD of hosts: 'Once again, old men and old women will sit in the squares of Jerusalem, each with a stick in their hand on account of their great age. The squares of the city will be filled with boys and girls playing in her squares.'

Thus says the LORD of hosts: 'If it will be a miracle in the eyes of the remnant of this people in those days, will it be a miracle in my eyes also?' declares the LORD of hosts.

There is a double merism here: old and young, male and female are depicted relaxing and playing in the open areas of Jerusalem — an idyllic picture of opposite extremes that implies peace for all ages and both sexes. Such healthy play and relaxed rest contrasted dramatically with the slave labour, malnutrition and starvation that had been the fate of the former Jerusalem, and even with their present straitened circumstances. The future holds blessing once more. Such a transformation may seem to Zechariah's hearers like a **'miracle'** (literally, a 'wonder', in the technical sense of something miraculous), but it is the sort of miracle that the Creator God of the universe does routinely. The normal interrogative marker is lacking on the last clause in Hebrew, perhaps expressing a sense of sarcasm: is anything really too hard for the Lord, even the miraculous?

8:7-8. Thus says the LORD of hosts: 'I am about to save my people from the land of the sunrise and from the land where the sun sets. I will bring them in, and they will dwell in the midst of Jerusalem. They will be my people and I will be their God, in truth and righteousness.'

Once again the Lord uses a merism to underscore the comprehensiveness of his salvation: he will save his people from the **'land of the sunrise'** (the uttermost east) and **'the land where the sun sets'** (the uttermost west), and everywhere in between. Normally, it is the Lord who will go **'in'** and **'dwell in … Jerusalem'**. But the Lord and his people are inseparable. It is not enough for him to return to Jerusalem unless all of his chosen ones are likewise brought in, so that the relationship which is the central goal of the covenant can be realized: **'They will be my people and I will be their God.'** Elsewhere the language of **'truth and righteousness'** is used to describe the faithfulness of David in 1 Kings 3:6, and the absence of these qualities depicts the unfaithfulness of Israel in Isaiah 48:1. The renewed Israel will not be like their forefathers.

8:9-11. Thus says the LORD of hosts: 'Strengthen your hands, you who hear in these days these words from the mouth of the prophets who [were] in the day when the house of the LORD of hosts was refounded, so that the temple might be rebuilt. Before those days, there were no wages for man or domestic animal. There was no peace from the enemy for going out or coming in, for I had turned loose every man against his neighbour. But now, I will not be to the remnant of this people as I was in former days,' declares the LORD of hosts.

The idiom **'from the mouth of the prophets'** normally refers to the reading aloud in public of written prophetic materials,[67] which is a mark of the fact that the prophetic writings were already regarded as having canonical authority among God's people. As in Haggai, the refounding of the temple marked a turning point in Israel's fortunes. This change in God's attitude to his people should result in bold activity on their part in serving him (cf. Hag. 2:4). In the past, there had not been the general peace and prosperity that were the necessary prerequisite for free travel and economic stability. Indeed, there were dangers from abroad (**'the enemy'**) and from near at hand (**'his neighbour'**). **'But now'** the state of affairs described in verse 10 is past history; a brighter future of favour and blessing lies ahead.

8:12-15. 'Seed will prosper, the vine will give its fruit, the land will give its produce and the heavens will give their dew. I will cause the remnant of this people to inherit all these things. Just as you have been a curse among the nations, house of Judah and house of Israel, so also I will save you and you will become a blessing. Do not be afraid; strengthen your hands.'

Indeed, thus says the LORD of hosts: 'Just as I planned disaster for you when your fathers made me angry,' says the LORD of hosts, 'and I had no compassion, so now I have turned. I plan in these days to do what is good for Jerusalem and the house of Judah. Do not be afraid.'

'Seed will prosper' is literally 'a sowing of peace'. Peace (*shalom*) occurs four times in this chapter, twice describing the state of God's blessing (8:10,12) and twice as part of the righteous lifestyle which Judah is called to pursue in response to that blessing (8:16,19). **'The vine'**, which is the first item in Haggai's list of four core agricultural products that are marks of God's blessing (Hag. 2:19), here stands as representative of total agricultural blessing. These agricultural blessings are themselves covenantal blessings, the result of **'the land [giving] its produce, and the heavens ... their dew'** (cf. Deut. 33:28). The situation of covenant curse, described in precisely these terms in Haggai 1:10, had been reversed, as had the **'disaster'** God brought on their fathers: the faithful **'remnant'** of the people would now inherit the fruit of their labours. This remnant is larger than merely the kingdom of Judah: it will include the **'house of Israel'**, the remnant of the northern kingdom, as well. Just as when they were under God's wrath, their name was often used by others as a **'curse'**, so now that they are under God's blessing their name will become a formula of **'blessing'** for the nations (cf. Ruth 4:11-12). God's faithfulness in judging their rebellion in the past should encourage them to be obedient as they look to the future. The goal of God's election of a people for himself in Genesis 12:2 will finally and certainly be realized: because they have turned to the Lord, they would find him turned towards them in blessing (see 1:1-6).

8:16-17. 'These are the things you shall do: Each of you shall speak truth to his neighbour; true and complete justice you shall render in your gates. No one shall plot evil against his neighbour in his heart, and you shall not love swearing what is false, for all these are things that I hate,' declares the LORD.

If Jerusalem is to be 'the City of Truth' (8:3), then its inhabitants will need to be transformed into people of **'truth'**. Truth is foundational for a stable society, as is **'justice'**. In the ancient world, the city **'gates'** contained seats where the prominent citizens would gather and where justice was dispensed. As in Zechariah 7:9-10, the prophet here gives a summary of the law in a style typical of the Pentateuch, even though it is not a direct quote of any passage in the Law. What God had earlier commanded their forefathers and they had refused to heed, to their cost, is now reiterated for the new generation. Their fresh start of divine favour and grace must issue in faithful covenant living on their part in order that God may once again dwell in their midst in the renewed temple. As with Israel's original deliverance out of Egypt, the experience of God's grace comes first, which forms the foundation for the call to obey his law (see Exod. 20:1-17).

8:18-19. The word of the LORD of hosts came to me saying, 'Thus says the LORD of hosts: "The fasts of the fourth, fifth, seventh and tenth months will become happy occasions for the house of Judah, times of rejoicing and joyful assemblies. Love truth and peace!"'

The Jews were at this time observing fasts each year on four dates that had significance in recalling the destruction of Jerusalem in 586 BC. The **'fourth'** month was when Zedekiah and the Judean leadership fled Jerusalem after the walls were initially breached, leading to the king's capture and death at the hands of the Babylonians (2 Kings 25:3-7). The **'fifth'** month was the date of the actual fall of the city of Jerusalem to Nebuchadnezzar (2 Kings 25:8). The **'seventh'** month commemorated the death of Gedaliah and the end of any kind of Judean rule (2 Kings 25:25), while the **'tenth'** month marked the date of the beginning of siege of Jerusalem (2 Kings 25:1). These solemn reminders of Judah's sin and its consequences would be transformed from times of fasting to feasting, from expressions of sorrow over sin and its fruits to celebrations of joy over salvation and its fruits. **'Love'** in the Bible is covenantal language, not emotional: to **'love truth and peace'** implies a dedicated commitment to pursue these things, rather than to have warm, fuzzy feelings about them. It is the opposite of loving to swear what is false (8:17). The blessing that would come from the work begun with the raising up of the temple should provide the motivation to lives of renewed obedience.

8:20-23. Thus says the LORD of hosts: 'Peoples will once again come in, along with the inhabitants of many cities.' The inhabitants of one will go to another, saying, 'Let us indeed go to entreat the face of the LORD and to seek the LORD of hosts. I myself am going.' Many peoples and mighty nations will go in to seek the LORD of hosts in Jerusalem and to entreat the face of the LORD. Thus says the LORD of hosts: 'In those days, ten men from nations of every language will seize the corner of the robe of one Jew saying, "Let us go with you, for we have heard that God is with you."'

The eschatological blessing of the future is not just for Jerusalem or Judah, nor even merely for the remnant of the house of Israel (8:13); it must extend more broadly to include the **'peoples'** — that is, the composite population of the surrounding area that was culturally akin to Judah, as well as also ultimately encompassing the **'mighty nations'**, their former enemies. Bethel-Sharezer and Regem-Melek are a kind of first fruits of this eschatological ingathering through their sending to **'entreat the face of the LORD'** (see 7:2). What is in view here goes beyond an ingathering of the Diaspora; it extends even to a bringing in of all nations, tribes and languages, as they recognize that God is indeed with his people. In that day, the judgement of the exile in which God was not with his people (at least, not in Jerusalem) would finally be over.

Application

To see the relevance of this passage, we first have to locate it in its original setting in redemptive history. Times were not simply hard for the Judeans in the way that they are often hard for God's people, but specifically as a result of God's curse on a nation of covenant-breakers. That is why they had been observing these fasts. Now that the temple had been rebuilt, was it time to stop fasting yet? The prophet's answer in the previous chapter was to remind his hearers of God's faithfulness in bringing upon the covenant-breakers the judgement they deserved. Since the fathers did not take to heart the words of the earlier prophets and live like covenant-keepers, they reaped the whirlwind. But his argument in chapter 7 is preliminary, setting up the point he is making in chapter 8. God's covenant faithfulness is determinative for the future, not the unfaithfulness of his people. He will fulfil his purpose in electing Zion. He will return to the city and dwell in the midst of his people again. The result will be the blessings of happy youth and blessed old age, peace for all ages.

The prophet anticipates a response of incredulity on the part of his hearers, which he meets with the question: 'Is even such a miraculous transformation really a wonder in the Lord's sight?' Clearly, the answer is 'No'. Our God can easily do things far harder than this.

What difference is this supposed to make to Zechariah's hearers? They are to be strong, remembering the prophetic word. They are to watch for the transformation that will flow from the restoration of the temple, which is the visible symbol of the return of God's presence to the midst of his people. Such a hope should free them from fear of the future and motivate them to live as those who have been redeemed by the Lord, living out the unmerited grace of God in holy lives. In the meantime, they should look forward to the consummation of God's blessing. Though they were now fasting because of the outworking of God's judgement, one day they would feast because of the outworking of God's salvation. One day, God's temple would be a centre for all creation, a place where every tribe, language and people group would go up and seek the Lord.

We too live in a fallen world that exists under the curse of God. We too feel the effects of that curse in sickness, pain, frustration and broken relationships. Therefore, we too can receive encouragement from the prophet's words. For us, that means that we must recognize that much of the pain around us is the result of the Fall and its associated curse. We are men and women of unclean lips who dwell in the midst of a people of unclean lips (Isa. 6:5). In recognition of the sin that is within us and around us, it is appropriate for us to fast to express our personal repentance and sorrow for sin and its bitter fruits. Yet the curse is not the end of the story because of God's electing grace. God will have those whom he has chosen for himself, and nothing in the world can prevent that purpose from triumphing. God will bring to completion his sanctifying work in our hearts and the hearts of all those who are his people; our present fasting will ultimately be turned into eschatological feasting in the marriage supper of the Lamb.

The prerequisite for the marriage supper of the Lamb, though, was the slaughter of the Lamb. The Lamb that will be exalted had first to become the Lamb that was slain. In him, the presence of God came and tabernacled among his people, yet his own would not receive him. Instead, they stripped him, beat him and mockingly crowned him with thorns. In so doing, they unwittingly opened the door of salvation to God's people from every tribe and language group, from north and south and east and west. These now gather at the heavenly Mount Zion, the holy mountain of God, where they celebrate the day on which the Holy One of God became the atoning sacrifice for our sins. In the Lord's Supper, we look back to the day of our deliverance and look forward to the glorious future that awaits us, when we will be done with our fasting and mortifying of our sinful flesh once and for all. On that day, death will finally be swallowed up in victory and the wedding feast of the Lamb will at last be consummated.

Prisoners of hope
(Zechariah 9:1-17)

Life was tough for Zechariah's audience. They lived in a backwater community, ruled by an alien government. They felt as though they had been thrown into a waterless pit, like their forefather Joseph (9:11). Where was God at a time like this? It is true that things were not as bad as they could have been. The pit could have been full of water, so that they drowned. At least they had been thrown into a waterless pit. But none the less they found themselves living in dark times, struggling to keep a grip on God. Into that situation, the prophet brings an unexpected message of hope for the future.

9:1-4. A burden: The word of the LORD is against the land of Hadrach, and Damascus is its resting place, for the eyes of mankind and all the tribes of Israel are on the LORD. [The word is against] Hamath also, which borders it, and Tyre and Sidon, though they are extremely clever. Tyre has built a stronghold for herself and piled up silver like dust and fine gold like the mud on the streets. Look, my Lord is about to dispossess her and strike her strength into the sea. She will be consumed by fire.

A **'burden'** is a technical term for an oracle, or a series of oracles, that often — though not always — has ominous import (see 12:1; Mal. 1:1).[68] As in 1:12, the oracle concerns the nations that are wrongfully at rest, who will now be subject to the Lord's judgement.

All humanity, including but not limited to **'the tribes of Israel'**, are watching the Lord, waiting for this climactic intervention. The **'word of the LORD'** will 'rest' in judgement upon Damascus and its surrounding area, modern Syria. The idea of God's Spirit finding rest through an act of judgement on the nations was also present in Zechariah 6:8.

The oracle begins with judgement on **'Hadrach'**, an area in northern Syria that encompassed **'Damascus'**, and neighbouring **'Hamath'**, after which it moves south along the coast to **'Tyre and Sidon'**. In spite of all its natural resources and its vast wealth gained through trade, this whole region will experience the fiery judgement of God that will leave it desolate. He will eliminate the wealth and power of Tyre. The phrase stating that he will **'strike her strength into the sea'** includes a play on words: the word for **'strength'** could also be translated 'army', or 'wealth'. The Lord will strike Tyre's army and in so doing sweep her wealth into the sea, which was historically both the source of Tyre's wealth and her strength (see Ezek. 27 – 28).

9:5-8. 'Ashkelon will look and be afraid, along with Gaza; she will writhe in great distress. As for Ekron, her hope will dry up. There will no longer be a king in Gaza, and Ashkelon will not be inhabited. The illegitimate will inhabit Ashdod; I will cut off the pride of the Philistines. I will remove his blood from his mouth and his abominable foods from between his teeth. The one who remains will belong to our God and will become like a tribal chief in Judah, while Ekron will be like a Jebusite. I will set up camp for the sake of my house [to protect it] against an army, against those who pass through and return. The oppressor will no longer pass among them, for now I am watching with my eyes.'

From Tyre and Sidon, the oracle continues southward following the route that Alexander the Great would later take, to the five cities of the Philistines: **'Ash-kelon'**, **'Gaza'**, **'Ekron'** and **'Ashdod'**. They too will face absolute destruction, which they will be helpless to avert. Their monarchy will come to an end; instead of their own children inheriting their land, their population will be replaced by **'the illegitimate'**, a word which may refer to people of mixed ethnicity (see Deut. 23:2).[69] Yet even from the destruction of those pagan nations, a remnant will emerge who will attach themselves to the Lord (see 8:22-23). The Lord will purify them from their unclean and idolatrous habits, such as eating meat still containing the blood (Gen. 9:4) and other unclean foods (perhaps here specifically food that had been offered to idols). The purified remnant will become leaders among the Lord's people, like tribal chieftains. Ekron will become like the Jebusites, the inhabitants of Jerusalem, who were incorporated into the social structure of Israel in David's time.

By the destruction and conversion of Israel's traditional enemies, and through his personal protective presence, the Lord will thus eliminate any future threats to the peace and safety of his **'house'** and his people. They will no longer have to fear marauding oppressors invading from the north, as they had so often in the past. Now his eyes would be upon them for their good (see 4:10).

9:9-10. 'Rejoice greatly, Daughter Zion; shout aloud, Daughter Jerusalem! Look! Your king will come to you. He is righteous and brings salvation; he is humble and rides upon a donkey, upon a colt of the she-asses. I will cut off the chariot from Ephraim and the horse from Jerusalem. The battle bow will be cut off and he will speak peace to the nations. His reign shall be from sea to sea and from the River to the ends of the earth.'

This campaign against Israel's enemies would culmin-
ate in the triumphal entry of her **'king'** to **'Jerusalem'**. The people of Jerusalem, personified as a young
woman, are summoned to acclaim their coming king,
just as the young women of antiquity would have
welcomed home a conquering hero (1 Sam. 18:6). This
king is described as **'righteous'**, like the ideal ruler of
Psalm 72. Through his personal obedience to the
Mosaic covenant, he will ensure God's blessing on his
people, thereby bringing about their **'salvation'**.

He is also **'humble'** and comes riding on **'a donkey'**, the mount of one who comes to bring peace,
rather than the standard military mount, a horse. A
donkey was not a particularly humble form of transportation in the ancient world: kings and rich people
would ride donkeys (see Judg. 12:14), while poor
people walked. However, people did not normally ride
to war on a donkey.[70] Through the coming of this king,
the Lord will bring to an end Israel's need for the
traditional instruments of war: the **'chariot'**, **'[war]
horse'** and **'battle bow'**.

The coming ruler will rule the whole earth, **'from
sea to sea'** and **'from the** [Euphrates] **River to the
ends of the earth'**, just as Psalm 72:8 anticipated.
The result of his rule will be universal **'peace'**. Unlike
Psalm 72, however, the focus on this chapter is entirely on the Lord as the one who brings about this
universal kingdom of peace, not on the Davidic king.

9:11-12. 'As for you, by the blood of your covenant, I will set
free your captives from the waterless pit. Return to the
fortress, captives of hope. Even today I announce that I will
return to you a double portion.'

The **'captives'**, or 'prisoners', those of God's people
still remaining in exile, would be set free from **'the
waterless pit'**, a dry well that could be used as a
temporary prison (see Gen. 37:24; Jer. 38:6). This

salvation would come because of **'the blood of your covenant'** — that is, the blood of the sacrifices that were offered to ratify the covenant (see Exod. 24:8). When a covenant was made in the ancient world, the sacrificial animals were symbolic of what should happen to covenant-breakers. Their blood formed a self-imprecatory oath that testified to the seriousness of the covenant bond between God and his people. When the covenant was made at Mount Sinai between the Israelites and God in Exodus 24, the people were sprinkled with blood from the sacrifices that ratified it as a sign of the death that would come to them should they break the covenant.

Yet behind the Sinai covenant lay an older covenant between God and Abraham established in Genesis 15. In this covenant, Abraham did not pass between the pieces of the torn-up animals, as the parties making the covenant normally did. Instead, God passed alone between the pieces in the form of a fiery torch. The commitment sealed in blood that confirmed the covenant with Abraham was not made by Abraham but by God. God himself would pay the price necessary for covenant-breakers to be received into his blessings. The blood of this covenant testified that, even though the people deserved death for transgressing the covenant made at Sinai, God himself would none the less bring to fruition his purpose to have a people for himself.

'Your' is feminine singular and refers to God's people, personified in 'Daughter Jerusalem' (9:9). The blood of the sacrifices testified to the seriousness of the covenant bond between God and his people. Though they were now captives in a foreign land because of the Lord's faithfulness to judge their sin, the sacrifices gave assurance of the enduring possibility of forgiveness. As captives of this hope, they should return to Jerusalem, their **'fortress'** (see 2:6-7),[71] for the Lord had committed himself to **'double'** their former prosperity, recompensing them for their sufferings (cf. Isa. 40:2).

9:13-17. 'For I will surely bend Judah as my bow and fill it with Ephraim. I will brandish your sons, O Zion, against your sons, O Javan, and I will make you like a warrior's sword.' The LORD will appear against them and his arrow will go out like lightning. The Sovereign LORD will sound the trumpet and he will ride on the southern storms. The LORD of hosts will be a hedge around them; they will consume and subjugate those who sling stones. They will drink; they will roar as with wine; they will be full like a basin, like the corners of the altar with sacrifices. The LORD their God will save them in that day. His people will be like a flock, like precious stones in a tiara, sparkling over his land. How great is its loveliness and beauty! Grain will make the young men thrive, and new wine the young women.

The prisoners of war are not the only ones who need to hear the news of the coming king. Their oppressors, personified as the **'sons'** of **'Javan'** (often translated 'sons of Greece'), are also addressed. The Greeks were not a world-threatening empire until long after Zechariah's time, but in Genesis 10 'the sons of Javan' is a more general term that encompasses many of the coastal Mediterranean peoples. These peoples included the Greeks, so that later it became natural to use this term to denote the Greeks, but here the more general meaning is in view. The day of all those who are oppressing God's people will soon be over.

In place of the earlier image of breaking the threatening bows and removing the chariots, God will make the Israelites into a **'bow'** against their enemies, uniting Ephraim and Judah together into a single weapon — a bow and its arrow — while he will make Zion's sons into **'a warrior's sword'**. The Lord will thus appear as the divine Warrior, sounding the **'trumpet'** to advance, riding on the threatening storm clouds (Ezek. 1:4) and shooting his deadly lightning arrows. He will surround his people with a hedge of protection, so that they defeat **'those who sling stones'**, which were potent weapons in antiquity. They will shout like those who have had too much to drink, and pour out the blood of their enemies, just as blood was poured out in the sacrificial ritual, where it drenched the altar. By destroying their enemies, he will rescue his people and shepherd his **'flock'**. They will be the jewels of his crown, his beautiful and treasured possession. They will never again go hungry and thirsty, but will receive the covenantal blessings of **'grain'** and **'new wine'** (see Deut. 33:28).

Application

Zechariah 9 brings the transforming message of a coming king (9:9). His hearers were called to be prisoners of hope because his coming was as yet a future reality. So too we await the return of our King from heaven. In the midst of an often difficult present, we must keep our eyes firmly fixed on the future, when God will fulfil all that he has promised. But hope also leads to action: the prisoners of hope are required to prepare God's house to receive royalty, because the king is coming.

The coming king is *a king of peace for his people*: he has come to take away the chariots and war horses, break the battle bow, proclaim peace to the nations and salvation to his own. Yet for their oppressors he would not be a king of peace. Instead, the Lord would appear as *the divine Warrior*, sounding the bugle to advance against them, shooting his deadly arrows, destroying and pouring out blood in abundance. By destroying their enemies, he will redeem and shepherd his people.

This king is also *the righteous one* (9:9). The blessings of the covenant that God promised to Moses — the blessings of grain and new wine — are promised only to the righteous, to covenant-keepers. Yet Zechariah's hearers had just returned from exile — an exile that came upon God's people because of Judah's long history of sin and covenant disobedience. How could there be hope and blessing for men and women like them? The answer is because of the blood of the covenant (9:11), which testified to the Lord's commitment to accomplish the goal of his covenant relationship with his people.

This passage forms the background to Jesus' triumphal entry into Jerusalem. The crowds and the disciples saw the coming king and thought that there would be a straightforward road to victory. Jesus knew how that mission would be accomplished, though. On the night before his death, as they sat down to their Passover meal, he said to his disciples, 'This is my blood of the covenant, which is poured out for many for the forgiveness of sins' (Matt. 26:28). The blood that would be shed to bring us peace was his blood. The righteous King had to die in place of his unrighteous followers, the Good Shepherd in place of his unfaithful flock, so that God could accomplish his eternal purposes.

There is another day coming, when the same King will return — no longer seated on a donkey, but on the white warhorse (Rev. 19:11-16). He will come to smash his enemies once and for all, including the last enemy, death itself. On that day, he will crush all those who oppose him and set all his prisoners of hope free. The King is coming! Blessed indeed is he who comes in the name of the Lord! In the meantime, as we experience a world of waterless pits and hostile foes, we are called to wait for this return with hope, confident that our King will come in victory to bring about our full salvation and the final establishment of his kingdom in all its glory.

The true source of blessing
(Zechariah 10:1-12)

In Zechariah's day, the returned exiles were once again seeking blessing in the wrong places, looking for hope in idols, dreams and divination. The result of their search for fulfilment was not satisfaction but empty wandering, like lost sheep. In this passage, from beginning to end, the focus is on the Lord as the only one who can meet their needs.

10:1-2. Seek rain from the LORD in the season of spring rain; the LORD makes thunderclouds and showers of rain. He gives to each one green plants in the field.
    The household idols say nothing and the diviners see a lie; dreams speak what is false; they provide empty comfort. Therefore [the people] wander like sheep; they are oppressed because there is no shepherd.

In view of the Lord's promise to provide them with grain and new wine (9:17), they should look to him in faith for **'rain'**. The Israelite agricultural economy was crucially dependent on rain for its success, especially the **'spring rain'**. Since pagan gods such as Baal also claimed to make the **'thunderclouds'** that controlled the rainfall, a crucial test of Israel's faithfulness to the Lord was the one from whom they sought the rain (see Deut. 11:13-17). In the past, their leaders had sought help from the **'household idols'**, like those that Rachel stole from Laban (Gen. 31:34), or from pagan **'diviners'** and the interpreters of **'dreams'**. Yet these

sources yielded only **'empty comfort'**, and the people
had been left wandering and leaderless, like sheep
without a shepherd. More precisely, as the following
verses make clear, they are not entirely without shepherds: what they lack is a *good* shepherd.

10:3-5. 'I am angry with the shepherds and I will confront the
male goats. The LORD of hosts will visit his flock, the house
of Judah, and make them like a majestic horse in battle.
From him will come the cornerstone, from him the tent peg,
from him the battle bow, from him will come every overseer.
Together they will be like warriors, trampling [their enemies]
underfoot in battle like the mud of the streets. They will fight
because the LORD is with them; they will put to shame the
cavalry.'

The Lord's anger was kindled against the leaders of
his people, described as **'the shepherds'** and **'male
goats'**. These two groups seem to represent different
levels of leadership, with the shepherds having official
control of the flock, while the male goats provided the
leadership from within the flock (cf. Jer. 50:8).[72] These
same elements appear together as an image of abusive
power in Ezekiel 34. As a result of their failures, the
Lord would remove them and provide a new and better
shepherd for his flock. The flock would be transformed
from wandering sheep into a majestic warhorse, while
the Lord himself would provide better leaders for
them.[73]

These leaders are described metaphorically as a
'cornerstone', the foundation around which a building was constructed. The cornerstone (*pinnâ*) recalls
Isaiah 28:16, where God declares, 'Behold I am laying
in Zion for a foundation a stone, a tested stone, a
precious cornerstone, of a sure foundation,' and
Psalm 118:22: 'The stone the builders rejected has
become the head of the corner.'

A **'tent peg'** (*yātēd*) is an image of solid stability, which recalls Isaiah 22:20-23, where Eliakim was given an authoritative role over Jerusalem and Judah and described as 'a tent peg fastened in a sure place'. The **'battle bow'** represents military power (see 9:10).

These images all have royal associations,[74] but the renovation of leadership extends down to the lower level of **'overseer'** (*nôgēś*; the same term was translated 'oppressor' in 9:8), an emphasis that fits with the twofold nature of the defective leadership that is being replaced. These new leaders would be triumphant against all foes because of the Lord's presence with them. A number of verbal connections ('battle bow,' 'overseer,' 'mud of the streets') tie their victory here to the Lord's triumph announced in chapter 9.

10:6-7. 'I will strengthen the house of Judah and save the house of Joseph. I will bring them back, for I have compassion on them. They will become as if I had not rejected them, for I am the LORD their God and I will answer them. Ephraim will become like a warrior; their hearts will rejoice as with wine. Their children will see it and rejoice; their hearts will delight in the LORD.'

The Lord's intervention on behalf of his people would result in their strengthening and deliverance. Whereas they were once like sheep without a shepherd, **'rejected'** by the Lord, he will now **'have compassion on them'** (cf. Ezek. 39:25), completing the process of restoration begun when he brought Judah back from exile. This restoration will extend beyond Judah to include **'the house of Joseph'**, the northern kingdom (also known as **'Ephraim'**, after the most significant of the northern tribes). This kingdom was defeated and exiled by the Assyrians in 722 BC. When they cry out to him in exile, he will **'answer them'**, and bring them home as well, resulting in strength and joy for all of God's people. Those who once were scattered sheep, ready to be slaughtered, will become mighty warriors, celebrating their triumphs with wine.

10:8-12. 'I will whistle for them and I will gather them. Surely I have redeemed them and they will become as numerous as they were. Though I sowed them among the peoples, in distant places they will remember me. They will survive with their children and they will return. I will bring them back from the land of Egypt; from Assyria I will gather them. I will bring them to the land of Gilead and Lebanon, but [enough room] will not be found for them. He will pass through the sea of distress and he will strike the waves of the sea; all the depths of the Nile will dry up. The pride of Assyria will be brought down and the sceptre of Egypt will be removed. I will make them strong in the LORD, and in his name they will patrol,' declares the LORD.

As a Near-Eastern shepherd whistles to summon his flock, the Lord will **'whistle'** for his people, bringing them back from the nations where he scattered them, as a farmer scatters seed across the ground. Earlier, he used the same signal to summon **'Egypt'** and **'Assyria'** to judge Israel (see Isa. 5:26; 7:18). Now it will be the signal for their restoration, the time for harvesting the scattered seed as the judgement of exile bears its fruit in the people remembering the Lord. To **'remember'** the Lord is more than a mere mental recollection: it implies the action that follows this mental state, repenting of their sin and rebellion. Though this action is still in the future, it is assured because the Lord has already redeemed them (the tense of the Hebrew is perfect).[75] Even though the Lord gave them into slavery for their sins, he never re-nounced his right of ownership over them, and he will certainly reclaim them from their bondage.

This restoration involves a second exodus, in which the Lord will pass through **'the sea of distress'** and strike down **'the waves of the sea'**, representing all the forces of chaos arrayed against Israel. The Lord will also gather his people from their more recent adversary, Assyria, bringing to an end their bondage. Egypt and Assyria are geographical opposites, with Egypt as the major military threat to the south of Israel and Assyria to the north. Both of these historic adversaries will be laid low by the Lord, when he restores his people to himself and brings them to the historic centres of fertility, **'Gilead and Lebanon'**. Yet even when their territory is expanded to include these areas, which were not part of post-exilic Judah, there will still not be enough room for all of them because of their number. He will strengthen them and send them out on patrol, just as he sent his angelic forces out in Zechariah 1:11.

Application

The Lord is the central character in this passage, *the one who meets his people's needs* for rain, leadership, unity, restoration and blessing. Rain in its season was the most basic necessity for life in Judah. Because rain was so foundational to life, the place where the people sought it was a key indicator of their spiritual health. For us, there are many things that we view as being essential to our lives, such as a fulfilling career or a loving relationship. These can act as diagnostics of our spiritual health. Are we willing to entrust these most precious aspects of our lives to the Lord, and to wait patiently for him to provide them? Or do we grow impatient with God and seek to fulfil our desires in other ways?

Secondly, *the Lord provides leadership*. Those who were leading God's people at this point had not been good leaders. The Lord would judge those false leaders who had led them astray, serving themselves and meeting their own needs instead of laying down their lives for the flock. He promised that he would take care of the flock himself and provide them with the godly leaders they needed, who would defend their people against their enemies and enable them to dwell in peace and security.

We too have a great need of godly leaders in the church. Sometimes we take that godly leadership for granted; at others, we seek people who will manage the church as if it were a corporation instead of a flock. What we need, however, is godly men who will fight for the flock under their care, not with sword and bow, but with the spiritual weapons described in Ephesians 6, especially prayer.

The promised restoration is not restricted to the remnant from Judah, but extends more broadly to include the remnant of the northern kingdom, who will be reunited with what is left of the house of Judah. Such a restoration was beyond the realms of what most Jews of Zechariah's day expected, but not beyond the power of God. His new people, the church, includes not only Jews but Samaritans from the former territory of the northern kingdom, as well as Gentiles and Jews from all over the Diaspora. God's vision for the kingdom and his power to accomplish his goals are always far beyond everything we can ask or imagine.

This glorious act of salvation is a new exodus in which the Lord himself passes through the troubled waters in order to bring back the scattered remnant and restore them to their true glory. The borders of the land will have to be expanded to make room for their vast numbers and to hold the full scope of their blessing. This is not a grudging master allowing his wayward servant to return to a menial position, but a compassionate father clothing the prodigal son in the best robe and feeding him with the fattened calf.

Our true shepherd is Jesus Christ, the Good Shepherd appointed by the Father to take care of his flock (John 10). He is the true cornerstone upon which his church is built (Acts 4:11; Eph. 2:20). He is the tent peg upon which our whole salvation rests. In him, God himself passed through the waters of distress, stilling the storm for his disciples (Mark 4:35-41), but undergoing the full assaults of the forces of chaos on the cross. It is because the Father had no compassion on his Son on that day that he can now have compassion on us, who were by nature rebels and sinners against him. In Christ, he unites together Jew and Gentile into one new temple, a place of strength and joy (Eph. 2:11-22). This is truly the new exodus that God has accomplished for his people (Luke 9:31), beginning with the cross and ending with our full and final salvation in the new Jerusalem, our heavenly Mount Zion (Heb. 12:22-24). In him, we have been blessed with every spiritual blessing (Eph. 1:3). Why should we feel the need to seek any good thing from any other source?

No compassion
(Zechariah 11:1-17)

'I will not show compassion.' These are chilling words to hear from the Lord, but they remind us that we cannot take God's grace for granted. We cannot simply presume that 'God will forgive; it's his job.' The same God who is 'compassionate and gracious, slow to anger and abounding in steadfast love and faithfulness ... forgiving iniquity, rebellion and sin' is also the God who will not leave the guilty unpunished (Exod. 34:6-7). If we spurn his good gift of godly leadership, then he may turn his back on us and leave us to the fate we so richly deserve.

11:1-3. Open your doors, O Lebanon, so that fire may consume your cedars. Wail, O cypress, for the cedar has fallen; the mighty [trees] are devastated. Wail, oaks of Bashan, for the inaccessible forest has been felled! Hear the sound of the shepherds wailing, for their splendour is devastated! Hear the sound of the roar of lions, for the thicket of the Jordan is devastated!

The glory of Israel's shepherds, who were the subjects of the Lord's judgement in 10:3, will be brought low. They are pictured in three horticultural images as massive **'cedar'** trees, for which **'Lebanon'** was famous, as the mighty **'oaks of Bashan'**, a fertile region of the Transjordan, and as the lush **'thicket of the Jordan'** valley. Glorious and prosperous as all of these trees were, they could be devoured by **'fire'**, or

'felled' and brought low, or made worthless by the
presence of fierce **'lions'**;[76] so too Israel's shepherds
will lose their glory when the Lord acts to deliver his
people. The background of this passage is Jeremiah
25:34-38, where the focus is on the judgement of the
shepherds as part of a larger judgement upon the
nations of the world. This suggests that the shepherds
in view here are leaders within Judah who have
betrayed their own people and are serving the interests of the Persians.

11:4-6. Thus says the LORD my God: 'Shepherd the flock to
be slaughtered, whose buyers will slaughter them and not
incur guilt, whose seller will say, "Blessed be the LORD, I
have become rich!" and whose shepherds have no compassion on them. For I will no longer have compassion upon
those who dwell in the land,' declares the LORD. 'Look, I
myself will hand over every human being into the power of
his neighbour and of his king. They will pulverize the land
and I will not deliver [it] from their power.'

These verses record a prophetic sign act that Zechariah was instructed to perform. He was to become
shepherd to a flock symbolically described as **'the
flock to be slaughtered'**, for neither their owners nor
their shepherds cared about them as anything other
than a means of acquiring wealth. The word for
'slaughter' used here is elsewhere found only in
Jeremiah, where it describes the forthcoming destruction of Jerusalem, so the prophet is warning of a
possible return to the dark days of destruction and
despair.[77] The reason for this judgement would be the
same as for the former devastation: the Lord's lack of
compassion on his people, abandoning them without
pity to abuse from their Persian overlords (their **'king'**)
and their fellow citizens (their **'neighbour'**). Because
the Lord had no concern for them, they could be
slaughtered by their enemies without fear for the

consequences. The result would be that the land would be **'pulverize[d]'**, a word used to describe the act of grinding or pounding something into pieces.

This is a surprising turn of events after the optimistic word of the previous chapter, where the Lord promised to have compassion on his people and provide a good shepherd for them (10:4-6), and even the opening verses of this chapter, which spoke of judgement on the unfaithful shepherds. However, the sign act that follows makes clear the reason for this change: they have despised and rejected the good shepherd that the Lord has sent, resulting in a change in the Lord's attitude to them. It is possible that the immediate historical context of these events reflects a rejection of Zerubbabel by his generation, in spite of the Lord's calling for him to lead his people (Hag. 2:23).[78] Since they rejected the shepherd God had chosen, they would face the consequences.

11:7-13. So I shepherded the flock to be slaughtered, thereby [becoming shepherd] of the afflicted of the flock.[79] I took for myself two staffs: one I named 'Kindness'; the other I named 'Unity'. Thus I shepherded the flock.

I eliminated three shepherds in a single month, but I grew impatient with them [the flock] and they also detested me. So I said, 'I will not shepherd you. Let the one who is dying die; and the one who is being eliminated be eliminated; and let those that remain eat one another's flesh.' Then I took my staff 'Kindness' and I broke it in pieces to invalidate my covenant which I had made with all peoples. It was invalidated on that day. Then the afflicted of the flock who were observing me knew that this was the word of the LORD.

Then I said to them, 'If it seems good in your eyes, pay my wages, and if not, don't.' So they weighed out my wages: thirty silver pieces. Then the LORD said to me, 'Throw it to the potter' — the noble price at which I was valued by them. So I took the thirty silver pieces and I threw them into the house of the LORD, to the potter.

The reason for the Lord's lack of compassion on his people becomes clear as the sign act unfolds. Zechariah tended his flock with the staffs, **'Kindness'** and **'Unity'**, symbolizing the Lord's initial positive intentions for his people. In a very short period, he removed **'three'** other shepherds and became the shepherd to this flock, symbolizing the complete purging that had taken place in the defective leadership of Judah. The number 'three' is symbolic of completeness rather than having in view any three particular post-exilic leaders, while 'one month' simply denotes a short period of time. Yet instead of a positive relationship developing between the shepherd and his flock, he **'grew impatient'** with them and they **'detested'** him. He therefore resigned from his position, and left the flock to tear itself apart and to suffer the depredations of their enemies all around. He broke his staff, 'Kindness,' breaking the **'covenant'** he had made with the nations around Israel that had resulted in the return of his people to Judah and protected them from the enmity of their foes. With this covenant broken, the flock was left unprotected against their rapacity. The **'afflicted'** ones, the weakest members of the community, were thus left exposed to the power of the strong, yet they recognized that this was the Lord's decree. This group of people may well have included many of Zechariah's supporters, for they in particular were observing his actions. That support did not protect them from the coming judgement on God's people as a whole, however.

Zechariah then asked for his wages and received the derisory sum of **'thirty silver pieces'**, the price of a slave, which epitomized the community's view of his value. He was instructed to reject this fee, throwing it to a **'potter'**, who worked at the temple, suggesting the Lord's rejection of the temple activities as well.

11:14-17. Then I broke in pieces the second staff, 'Unity,' invalidating the brotherhood between Israel and Judah.

Then the LORD said to me, 'Once again, take the equipment of a wicked shepherd. For look, I am going to raise up a shepherd in the land who will not protect those being eliminated, nor seek the scattered, nor heal those being destroyed, nor support those who are standing firm. Instead, he will consume the flesh of the fat [sheep] and he will tear off their hoofs. Woe to my worthless shepherd, my forsaker of the flock! A sword against his arm and his right eye! May his arm wither completely and his right eye become completely blind!'

At this point, Zechariah broke the second staff, **'Unity'**, destroying the **'brotherhood'** that existed between the northern and southern kingdoms of **'Israel'** and **'Judah'**. He was then told to leave the flock to the tender mercies of a **'wicked shepherd'**,[80] who would not care for the flock but would exploit it for his own benefit. The sign acts in this chapter completely reverse the pictures of Ezekiel 34 and 37, in which the Lord promised to be Israel's Shepherd, judging their present bad shepherds and providing a good shepherd, a new David, who would reunite his people. Instead, because of their failure to respond positively to the shepherd he provided, the Lord declares that he will no longer have compassion on them and deliver and reunite them. Now they will be given over once again to a wicked shepherd, an 'anti-shepherd' who behaves in a manner exactly opposite to the good shepherd's behaviour, as described in Ezekiel 34.[81] Because they rejected the shepherd whom the Lord had raised up, God's people would once again return to the situation that led up to the exile. The New Testament sees in the rejection of the good shepherd by the flock and the derisory wages paid to the prophet a foreshadowing of the rejection and betrayal of Jesus by the Jews of his day (Matt.

27:3-10; John 10). This rejection led to the destruction of Jerusalem by the Romans in AD 70, a return to
the situation of 586 BC. Some have therefore sought to
identify the wicked shepherd as one or more of the
emperors of Rome, who dealt so savagely with the
Jewish nation in AD 70.[82]

Yet the handing over of the Lord's people to a
worthless shepherd cannot be the end of the story.
The Lord could never abandon them fully and finally.
As a result, he declares that he will ultimately act to
bring judgement on the worthless shepherd that he
has installed, striking his **'right eye'** and his **'arm'**,
parts of the body essential to carry out warfare and to
exert control over the flock. This leaves open the
possibility of a return to the positive promises of
Ezekiel 34 and Jeremiah 23 of a reunited community
under the tender care of a good shepherd.

Application

The Lord provides good leadership for his people in spite of their
history of sin. This was his promise in Ezekiel 34 — a promise
reiterated in Zechariah 10 and which had apparently found a
measure of historical fulfilment. By raising up Zerubbabel, the Lord
had given the returned exiles a fresh start under a shepherd who
really cared for their welfare. However, the people failed to appre-
ciate this gift of God's grace and rejected Zerubbabel. Such a
rejection of the Lord's shepherd would have dire consequences,
as the acted out parable of Zechariah 11 makes clear.

This prophetic sign act has relevance for God's contemporary
flock, the church, as well as for Zechariah's hearers. The Lord has
declared his purpose to raise up godly leaders for his church who
will act as their shepherds (1 Peter 5:2-3). It is their responsibility
and privilege to proclaim the gospel news of God's favour towards
us in Christ to the flock and to unite it through the teaching of sound
doctrine (Eph. 4:11-16). They are to care for the weak and protect
them against those who are stronger and against marauders from

the outside. Such leaders are a gift of God to the church, and their ministry is to be cherished and encouraged by those whom God has placed under their care. If we despise those leaders and fail to value their ministry, God may remove his good shepherds and replace them with uncaring leaders who divide the church and allow it to tear itself apart by teaching false doctrine and by failing to admonish and encourage the weak.

The primary fulfilment of this prophetic sign act occurred in the life and ministry of Jesus. He was truly the Good Shepherd (John 10:11-18), sent to earth to shepherd the flock otherwise destined to destruction, rebellious humanity (Eph. 2:1-3). He came to his own sheep, to the Jews, but they refused to receive him (John 1:11). He came to bring the Gentiles too into his flock (John 10:16), but the Jews and Gentiles instead conspired together to reject and crucify him. At his greatest hour of need, his own disciples abandoned him and fled, while Judas, one of the Twelve, betrayed him for thirty pieces of silver (Matt. 26:14-16). This sum, the price of a slave, was the noble price at which Jesus was valued by the Jewish authorities. Judas was later gripped by remorse, so he took his wages and tried to return them to the religious authorities. They refused to receive the payment, however, being more concerned over the ethics of placing blood money in the temple treasury than they were about using that money to condemn an innocent man to death. Instead, they bought with it a field in which to bury foreigners. Providing a further connection to Zechariah 11, this field was known as 'the Potter's Field' (Matt. 27:7-10).

If Jesus is the true Good Shepherd, what will be the fate of those who reject and despise him? They will hear the most fearsome declaration that God can make: 'I will not be your shepherd, and I will not have compassion on you.' Such a rejection of the Messiah by the Jews of Jesus' own day led to the destruction of Jerusalem in AD 70 by the Romans. Yet even that terrible holocaust was a minor tragedy in comparison with the eternal judgement that awaits all those who reject the Christ, Jew or Gentile alike.

Yet the final words of the passage return our thoughts to hope. The Lord cannot and will not abandon his promise to have a flock of his own whom he will shepherd, judging all their enemies from within and without. The disciples who abandoned Jesus and fled were graciously restored by him. Many of those same Jews who rejected Jesus and called for him to be crucified were converted on the Day of Pentecost and brought from death to life. Many more, both Jews and Gentiles, have been redeemed from eternal death through Jesus in the days since then, and will continue to be until the full number of God's flock is brought in and united under one shepherd, even Jesus himself. While we may never presume upon his mercy, none the less even our sin cannot ultimately triumph over God's gracious promise.

The final frontier
(Zechariah 12:1-9)

The last section of the book, Zechariah 12 – 14, describes the complete restoration and renewal of the Lord's people: its focus is on the Day of the Lord (**'that day'**), the cataclysmic and climactic resolution of the whole of world history, when the Lord brings all his purposes to final consummation.

12:1-3. A burden: the word of the LORD concerning Israel. This is a declaration of the LORD, the one who stretches out the heavens and lays the foundations of the earth and forms the spirit of man within him: 'Look, I am about to make Jerusalem a cup of staggering to all the peoples who surround [her]. Judah will also be [involved] in the siege against Jerusalem. On that day, I will make Jerusalem a heavy stone to all peoples; all who try to lift her will gash themselves, though all the nations of the earth gather against her.'

The phrase, **'A burden: the word of the LORD'**, marks this as the beginning of a new section in Zechariah's prophecy (see 9:1; Mal. 1:1). The Lord is the creator both of the universe and of individual human beings: in the beginning, he **'stretch[ed] out the heavens'**, as though the sky were like a tent, and laid its **'foundations'**, as though it were a building. As creator of everything out of nothing in the beginning, the Lord is able to re-create a new heavens and a new earth, including forming a new society in the prophet's own day out of the existing chaos of post-exilic Judah. He also creates individual human beings, **'form[ing] the spirit of man within him'**, which means that he can remake individuals as well as society as a whole. In that re-creating work, Jerusalem will be the instrument of his judgement upon the nations. Though they **'surround'** her in military array, ready to besiege her and Judah too, she will be **'a cup of staggering'** for them, a cup filled with intoxicating liquor, the consumption of which results in shame, disorientation and destruction (cf. Jer. 25:15-29). She will be like **'a heavy stone'**, of the kind used in ancient weightlifting competitions, that will hurt, or more specifically, **'gash'**, or cut (see Lev. 21:5), those nations that try to move her.[83] In the past, the Lord had promised to protect Jerusalem as the city where he dwelt (Ps. 46:4-8). Though Jerusalem's sin led to her abandonment by the Lord during the exile and subsequent destruction (Ezek. 8 – 11), on the final day of consummation, his presence would once more maintain the safety of the city. This promise of protection for his dwelling place implies that the earlier promises to purify his people have been effective.

12:4-6. 'On that day,' declares the LORD, 'I will strike every horse with panic and his rider with madness, but I will open my eyes towards the house of Judah. All of the horses of the people I will strike with blindness. Then the leaders of Judah will say in their hearts, "The inhabitants of Jerusalem are my strength through the LORD of hosts, their God." On that day, I will make the leaders of Judah like a fire pot among trees, or a flaming torch among straw: they will consume all the peoples around them on the right and the left. Jerusalem will dwell once again in her proper place — [that is] in Jerusalem.'

When the nations of the earth gathered together for war against Jerusalem, the Lord would strike their elite cavalry troops with **'panic'**, **'madness'** and

'**blindness**', images drawn from the covenant curses
of Deuteronomy 28:28. Those who assault his people
are under his curse, as the covenant made with Abraham had promised (see Gen. 12:1-3). In stark contrast
to the blindness of the threatening warhorses, the
Lord's gaze would be fixed upon his people, the house
of Judah, for their blessing (see 4:10; 9:8). Empowered
by the Lord, the leaders of Judah would become like a
blazing '**fire pot**' located among the '**trees**', or a
'**flaming torch**' among the intensely flammable
sheaves of grain (see Judg. 15:1-8), devouring the
nations all around them. In their moment of victory,
the leaders of Judah would recognize that the inde-
structible strength of Jerusalem comes not from
themselves, but from their trust in the '**LORD of
hosts**', God's military title. This final triumph over the
nations will allow Jerusalem to dwell undisturbed in
her proper place.

12:7-9. 'The LORD will save the tents of Judah first, so that
the glory of the house of David and the glory of the inhabitants of Jerusalem may not be greater than [that of] Judah.
On that day the LORD will be a hedge around the inhabitants
of Jerusalem. The one who stumbles among them on that
day will become like David, and the house of David will
become like God, like the angel of the LORD before them. On
that day, I will search to destroy all the nations that come
against Jerusalem.'

Just as the Lord promised Abraham, he would bless
Judah and Jerusalem while cursing those who raised
themselves against them (Gen. 12:1-3); there will be
'**glory**' for Jerusalem and the whole of Judah, and
destruction for the nations that come against her,
while the Lord will provide a protective shield around
them (cf. 9:15). All of Jerusalem's inhabitants will be
raised to the highest status of human glory, that of
David, the man after God's own heart (1 Sam. 13:14),

while the line of David will attain an even greater, godlike glory. On that day, the descendant of David will lead them triumphantly into battle, just as the angel of the Lord did in days of old (see Josh. 5:14).

Application

In spite of their past sin, the Lord has not abandoned his chosen ones and will never do so. As the covenant with Abraham made clear, God's purpose for Israel was that they would be a blessing to the nations. Yet there was also the threat in that covenant that if the nations attacked them, then their enemies would find themselves under the Lord's curse. The Lord who created all things out of nothing, and each of us individually, is able to re-create his people and defend them against all threats. Even though in the past the nations had invaded Judah and successfully assaulted Jerusalem, the future would be different from the past. Now that the Lord had returned, they could rest assured that he would keep them safe and glorify them through his protection.

This message is relevant for God's people in all times and ages, even though the earthly city of Jerusalem is no longer the centre of our hope. In our times, God no longer dwells by his Spirit in an earthly temple, but in the midst of his people whenever they gather for worship. The promises made to Jerusalem and Judah have continuing significance for believers because trials and tribulations are not restricted to a special period in the church's history. On the contrary, Jesus assured us that in this world we will have tribulation (John 16:33), which has certainly been a faithful description of our situation. Nevertheless, there are particular periods of the church's history that are even more trying than normal for the saints. Yet these trials should not cause us to despair, no matter how intense they may be, because the Lord is committed ultimately to deliver his elect and judge their enemies. However weak we are in ourselves, the Lord is able to strengthen us and enable us to stand, giving us a glory far beyond anything that comes from ourselves.

Repentance and cleansing
(Zechariah 12:10 – 13:9)

The previous oracle dealt with the protection of God's people in the midst of many trials and tribulations; this oracle focuses on their purification. These two motifs are regularly connected in the prophets: God's promise is never an abstract commitment to side with an ethnic or cultural group, but is always an assurance that he will transform them into a holy people as well as preserving them from all their enemies.

12:10-14. 'I will pour out on the house of David and the inhabitants of Jerusalem a spirit of favour and supplication. They will look at me, the one whom they have pierced, and they will lament for him as one laments for an only child. They will grieve bitterly for him as one grieves for a firstborn. In that day, the lamenting in Jerusalem will be as great as the mourning at Hadad-Rimmon in the valley of Megiddo. The land will mourn, each clan by itself. The clan of the house of David [will mourn] by itself, with their women by themselves; the clan of the house of Nathan [will mourn] by itself, with their women by themselves; the clan of the house of Levi [will mourn] by itself, with their women by themselves; the clan of the house of Shimei [will mourn] by itself, with their women by themselves; all the rest of the clans [will mourn], each clan by itself and their women by themselves.'

The 'pouring out' of **'spirit'** in the Old Testament always indicates the pouring out of God's Spirit (see Ezek. 39:29; Joel 2:28-29).[84] The Spirit will give to the house of David and the inhabitants of Jerusalem **'favour and supplication'**, which implies both repentance on the part of the people and forgiveness from the Lord. The sin which they will lament involves mourning because of the one whom they have **'pierced'**, a word which usually connotes being fatally stabbed by a sword or spear (see Num. 25:8). The person who is pierced is clearly the Lord (**'... me, the one whom they have pierced'**). In its original context, the piercing was metaphorical: the Lord was stabbed in the heart, as it were, by his people's abandonment of him. Yet, as redemptive history unfolded, that rejection of God found its culmination in a literal piercing of the Son of God with a Roman spear (John 19:34,37).

In the future, however, his people will demonstrate their repentance of this sin by means of intense mourning. That mourning is likened to the mourning for an only child, upon whom all hope for continuation of the family line rested, or like the **'mourning at** [or 'for'] **Hadad-Rimmon'**. Hadad-Rimmon could be the name of a town near **'Megiddo'**, which would make this a reference to the deep national mourning that followed King Josiah's death in battle there (see 2 Chr. 35:24). Alternatively, Hadad-Rimmon may be another name for the Canaanite god Baal, whose worship involved lament for his death and descent into the underworld. In this case, it could be a reference to the intensity of mourning that marked those rites of pagan worship with which Judah was all too familiar. The mourning over this sin will affect the entire community, family by family, men and women alike. Two particular lines are singled out: the royal line of **'David'**, by way of his son **'Nathan'** (1 Chr. 14:4), and the priestly line of **'Levi'**, by way of his grandson, **'Shimei'** (1 Chr. 6:16-17). These two lines represent the royal and priestly leadership of the community, who together will lead the people in their public expression of repentance.

13:1. 'In that day, a fountain will be opened to the house of David and to the inhabitants of Jerusalem to remove guilt and defilement.'

The repentant people need to be cleansed from their iniquity, so God will open up for them **'a fountain'**, or 'spring', from which will flow the running water necessary for ritual purification (see Lev. 14:5). Like the purifying waters that resulted from the sacrifice of the red heifer in Numbers 19, this flowing spring of purification would effectively cleanse away their guilt and defilement.

13:2-6. 'On that day,' declares the LORD of hosts, 'I will cut off the names of the idols from the land and they will be remembered no more. I will also remove the prophets and the spirit of uncleanness from the land. If someone still prophesies, his father and mother who gave him birth will say to him, "You shall not live, for you have spoken a lie in the name of the LORD." His father and mother who gave him birth shall pierce him when he prophesies.

'In that day, the prophets will each be ashamed of his vision in his prophesying. He will not put on his garment of hair in order to deceive. He will say, "I'm not a prophet. I am someone who works the soil; indeed the soil has been my property from my youth." When someone says to him, "What are these wounds between your hands?", he shall say, "[The wounds] with which I was struck at the house of my friends."'

The people's need for cleansing comes from their devotion to **'idols'**. This attachment to idolatry is the sin that 'pierced' the Lord in 12:10, metaphorically in its original context and actually in the person of Jesus. As he does consistently in the book of Zechariah, the Lord promises not merely to cleanse his people from the guilt of their sin, but to break its power over them as well. Here he declares that he will excise the **'names'** of the idols from the land, terminating their influence, and even their memory. Since much of the influence of the idols was exercised through false prophets, who told the people what they wanted to hear (see 10:1-3), they too will be removed from the land. Their own parents will execute them, in line with Deuteronomy 13:6-10. The punishment of 'piercing' — fatally stabbing — fits the impact that their sin had of 'piercing' the Lord (12:10).

This public antipathy will make the false prophets eager to conceal their activities. They will no longer dress in a **'garment of hair'**, as did Elijah (see 1 Kings 19:13; 2 Kings 1:8). The exact phrase 'garment of hair' is found in Genesis 25 to describe Esau's skin, which Jacob later mimicked in order to trick his blind father, an allusion that underlines their intent to deceive the people. If confronted, they will explicitly deny that they are prophets: instead, they claim to be workers of the soil (Gen. 4:2), a profession they have followed from their youth. Yet the true nature of the false prophet's activity will be exposed by the **'wounds between [his] hands'** — that is, on his back (see 2 Kings 9:24). These are the ritual scars related to pagan practices which he will confess that he received at the **'house of [his] friends'** (or 'lovers'), the fellow-idolaters with whom he practised pagan worship (see Ezek. 16:33-37).

13:7-9. 'O sword, awake against my shepherd, against the man who is my fellow,' declares the LORD of hosts. 'Strike the shepherd and the flock will be scattered. I will turn my hand against the little ones and it shall be against the whole land,' declares the LORD.

'Two measures will be cut off from it, but the third will remain in it. This third I will bring into the fire and I will refine them as one refines silver and test them as one tests gold. They will call on my name and I will answer them. I will say, "They are my people," and they will say, "The LORD is our God."'

As in 11:17, the **'sword'** of the Lord's judgement goes out against a shepherd, but this time it is directed against the good shepherd, something that could have been barely comprehensible to the prophet's original audience. Why would God judge his own good shepherd? The earlier symbol of water for purification is now replaced by the sword and by fire, and the judgement begins with the leader of the community. His death results in the scattering of the flock and a time of great trial and testing for God's people, during which many will perish. Yet the ultimate result of that period of testing is not their destruction, but their refining. They will emerge from the fire of tribulation refined like gold or silver (see 1 Peter 1:7), with a renewed dedication to worship (calling on the name of the Lord) and experiencing the Lord's responsiveness.

Application

Repentance is a gift from God, worked in us by his Spirit, not an attitude that we can drum up within ourselves. It involves not merely an abstract recognition that we have done wrong, but a clear acknowledgement that the one against whom we have sinned is the Lord (see Ps. 51:4). From the perspective of our position on this side of Calvary, we can see that our sins have not merely pierced the Lord's heart metaphorically but literally, as each of our sins was paid for individually on the cross of Christ. If, by God's grace, that reality penetrates our hearts, then we shall certainly mourn over our personal sin and weep for its cost.

Yet our sin is not just a private reality; our sins have a corporate dimension that makes it appropriate that we should mourn and lament them publicly. Christians are kings and priests in God's kingdom (1 Peter 2:9; Rev. 5:10), so it is fitting that we should provide leadership to our communities in mourning and lamenting the sins that mar our cities and towns. We cannot simply respond to the sins of our culture and the church of our day in the way that the Pharisee did in Jesus' parable, thanking God that we are free from their stain. Rather, like Daniel (Dan. 9) and Ezra (Ezra 9), we should be on our faces before our God lamenting these sad realities in repentant prayer and pleading for God's mercy upon us and our people.

Yet the cross denotes not merely the sad reality of what we have done to God, but also the triumphant reality of what he has done for us in Christ. At the cross, my sins pierced Christ, but the blood which flowed from those wounds forms a cleansing fountain that washes them all away. As we confess our sins in true repentance, the blood of Christ purifies us from all of our unrighteousness (1 John 1:9). For that reason, when we fix our eyes on the cross, we not only weep and mourn for our sins; we glory and triumph in the grace of God that has saved us and is transforming us, and which will ultimately renew all creation.

Part of that renewal of creation lies in purifying us from all the idols that so easily bind us and from the false prophets that lead us astray from his Word. These motifs are connected in Deuteronomy 12:29 – 13:11, where the Lord declares that he will test Israel's faithfulness to him by allowing false prophets to come among them. However, here he promises that in the days to come, the people's single-minded devotion to him will be such that all false prophets will be put out of business or driven underground.

Yet even this purifying work of God does not free his people from trials. The good shepherd that he provided would be struck down by the Lord, resulting in difficult times of testing and purification for the flock. In the New Testament, it becomes clear that this prophecy relates to the death of Christ and the scattering of the disciples that followed (Matt. 26:31). Indeed, the Christian life is a constant experience of trials and difficulties, yet these afflictions are God's means of refining us and setting our hearts firmly on our heavenly home.

Through trials to glory
(Zechariah 14:1-21)

The prophet has painted many word pictures of the glorious future that lies ahead for the people of God. None the less, his last oracle is a sobering reminder that this glorious future does not lie at the end of a smooth and easy pathway, but on the far side of many dangers, toils and snares. In particular, it appears that the period immediately preceding the Lord's final victory will be a time of great trial for his people.

14:1-5. Look! A day is coming for the LORD when your plunder will be divided in your midst. I will gather all nations against Jerusalem for war. The city will be captured, the houses plundered, the women raped. Half of the city will go out into exile, while the remainder will not be cut off from the city.

Then the LORD will go out and fight against those nations as he fights on the day of battle. His feet will stand on that day on the Mount of Olives, which faces Jerusalem to the east. The Mount of Olives will be split in half from the east to the west [forming] an exceedingly great valley: half of the mountain will withdraw northwards, and half southwards. You will flee by the valley of my mountains, for the valley of the mountains will reach to Azal. You will flee just as you fled from the earthquake in the days of Uzziah, king of Judah. The LORD my God will come, along with all the holy ones.[85]

A time of climactic trial is described in the beginning of chapter 14. The Day of the Lord will be a difficult time for the Lord's people as well as for their enemies. The 'testing' of the community anticipated in 13:9 takes concrete shape here. Judah's possessions will be divided by her enemies in front of her, and Jerusalem will again be captured, with horrific consequences in terms of rape, plunder and the exile of a significant portion of her population. Yet even this level of trauma is not beyond the Lord's power and plan to control. At the height of her distress, the Lord will go out once more as a warrior to win the final victory.

He will arrive by way of the **'Mount of Olives'**, across the Kidron Valley to the east of Jerusalem, the same route by which he abandoned the Jerusalem temple in Ezekiel 11:23. Typically of such appearances of God, this theophany will shake the natural order, splitting the mountain in two. The two halves will move north and south, creating a **'valley'** aligned **'from the east to the west'**, along the sacred axis of the temple. This valley will provide a way of escape for the inhabitants of Jerusalem to **'Azal'**, an unknown location, and an access road for the divine Warrior to return to his city. He comes accompanied by **'all the holy ones'** — either his angelic army (see Deut. 33:2) or his returning people (1 Thess. 4:16-17).

The **'earthquake in the days of Uzziah, king of Judah,'** was a traumatic event also mentioned in Amos 1:1-2.

14:6-9. In that day, there shall be no light, cold, or frost. It will be [a return to] day one, a day known [only] to the LORD, when there will not be day or night. At the time of evening, there will be light. On that day, living water will flow out from Jerusalem, half to the eastern sea and half to the western sea. It will flow both in summer and in winter. The LORD will be king over the whole earth. In that day there will be one LORD, and his name will be unique.

The transformation of the natural order at the coming of the Lord continues with a return to the primordial conditions. That day will be like the first day of history (**'day one'**), a unique day **'known [only] to the LORD'**, for he alone was present on that day. The phrase rendered **'there shall be no light, cold, or frost'** is difficult to translate: literally, it reads, 'There will be no light of splendour; they will congeal,' perhaps suggesting that the heavenly bodies will be extinguished. Just as on the first day, when light and darkness had not yet been separated (Gen. 1:3-4), so on that day there will be neither **'day'** nor **'night'**, but **'at ... evening, there will be light'**. Instead of the world that we experience of alternating light and darkness, in that final world permanent light will prevail, whose source will be God (see Isa. 60:19).

The focus of this oracle is thus not on the trials that face God's people, intense though those may be, but on the certain victory that awaits them on the far side of these things. A perpetual supply of **'living** [or flowing] **water'** will also emanate from Jerusalem, reaching out both east and west, to the Dead Sea and to the Mediterranean. Such a life-giving river is a common feature of depictions of sanctuaries, from the Garden of Eden to the new Jerusalem. From his sanctuary in Jerusalem, the Lord will exercise his reign over the whole earth. Israel's familiar affirmation of the Lord's uniqueness in the *Shema* (Deut. 6:4) will finally be universally recognized.

14:10-11. The whole land will become like the Arabah, from Geba to Rimmon, south of Jerusalem. She [Jerusalem] will be exalted and will return to her proper place, from the Benjamin Gate to the site of the First Gate, as far as the Corner Gate and from the Tower of Hananel as far as the winepresses of the king. They will dwell in her and it will never again be devoted to destruction: Jerusalem will dwell securely.

The territory of Judah will be turned into a flat plain, from **'Geba'** on its northern border to **'Rimmon'**, thirty-five miles to the south-west of Jerusalem, in order that the city of **'Jerusalem'** can tower over its surrounding countryside. The significance of this transformation is theological rather than topological, making clear Jerusalem's exalted status before the Lord (cf. Isa. 2:2-4). It will be fully inhabited and secure, without fear of a further decree of utter destruction from the Lord because of the sins of its inhabitants.

14:12-15. This will be the plague with which the LORD will afflict all of the people who went to war against Jerusalem. Their flesh will rot while they are still standing on their feet; their eyes will rot in their sockets and their tongues will rot in their mouths. On that day, there will be a great panic from the LORD among them. Each man will seize the hand of his companion and raise his hand against his companion. Judah too will fight at Jerusalem.[86] The wealth of all the nations on all sides will be gathered — gold, silver and clothing in great abundance. A similar plague will be upon horse and mule, camel and donkey, and every domestic animal that is in those camps.

Instead of judging his own city, the Lord's curse will now fall upon the nations that have come against it. Their bodies will instantaneously rot, under the effects of a hideous curse, especially their eyes and their tongues, the organs of vision and speech. In addition, they will fight among themselves, a common motif in accounts of holy war. The same curse will affect the military animals within their camp — the horses, mules, camels and donkeys. Judah too will be involved in this conflict, fighting alongside Jerusalem against the other nations on a united front. In contrast to the plunder that the nations took from Jerusalem in 14:1,

now Judah will collect vast spoil from the nations who
assaulted her.

14:16-19. All those who survive from all those nations which
went up against Jerusalem will go up from year to year to
worship the King, the LORD of hosts, and to make a pilgrimage for the Feast of Tabernacles. Those from the families of
the earth who do not go up to Jerusalem to worship the King,
the LORD of hosts, will not receive rain. If the family of Egypt
does not go up and enter, there will not be [rain] upon them.
This will be the plague with which the LORD will afflict the
nations that do not go up to make the pilgrimage to the Feast
of Tabernacles. This will be the punishment of Egypt and the
punishment of every nation that does not go up to make the
pilgrimage of the Feast of Tabernacles.

The nations that once came up against Jerusalem for
war will now come to her for the three annual festi-
vals, especially the climactic autumn **'Feast of Tabernacles'**, a celebration which particularly focused on
the Lord's kingship. The reign of God would thus be
demonstrated both by the destruction of his enemies
and by their submission to him. As Psalm 2 asserted,
all the kings of the earth must ultimately submit to
the Lord and his anointed, or be crushed.

This requirement will be enforced by the threat of
the judgement of a lack of rain, which would cripple
their harvests. This is a classic covenantal curse (see
Deut. 28:22-24), and prayers for rain may have become part of the liturgy of the Feast of Tabernacles.
Just as in Elijah's day, the ability to control the presence or absence of rain is a key indicator of the Lord's
existence and power (see 1 Kings 17 – 18).

The old enemy Egypt is singled out for mention
with a separate plague, since their harvests were
watered by the Nile, without need for local rainfall.
The mention of Egypt and plagues evokes the Lord's

earlier judgement upon Egypt and her gods at the time of the Exodus.

14:20-21. On that day, upon the bells of the horses will be [inscribed] 'Holy to the LORD,' while the cooking pots in the house of the LORD will become like the sprinkling bowls in front of the altar. Every cooking pot in Jerusalem and Judah will be holy to the LORD of hosts, and all those who sacrifice will go in and take some of them and they will cook with them. There will no longer be a trader in the house of the LORD of hosts on that day.

While a severe curse will be inflicted on the Lord's enemies, his people will experience complete sanctification. An elevated state of ritual holiness will then affect everything within Jerusalem, down to the most humble of artefacts. Even common items like the **'bells of the horses'** would now be inscribed with the phrase, **'Holy to the LORD'**, which was previously inscribed on a plate on the high priest's turban (Exod. 28:36-38). Ordinary cooking pots would now share the special status of the consecrated **'bowls in front of the altar'**; indeed, this will be necessary in order for there to be enough utensils to boil the meat from all the sacrifices that will be offered. On that day, there will no longer be **'a trader'** (literally, 'a Canaanite') in the Lord's house, a reference to those Gentiles who had been there in the temple merely for business reasons, whose presence defiled the holiness of the Lord's house (see Ezek. 44:9). The temple would finally become a fit place for the Lord to live among his people, a holy dwelling for the Holy One of Israel.

Application

Through many dangers, toils and snares,
   we have already come.

'Tis grace has brought us safe thus far,
    and grace will lead us home.

This stanza from John Newton's famous hymn, 'Amazing Grace', is a fitting summary of Zechariah 14. The prophet warns his hearers, who are wrestling with the challenge of remaining faithful to God in the day of small things (4:10), of far greater trials yet to come. However, even trials as horrific as those that he describes in this chapter cannot extinguish the Lord's people, for God will certainly deliver them in the end. In fact, those who inflict such persecution on God's people are more to be pitied than the martyrs whom they slaughter, for they will themselves be victims of divine judgement of truly terrible proportions. On the last day, every knee will indeed bow before the Lord and his Anointed, willingly or unwillingly. How much better to bow willingly, no matter what the cost in persecution may be, than to be found holding out against the Lord when the sands of time finally run out!

If the Lord is thus able to protect and preserve his own during the worst of all assaults, through martyrdom or deliverance, how much more is he able to protect us during the 'light and momentary afflictions' (2 Cor. 4:17) that we experience during our earthly pilgrimage. Of course, the person who first called them 'light and momentary afflictions', the apostle Paul, himself experienced his fair share of trials and tribulations. Yet when he compared them with the sufferings of Christ on the cross, his own sufferings were put into their proper perspective. Since Christ has died to bear the wrath of God in our place, any suffering that God calls us to endure cannot destroy us and must ultimately equip us to serve and enjoy him better. The 'many dangers, toils and snares' that we endure in this life provide us with opportunities willingly to bow our knees before the holy wisdom of our Creator, which is so much richer and more profound than our own. In the end, too, they will make the peace and security of dwelling as God's holy people in heaven all the sweeter.

In the meantime, all of life is raised to the level of the sacred for those who are redeemed in Christ. Under the old covenant, some Israelites were called to be especially devoted to the Lord, as priests or as Nazirites — those who made a temporary vow of consecration (see Num. 6). In Christ, however, we are all called to exhibit supreme holiness, as living stones in God's temple and a holy priesthood (1 Peter 2:5). As temples of the Holy Spirit, we are to be separate from all uncleanness so that we can be wholly devoted to God's service (2 Cor. 6:16 – 7:1). There are no trivial actions that we perform, no secular duties: in the light of God's supreme love for us in the gospel, our whole lives are to be placed on the altar as living sacrifices, holy to the Lord (Rom. 12:1).

Malachi

'I have loved you'
(Malachi 1:1-5)

'You hate me!' Probably every parent of teenagers has heard that phrase at some point. When a child is kept at home because of bad behaviour, or a parent decides that the family budget will not stretch to a certain new item of clothing, or that attendance at a particular film or concert does not fit the family goals of propriety, that phrase easily rears its ugly head. 'If you really loved me,' the teenager says, 'then you wouldn't be doing this to me.'

More seriously, however, many people express this attitude towards God. Something has happened in their lives — something by no means trivial — and because of it they have concluded that God hates them. That raises the question: 'How can we know that God really loves us?' Is there something more than a glib assurance that 'God loves you and has a wonderful plan for your life'? Where is the evidence for that statement when you find yourself wrestling with discouragement or divorce, loneliness or abandonment, profound physical distress or deep spiritual turmoil? How can you know that God really loves you? This is the question with which Malachi's prophecy begins.

1:1. A burden. The word of the LORD to Israel by means of 'Malachi' ['my messenger'].

A **'burden'** (*maśśâ*) is a technical term for prophecy (see 2 Kings 9:25,26, where *maśśâ* is parallel to 'the word of the LORD'). This title connects the book of Malachi together with the latter part of Zechariah, the two main sections of which each begin in exactly the same way (Zech. 9:1; 12:1). Though this is not always the case, the term 'burden' often seems to carry overtones of judgement; thus when a prophet comes to you with a burden, it is not necessarily good news.[1]

The designation of the prophet, **'Malachi'**, could be either a personal name or a title ('my messenger'). Plausibly, either would fit equally well in this context. However, in all the other biblical instances of the phrase, **'the word of the LORD ... by means of [X]'**, X represents a personal name, so that is probably its signification here. As with some of the other prophets (e.g. Ezekiel), the prophet's personal name fits perfectly the task to which he has been called.

1:2-3. 'I have loved you,' says the LORD.
    But you say, 'In what way have you loved us?'
    'Was not Esau the brother of Jacob?' — oracle of the LORD — 'yet I loved Jacob. But Esau I hated, so I made his mountains desolate and [gave] his inheritance as a wilderness for jackals.'

The book of Malachi is structured around a series of prophetic disputation speeches, in which the prophet cites a contemporary saying which he then goes on to refute (similar forms of speech may be found in Ezek. 11:3-12;18:2-32). In Malachi, the pattern normally begins with the Lord making a statement that the people challenge and the Lord then vindicates. The people's challenge may not necessarily be a verbatim citation of an actual response, but it clearly represents the world view of the prophet's hearers, whether or not their thoughts were expressed aloud.

The Lord's opening declaration is **'I have loved you'**, which Israel immediately challenges with the question, **'In what way have you loved us?'** 'Love' in this context is not an emotional feeling, but rather a covenantal term that expresses the behaviour that flows out of a committed relationship. It can thus express the friendly relationship between kings engaged in a mutual alliance (e.g. 1 Kings 5:1), as well as the more intimate commitment of heart and life in marriage (e.g. Hosea 3:1). So to question the Lord's love is not to voice doubts about his inner emotional state, but to impugn the faithfulness of his actions towards his people.

That Israel should thus question the Lord's love for them at this point in redemptive history might at first seem surprising. Should the God who brought their forefathers out of the land of Egypt and gave them the land of Canaan have to prove afresh his love to his people? Was there any doubt of the Lord's attitude towards them, given the fact that, in spite of their sinful rejection of him which led to the exile, he had redeemed them out of their bondage in Babylon? Yet in another sense it is perhaps not so surprising that they should express doubts concerning his care for them at this point, perhaps a century after the return from exile. Essentially, the question boiled down to this: 'Lord, what have you done for us lately?' Life as a vassal state of Persia was hard for those who had returned from the exile. Their situation seemed far from the golden age of peace and prosperity anticipated in Isaiah 40 – 66, or even in the book of Haggai. In the midst of a generally disappointing and frustrating experience of life, they questioned God's interest in their plight, and thus his commitment to fulfil his covenant promises.

The Lord's response to their question may seem equally surprising to us, centring as it does on the contrast between the Lord's attitude to Jacob and

Esau. Jacob and Esau were the twin sons of Isaac and Rebekah. Yet before the twins were born, the Lord declared that the older son, Esau, would serve the younger, Jacob (Gen. 25:23). Instead of following the normal human pattern of heredity according to the order of birth, the line of promise would run through the younger son. This pattern of election was not based on anything in the boys' behaviour, but rather on the Lord's sovereign election of the one, Jacob, and the rejection of the other, Esau. Thus, the Lord declares, **'I loved Jacob. But Esau I hated.'** 'Hate' is the antonym of love and, like the latter, it is a covenantal term that includes the behaviour that flows from a rejection of relationship. Thus Deuteronomy 21:15-17 deals with the situation of a man with two wives, one of whom is 'loved' while the other is 'hated', an attitude that leads him to reject her child by him from his position as firstborn — a rejection that this law forbids. The Lord's hatred for Esau is thus a sovereign rejection of him and his offspring from the undeserved privilege of relationship with the Lord for which Jacob has been chosen. This divine election and rejection worked itself out in history, with Jacob's descendants, Israel, becoming God's chosen people while Esau's descendants were outsiders to his promises. As a result of this committed negative attitude on the Lord's part, Esau's descendants were now experiencing his judgemental curse on their land.

How, though, do the negative judgements that the Lord has wreaked on the descendants of Jacob's brother, Esau, prove his enduring love for the descendants of Jacob? The answer is that the personal experiences of Jacob and Esau form a paradigm through which to understand the experiences of Malachi's hearers. Neither Jacob nor Esau deserved God's love, before or after it was bestowed on Jacob. In fact, both thoroughly deserved to be 'hated' — rejected and cast off — by God, with all the consequences that flow from that decision. For his part, Esau despised the birth-right that ought to have been his and regarded it as something of so little value that he traded it for a bowl of soup (Gen. 25:29-34). Meanwhile, Jacob sought to trick and manipulate his way into the blessing that the Lord had promised him, instead of trusting God to provide it by faith (Gen. 27).

As a result of the poisonous family relationships that ensued, Jacob was exiled from his home and family and left with nothing other than his clothing and his staff. Yet, at that lowest point, the Lord appeared to him at Bethel and assured him of his continuing presence with him and care for him or, in the language of Malachi, his love for him (Gen. 28:10-15). The Lord was faithful to his promise, in spite of Jacob's continuing scheming tendencies, and he brought him back from his exile with twelve children and great possessions (Gen. 35). Over the same period of time Esau prospered materially in his homeland, but he never personally encountered the Lord, nor did he feel that absence as a loss (Gen. 33).[2] The Lord's electing love takes his people safely through their trials and sanctifies them through that means, while those who are 'not elect' experience no such intervention in their lives (cf. Heb. 12:5-6).

This was exactly the experience of Malachi's generation. They had seen their forefathers go into exile for their sins and were currently facing many difficulties which they interpreted as evidence that the Lord had abandoned them, while their Edomite neighbours seemed to have had a much easier history. Edom survived and prospered through the destruction of Judah in 586 BC by siding with the Babylonians and aiding them against Judah. Where was the Lord's justice to be seen in that? Yet the Lord's answer was that Israel's continuing existence after the judgement of the exile was proof of his love: he was committed to them, in spite of their history of sin, and would never abandon them totally. In contrast, unloved Esau's descendants were now facing a destruction from which there would be no return. Picking up the language of the covenantal curses at Sinai, the Lord declared of Edom that **'his mountains'** were made **'desolate'** (see Lev. 26:33). **'His inheritance'** (a term with strong Abrahamic overtones) would be given to the **'jackals'** of the wilderness. This judgement on Edom for their sin of aiding the Babylonians against the Lord's people in their hour of greatest need had been anticipated by a series of oracles during the exilic period predicting Edom's demise (Jer. 49:7-22; Lam. 4:21-22; Ezek. 25:12-14; Obad. 1-21). Malachi declares that what was prophesied in those passages is now beginning to take effect. It is known that Nabonidus, the last of the Babylonian kings (559–539 BC) had a strong interest in the trade routes to the Red Sea and campaigned in the area of Edom, though the final demise of Edom seems to have come at the hands of a coalition of semi-nomadic Arabs during the fifth century BC.[3] These semi-nomadic raiders would aptly fit the description of desert 'jackals', though it is hard to be certain whether such a reference is intended.

1:4-5. Though Edom says, 'We have been beaten down, but we shall return and we will rebuild the ruins', thus says the LORD of hosts: 'They may rebuild, but I will tear down and they will be called "Territory of Wickedness" and "the people with whom the LORD is angry for ever". Your own eyes will see [this] and you yourselves will say, "Great is the LORD beyond the territory of Israel."'

The backdrop for this prophecy is Ezekiel 35 – 36. Ezekiel 35 contains a prophecy against Mount Seir, the ancestral home of Edom, declaring that her towns will be made into ruins (*ḥorbâ*) and desolate (*šᵉmāmâ*, Ezek. 35:3-4) because she rejoiced when the inheritance (*naḥᵃlâ*) of the house of Israel was made desolate

(Ezek. 35:15). Yet the Lord promised that he would cleanse Israel of their sins, return them to their homeland and rebuild the ruins (Ezek. 36:33). There was a future for the Lord's people beyond his historical acts of judgement. In contrast, Edom's self-confidence that they could bounce back from current setbacks and restore their former glory was unfounded. Whatever they rebuilt, the Lord would once again **'tear down'**. In this contrast of ultimate fates lay the undeniable demonstration of the Lord's love for Israel: even after they were judged for their sins and their land made desolate, the Lord had brought them back and enabled them to rebuild their ruins. His purposes transcended their sins, while when Edom fell, their fall would be ultimate.

The Lord's election, both for blessing and curse, is irrevocable. Even in the post-exilic period, when all that is left of God's historic people is Judah, the Lord still describes their land as **'the territory of Israel'**. The remnant that remained after the exile genuinely represented the whole people of God, the true Israel, and they were therefore heirs to all of the great promises of God. On the other hand, the descendants of 'hated' Esau would be known as **'people with whom the LORD is angry for ever'**. When they were judged, there would be no remnant left behind: Esau's line would be cut off completely. Yet even though God's election of one group to be his while another was rejected was based on God's sovereign choice prior to the birth of their ancestors, his election is not arbitrary. God will certainly sanctify those he has chosen to call his own (Ezek. 36:24-27), while the land of those whom God has rejected is aptly called **'Territory of Wickedness'**. Like their forefather Esau, those whom God has not chosen do not secretly long to be included among the elect; on the contrary, they are content to live their entire lives without reference to God or his righteousness.

When it becomes clear that this distinction between those whom God has chosen and those whom he has passed over is not based on anything in them, the result is not pride and boasting on the part of God's chosen ones, but astonishment and praise that acknowledges God's universal greatness — a greatness that extends far beyond the territorial borders of Israel to encompass not merely Edom but all nations. Salvation is truly of the Lord, not of man: all we contribute is the sin of which we are so ashamed (Ezek. 36:31). How amazing is our salvation, and how great is the grace of our God!

Application

How do you know whether God really loves you? When you find yourself tempted to doubt, compare your situation with that of those whom the Lord does not love, and you will soon see the difference. Judah had experienced the curses of the Sinai covenant because of their sin, culminating in exile. Edom was about to experience the same severe judgement of God, which itself was the fulfilment of earlier prophecy. The difference between the two peoples is not whether they experience trials and difficulties in this world, but whether those trials and difficulties terminate in their destruction, or whether they have a future beyond the judgement. For Israel, after the judgement of the exile comes the free and unmerited grace of restoration to the land, a grace based not on anything worthy in them, but solely on God's faithfulness to his commitment to the promise made to the patriarchs and to the honour of the Lord's name. God's grace is not based on our works, but solely on predestining love, which is itself based on God's sovereign choice. This not only explains God's continuing grace to his own people, Israel, when Edom is cut off for their sins, but also the fact that in Jesus Christ God's grace comes ultimately to the Gentiles themselves. Since election is election to grace, God can have mercy upon whomever he chooses, Jew or Gentile (Rom. 9).

The foundation for God's grace is his judgement on sin. Often sermons on this passage ask, 'How can God hate Esau?' — a question that is usually answered by saying that he doesn't *really* hate Esau; he just loves him less. Yet to be 'not chosen' by God is to be destined for eternal destruction: to adopt the language of the apostle Paul, the non-elect are 'vessels of wrath' (Rom. 9:22). If you minimize God's hatred for Esau, which results in his eternal destruction, then at the same time you have undercut the effectiveness of this oracle as an answer to the people's question concerning God's love. God's implacable hatred of Edom is the proof of his undeniable love for Israel, for whom even severe judgement is not terminal but a purifying fire. The real question that the passage poses is not, 'How can God hate Esau?'; it is, 'How can God continue to love Jacob, in the light of his ongoing rebellion and covenant-breaking?' The answer that the New Testament shows us is that his enduring faithful commitment to his people is possible because the destruction that we deserved has been poured out on Christ in our place. The Lord's terrible wrath and his hatred against sin were poured out on him on the cross, so now we experience the love that his obedience merited.

God's sovereign election is not an abstract idea, but works its way out in redemptive history. Jacob himself came through many sins to a point of repentance and faith, which was concretely marked by his burial in the patriarchal tombs of the promised land (Gen. 50:13), while Esau never cared about the birthright, even to the end of his life. Likewise, the Israelites went through much sin and judgement but remained the covenant people, while Edom's end was to become the territory of wickedness. Election is election unto life and sanctification, albeit through a slow and tortuous process in which we never outgrow our need for grace, while reprobation simply confirms sinners in their natural sinful tendencies.

It is striking too, that the prophet begins his message with a reaffirmation of the electing love of God for his people, before he begins to condemn their sins and failures. He starts with a reminder of the truth of the gospel before he applies the law to them. In fact, God's faithfulness to his promises further underlines the sinfulness of Israel's unfaithfulness to their covenant obligations, which is the focus of the rest of Malachi's oracles. Without God's electing love, their law-breaking would not have been nearly so heinous. Yet if God has been faithful in spite of Israel's repeated covenant-breaking, why haven't they been faithful to him? They are left without excuse. In the same way, we frequently blame God's perceived unfaithfulness or unfairness towards us to justify sin in our hearts, but we too are without excuse. God has been faithful to all of his promises.

Finally, the goal of electing grace is that God's glory should be made evident before the eyes of his people. We were created and redeemed to glorify God and enjoy him for ever, and the plan of our salvation and sanctification has been distinctly designed with that end in mind. All is of God, from beginning to end, so that he might receive all the praise that is his due.

Defiled worship
(Malachi 1:6-14)

Is our worship truly offered from our hearts, or are we just going through the motions? This is the key concern in this oracle, which flows naturally from the previous one. When we begin to doubt God's love, our worship becomes perfunctory, merely a matter of habit. The attitude that asks, 'How have you loved us?', questioning whether God has really shown his care towards us, leads quickly to 'What a weariness!' and then to 'What is the bare minimum that I can get away with?' On the contrary, however, when we recognize that he has indeed shown us his grace and that everything we have comes from his hands, our hearts are easily ignited with love and true reverence for God.

1:6. 'A son honours [his] father and a servant his master; if I am a father, where is my honour? If I am a master, where is my reverence?' the LORD of hosts says to you, 'O priests, despisers of my name.'
But you say, 'In what way have we despised your name?'

The initial assertion in this oracle is the truism that in normal, healthy relationships sons honour their fathers and servants respect their masters. Indeed, sons are required to honour their fathers and their mothers in the Ten Commandments (Exod. 20:12), and Paul instructs servants to respect their masters in Ephesians 6:5. Yet the Lord complains that his people show no **'honour'** or **'reverence'** in their hearts towards him, the greatest of fathers and masters. If the fear of the Lord is the beginning of wisdom (Prov. 1:7), there was no wisdom to be found in Israel. These images of son to father and servant to master combine hierarchy with relationship, reverence with closeness, and thus provide an apt model for Israel's relationship with their covenant Lord. 'Reverence', or awe and respect, is the appropriate response on the part of Israel to the God who has faithfully demonstrated his love towards them in graciously redeeming them from their sins while destroying those who assaulted them.

The Lord's rebuke is particularly addressed to the **'priests'**, who, by teaching the law and overseeing the sacrifices of God's people, should have provided them with ethical and religious instruction that would have guided their steps in the truth. These were the two most important aspects of a priest's calling in the Old Testament (Deut. 33:10). In fact, the priests of Malachi's day had failed in both of these key areas: in these verses the spotlight rests on their failure in the overseeing of sacrifices, while in the passage that follows it turns to their failure to teach God's law (2:5-9). This outward unfaithfulness revealed the attitude of their hearts towards the Lord: they despised his name. The **'name'** of the Lord is a key theme in this oracle and expresses the Lord's character and attributes, especially his gracious and compassionate love for his people (see Exod. 34:6-7). The priests were called to act as the Lord's representatives in placing his sacred name on the people in blessing (Num. 6:22-27), but instead they themselves were bringing that name into disrepute by their slipshod approach to their sacred duties.

As with the other disputations, the prophet anticipates an immediate objection from the priests challenging the Lord's assertion. They responded: **'In what way have we despised your name?'** In other words,

'How, specifically, have we failed to show you fear and honour?'

1:7-9. 'By offering on my altar food that is defiled. Yet you say, "In what way have we defiled you?" When you say, "The table of the LORD may be despised." When you bring blind [animals] to sacrifice, is that not evil? When you bring crippled and sick [animals], is that not evil? If not, take it to your governor: will he show you favour or acknowledge you?' says the LORD of hosts. 'Now entreat the favour of God so that he may be gracious to us: This is your responsibility. Will he acknowledge you?' says the LORD of hosts.

In response to the priests' challenge, the Lord lays out the specifics of the charge. A significant part of the ministry of the priests was to offer the sacrifices on the great bronze altar of sacrifice in the outer court-yard of the temple, which the Lord calls **'my altar'**. These sacrifices were supposed to be unblemished, as were the priests who offered them, for only the very best was good enough for Israel's Great King (Lev. 1:3). There were a number of different symbolic dimensions to Old Testament sacrifices, one of which was the celebration of a fellowship meal with the Lord. Thus the regular daily burnt offerings were accompanied by appropriately-sized grain offerings and drink offerings, which symbolically provided the food for the palace of the Great King (Num. 28:3-6), whereas in the fellowship offerings part of the animal was burned on the altar, while the rest was returned to the worshipper so that he could feast with his family and friends in the presence of the Lord.

The priests were failing in their responsibility to oversee the sacrificial system by offering on the altar **'food that is defiled'** — that is, animals that were in some way defective, those that were **'blind'**, **'crippled'** or **'sick'**. In so doing, they allowed, and even encouraged, the people to offer second best to God, as though there were no evil in thus despising the Lord's table.

Yet the hypocrisy of the priests (and the people who brought these damaged animals) was exposed by the rhetorical question: **'Take it to your governor: will he show you favour?'** The Hebrew phrase is literally, 'Will he lift up your face?', an idiom that means to show someone favour and acceptance.[4] If they were to appear before their civil leader to request a favour or to ask for a decision, they would be expected to bring a gift. To present a second-rate gift to such an important person in the secular realm would be regarded as a personal insult, and would almost inevitably spell disaster for their appeal. Yet when it came to making their petitions and requests to the Lord, a decision-maker of far greater power and authority than the secular governor, they had no qualms about bringing such second-rate offerings. The result of this state of affairs was predictable: would God really bless such a half-hearted approach? Surely not. The worshippers would face rejection by God, and the blame for this situation rested with the priests (**'This is your responsibility'** is literally, 'This is from your hands').

1:10-11. 'If only someone also among you would close the doors, so that you would not light up my altar in vain! I have no pleasure in you,' says the LORD of hosts, 'and I have no delight in tribute from your hands.

'Indeed, from the rising of the sun to its setting, my name [will be] great among the nations. In every sacred place, incense will be offered to my name and pure tribute, for my name [will be] great among the nations,' says the LORD of hosts.

In fact, their offerings to the Lord were so defiled by the attitude of heart that they exposed that it would have been better not to offer such sacrifices at all. The priests daily lit the fires on the altar of the Lord to burn the sacrifices, but it was all **'in vain'**. It would have been better if someone — anyone — had shut the doors of the temple to prevent the vain sacrifices from being offered. The best contribution any of the priests could have made to the task of ensuring that pure offerings were made would have been to shut down the whole enterprise. Even though that action would have breached the laws in the Pentateuch that required the offering of daily sacrifices, it would have been better to break those laws than to keep on observing the letter of them when the intent of the whole sacrificial system was being flouted so profoundly. After all, the reason for these offerings was to please the Lord, but the Lord could hardly take pleasure in offerings which assumed that God necessarily owed a blessing in return for sacrifice, no matter how flawed that offering might be. If it was intended to be **'tribute'** (*minḥâ*)[5] to a superior, it was a wasted offering, for it brought the Lord no delight.

The word 'tribute' (*minḥâ*) recalls the very first offerings in history, those of Cain and Abel (Gen. 4:3-4). Abel offered the very best that he had, the fat portions from the firstborn of the flock, while Cain merely gave 'some of the produce of the land'.[6] Cain and his token offering were rejected by the Lord, while the younger brother, Abel, was accepted along with his faith-filled offering. Though humanly speaking the older brother might have expected to be the favoured one, God chose instead the less favoured younger brother, just as he would later choose Jacob over Esau. However, in this case, faithless Israel fills the role of the rejected brother while the nations throughout the world will[7] undertake the role of the favoured younger brother.

'From the rising of the sun to its setting' is a comprehensive merism, a literary feature that uses two extremes to incorporate everything in between: the Lord's name will be revered from the uttermost east to the most distant west and everywhere between those horizons. The purity of the future worship of the nations, which will flow out of a true appreciation of the greatness of the Lord's name, forms a sharp contrast to Israel's defiled and half-hearted offerings and should further compound their sense of shame. This anticipation finds its fulfilment in the New Testament, where Jesus Christ comes to his own people and is rejected by them (John 1:11), yet through that very rejection the message of life comes to the nations, who gladly receive it (Rom. 11:25).

1:12-14. 'But you profane it when you say the Master's table is defiled and its food is contemptible. You have said, "What a nuisance!" and you have turned up your nose at it,' says the LORD of hosts. 'You bring the stolen and the crippled and the sick; thus you bring the offering. Should I delight in it from your hands?' says the LORD. 'Cursed is the deceiver who has in his flock a male, who vows [to sacrifice it] and sacrifices a damaged [animal] to the Lord, for I am a great King,' says the LORD of hosts, 'and my name [will be] revered among the nations.'

The evidence of the broken relationship between the Lord and his people lies in their defiled worship: the priests are going through the motions, and the worshippers are offering second-rate sacrifices. Here the sacrificial altar is called **'the Master's table'** (*šulḥan ᵃdōnāy*), rather than 'the LORD's table' (*šulḥan yhwh*, as in 1:7) linking Israel's sin back to the heart issue of lack of reverence for the Lord that was identified in 1:6. The problem was not a flaw in the *form* of Israel's worship, but rather in its *substance*. The phrase, **'What a nuisance!'**, is an idiomatic rendition of the exclamation, 'Behold, what trouble!', which was accompanied by a gesture of derision — literally, 'You sniffed at it.' Merely fulfilling the form of godliness is not enough: the right attitude of heart must be there, or the whole enterprise is defiled and worthless (cf. Hag. 2:10-14). It would have been better for the priests and people not to offer anything at all instead of offering such vain worship.

Often in ancient Israel, prayers for help were associated with a vow promising praise to God in the assembly when the Lord answered the petitioner's request.[8] Fulfilment of that vow was a public acknowledgement of God's deliverance, a testimony to his faithfulness, and it would often, though not always, be accompanied by a votive offering (e.g. 1 Sam. 1:24-25). Yet in this case, there were those who were making vows to sacrifice a fellowship offering when in need, but then reneging on their commitment. Such an offering had to be unblemished (Lev. 3:6), yet even though those who made the vows had such unblemished male animals in their flocks, they were instead offering animals that were in some way blemished, and therefore less valuable, or even ones that were **'stolen'**, and therefore did not cost the one offering them anything. Again this practice is a functional denial of the Lord's kingship and is in stark contrast to the reverence in which the Lord's name will be held among the Gentile **'nations'**.

Application

This passage challenges the casual attitude with which we often come to worship God. Is it possible that there are Sundays when it would be better for us not to go to church at all? We too can be going through the motions of worship — even orthodox, correct motions — but none the less be wasting our time and wearying the Lord. We may come to church as though we were the central characters in the drama, weighing the success of our time there by how it made us feel. We may saunter in late and allow our minds to drift throughout the service, practices we would never expect our employers, or honoured guests in our homes, to tolerate.

If this passage challenges ordinary Christians as to our worship, how much more does it challenge pastors! We who are called to lead God's people are in far more danger than are the ordinary members of the congregation. On Sundays, we have to be there professionally, and sometimes that is precisely why we are there — as professionals. Do we worship God ourselves, as well as leading others in worship? Do we set a pattern of reverence and awe before a holy God who judges sin? (Heb. 12:28-29). We are accountable for what we let others get away with in the services — and that includes not merely permitting someone to sing a tasteless solo, or to incorporate other inappropriate elements into worship, but creating an environment in which people are able to mouth their way through a beautiful, scripturally-driven liturgy without its ever engaging their hearts and minds in devotion to Almighty God.

This failure of true worship to engage the heart and mind invariably flows out of a failure to recognize and remember God's love to us in the gospel. That is why this passage cannot simply be preached as law and used to shame the hearers for the poverty of their worship. Otherwise, all that will happen is that people will feel the need to fake it better. Worship cannot simply be commanded; it has to be drawn out of us as we contemplate the gospel and our hearts are stirred afresh by God's amazing grace to us. The truth concerning all of us is that our worship is defiled and we are worthy of being rejected by God. Even our very best acts, our supreme moments of religious obedience to the Lord of hosts, are defiled and spoiled by our hard hearts. How else can we explain our ability to hear God speak to us through his Word and be scarcely able to stifle a yawn? Have we so quickly forgotten what our God has done to demonstrate his love for us? He has sent Christ to be the perfect worshipper in our place. There was nothing defiled or hard-hearted about his giving of himself. It is the perfect offering, a sacrifice utterly without flaw or blemish, whose merit is now credited to us by faith.

The result of Jesus' offering is not simply a restoration of God's own people to worship; it is the fulfilment of what Malachi foresaw: the extension of the true worship of God around the world. It turns out that God has not only loved Jacob and chosen to bless him and his descendants, but also that he has chosen to love a multitude of men and women from every tribe and nation. Jesus Christ came not merely to be a light to Israel, but a light to the Gentiles as well (Luke 2:32). Because of his ministry, the incense of believing prayers and the worship of devoted hearts is now offered not just in Jerusalem, but from the rising of the sun to its setting, all over the world (Acts 1:8). It is this undeniable love of God in Jesus Christ that, when properly understood, transforms our hearts from reluctant worship to joyful praises. Grasping the gospel turns us from haters of God into those whose chief delight is to glorify and enjoy God.

Give God the glory!
(Malachi 2:1-9)

2:1-3. 'Now, this commandment is for you, O priests. If you do not listen and set [your] heart to give glory to my name,' says the LORD of hosts, 'then I will unleash⁹ against you a curse and I will curse your blessings. Indeed, I have already cursed them because you are not taking it to heart. Look, I am rebuking the seed because of you and I will spread offal on your faces, the offal of your feasts, and you will be carried to it [the dungheap].'

The prophet continues to deliver God's rebuke to the priests. It was the priests' job to apply the Lord's commandments to his people; now he would apply a **'commandment'** to them, convicting them of their guilt.¹⁰ They are charged with not giving **'glory'** to his **'name'** — that is, they have not shown adequate respect to the Lord's power and holiness, as the previous oracle made clear (see 1:6). As a result, they will experience God's **'curse'** on their **'blessings'**. This could refer either to the blessings that they received from the Lord, or the blessings that, as priests, they issued in his name. Most likely it was the latter: the blessings that they pronounced on the people would be turned into a curse, rendering them futile and ineffective. Similar futility curses were pronounced on Israel in Haggai 1:6.

In fact, the priestly blessings were already under a curse, a curse that was affecting their **'seed'**. Many modern translations take this as a reference to the priests' offspring, which is plausible; however, given the references to literal seed in the covenant curses of Leviticus 26:16 and Deuteronomy 28:38 (especially combined with 'rebuke' in Deut. 28:20), it seems more likely that agricultural disaster is the primary judgement in view here (compare Hag. 2:19). A failure of the crops would also affect the priests, since their income depended in large measure on the tithes and offerings of agricultural produce brought by the people to the temple. There may also be a play on words here, however, in that this disaster will have ongoing effects on the priests' families (their 'seed') as well.

God's judgement would not merely have a financial impact on the priests. Since they have not honoured the Lord, he will in turn expose them to shame. This disgrace is graphically described by the disgusting (and defiling) metaphor of the priests having their faces covered with **'offal'** — that is, the internal organs of animals and their excretory contents. This term always refers to a waste by-product of the sacrificial process, and this would be especially plentiful at the three great annual **'feasts'**, on account of the vast numbers of sacrifices offered. Their **'faces'**, which were supposed to be lifted to the Lord in prayer, would instead be spread with this defiling muck, a vivid symbol of the total rejection of their ministry by the Lord. Instead of being accepted in the Lord's presence, they would be unceremoniously carried out and dumped on the dungheap with the defiling detritus of the sacrificial procedure. It would be no more than their lack of respect for the Lord deserved.

2:4-7. 'Then you will know that I unleashed against you this commandment so that my covenant with Levi might continue,' says the LORD of hosts. 'My covenant with him was life and peace and I gave them to him; [it was] reverence and he feared me and before my name he stood in awe. True instruction was in his mouth and injustice was not to be found on his lips. He walked with me in peace and uprightness and he brought many back from iniquity. For the lips of a priest should guard knowledge and people should seek instruction from his mouth, for he is the messenger of the LORD of hosts.'

Even though the Lord had rejected this present generation of priests, that did not mean that he had finished with the line of Levi. On the contrary, he had made a **'covenant with Levi'**, or more precisely with Levi's descendants, giving to them the hereditary right of the priesthood (see Exod. 32:29; Num. 25:11-13; Jer. 33:20-21). The goal of that covenant with the Levitical priesthood was to provide **'life and peace'** to God's people — that is, a life lived to the fullest in the light of the Lord's favour and blessing. The Levitical priesthood was essential to that goal through providing **'true instruction'**; teaching *torah*, or divine instruction, was one of the central responsibilities of the priests (see Deut. 33:10). Such true instruction flowed out of a **'reverence'** and fear of the Lord and **'awe'** of his holy **'name'** — precisely the qualities that the Lord found lacking in the priests of Malachi's day.

The people regularly brought their questions to the priests and received **'instruction'** in how God's law, as delivered to Moses in the Pentateuch, should be worked out in their situation (cf. Hag. 2:11). In that role, the priest functioned as the very **'messenger of the LORD of hosts'**. The Hebrew word for 'messenger' is the same as that used for 'angel', conveying the authority with which the priests spoke God's word to their contemporaries. Their role was not dissimilar to that of the expository preacher in our day: someone who takes God's inspired Word and applies it authoritatively to his hearers. It was crucial that in that role of moral guidance the priests should speak what was true, not counsel that endorsed and encouraged injustice. Without that ministry of turning **'many ...**

from iniquity', the people would follow their own instincts and the priests' false teaching, and would end up experiencing death and destruction instead of life and peace.

2:8-9. 'As for you, you have turned aside from the way; you have caused many to stumble with respect to the law. You have violated the Levitical covenant,' says the LORD of hosts. 'Therefore, I myself will certainly make you despised and low before all the people, because you are not observing my ways, but are respecting persons in [your] teaching.'

Yet the Levitical priests had failed in their commission. Instead of fearing the Lord, guarding the revealed truth and teaching it to the people, they themselves **'turned aside from the way'**, a phrase which echoes Israel's apostasy with the golden calf (Exod. 32:8). They had been teaching what their audience wanted to hear. They were **'respecting persons'** (literally, 'lifting faces', which implies showing favour to someone, cf. 1:8). This probably means that they were rendering different judgements in similar circumstances, depending on who was asking the question. A rich man might be told that the law of Moses permitted his divorce, while the poor man might be told that his situation did not qualify.

As a result, the law's reputation and authority were tarnished among the people and, far from their ministry of teaching resulting in bringing 'many' to repentance (2:6), they instead **'caused many to stumble with respect to the law'**.[11] In so doing, they had violated the terms of the covenant, and so could expect to receive a curse, rather than blessing, from God. Because they were showing favour to man, they would not receive favour from God (see 1:8). Malachi uses a prophetic perfect here to indicate the certainty of the fitting judgement that is coming on the priests. They sought honour and position in the community by shaping their instruction to the desires of their hearers, but since they failed to honour God and violated their covenantal obligations before him, they would end up **'despised and low'**, both in God's sight and also in the sight of their fellow-men.

Application

This section develops further the prophet's complaint in 1:6 that the priests were not giving God the glory he deserved because they were not teaching the law accurately and impartially to all. We are not priests of the Levitical order, yet as New Testament believers, we are all part of a new kind of priesthood (1 Peter 2:9). As such, we all have a duty to declare God's word to our neighbours and to the nations around us. We are called to be ambassadors of Christ (2 Cor. 5:20), charged as his messengers with applying his word rightly to those around us, so that many might be turned away from iniquity and be reconciled by God through Christ. If we fail to declare that message of challenge and good news faithfully because we fear human beings more than we fear the living God, then we are guilty of the same offence as the priests of Malachi's day. Alternatively, if we are only willing to confront some of the people some of the time with their need to repent, while allowing others to continue on unchecked in their sin, we have failed in our priestly calling.

This priestly duty is incumbent on all believers, but it is especially profound for those who are charged with the regular ministry of preaching God's Word. It is easy to play down the force of a biblical passage that we know will offend some of our hearers. It is hard faithfully to challenge the lifestyle and actions of people who are influential in our congregations, or those who are our own personal friends. We need to fear God more — and as a result to be less fearful of man.

Yet the good news of the passage lies in God's unshakable purpose to maintain the covenant with Levi. God's desire to grant his people life and peace would not be frustrated by the sins and failures of their fickle religious representatives. What Israel needed was a perfect priest who would offer right sacrifices on their behalf and teach them the law accurately and fairly, making judgements that were truth-filled, not based on a respect for persons. This was a goal that the Levitical priesthood could never attain.

That is why Jesus had to come as our great High Priest and just lawgiver (Matt. 5). He not only offered the perfect, once-for-all sacrifice towards which the covenant with Levi had pointed; he also taught us the perfect law of freedom. The work of the Levitical priesthood came to an end in the New Testament era, not because the covenant with Levi failed but because it fulfilled its ultimate purpose of pointing us to Christ (Heb. 7:11-28). Far from respecting persons, Jesus was devastating in his judgements on the rich and religiously respected (Matt. 16:1-4; 19:16-22), while at the same time gentle and gracious to the poor and the outcast (Luke 7:36-50). His ministry took the mighty and brought them low, while taking the low and lifting them up out of the gutter, seating them with princes (Luke 1:51-53). The only way into his kingdom is to stoop down and become like a little child (Matt. 18:2-5). It is in Christ that the covenant of life and peace made with Levi finds its fulfilment: life and peace come to us through his suffering and death. Blessing comes to us through his carrying of our curse.

It is as we ponder the awesome reality of the gospel, and the undeserved favour that God has shown to us at the cross, that we find the source of power that we need to recover from our fear of man. If the mighty, awe-inspiring God has favoured us in this way, then who can be so low as to be beyond the help of the gospel? Who can be so important as to be above its claims? This reality is what must empower and direct all of us, as we seek to fulfil our calling as priests of the new covenant. In the light of the cross, we must all be faithful in our calling to declare the message of the sacrifice of Christ to the nations, accurately teaching them to observe all of his law to the very end of the age (Matt. 28:20).

Our faithlessness to the faithful God (Malachi 2:10-16)

The prophet brings two related complaints against God's people in this section: marriage outside the covenant (2:10-12) and the divorce of covenantal wives (2:13-16). The connection between these charges and the preceding section lies in the fact that their worship was not being accepted because their marriages were not in order (see 1 Peter 3:7). We cannot relate to God pleasingly if our relationships within our own families are a mess. No acts of religious observance can cover over that fundamental problem.

2:10-12. 'Do we not all have one Father? Did not one God create us? Why then are we each acting faithlessly with his brother so that the covenant of our fathers is violated? Judah has been faithless; an abomination has been committed in Israel and in Jerusalem. Judah has profaned that which is sacred to the LORD, by loving and marrying the daughter of a foreign god. May the LORD cut off the man who has done it — whoever he may be — from the tents of Jacob, even though he brings tribute to the LORD of hosts.'

A rhetorical question is a more intense way of making a statement. Here two rhetorical questions force Malachi's hearers to concede two affirmations that make a single point: they all have one Father, namely God himself, who created them as a nation (cf. 1:6). If one God made them into a people at the beginning and entered into a fatherly relationship with them

(Deut. 32:6), then they owe covenant loyalty to him alone. If they all have one Father, they may expect him to exercise fatherly discipline on the disobedient.

'Acting faithlessly' means being unfaithful in keeping covenantal obligations. Since marriage is itself a covenant, the term can be applied to marital infidelity (Exod. 21:8), or more broadly in relation to any covenant, whether the latter was made with humans or with God (Hosea 6:7). Given the marital overtones in this context, where inappropriate marriage and divorce are key issues, it is possible that we should translate **'with his brother'** in a more generic way, such as 'with one another', since it seems that it is primarily the sisters, rather than the brothers, who are being betrayed.

If the Lord was Israel's Father, then it was his responsibility and right to choose a husband for her and arrange her marriage. Instead, Judah was marrying **'the daughter of a foreign god'** — that is, intermarrying with women from different religious backgrounds. This was an **'abomination'**, a term reserved for serious breaches of the covenant that cry out for judgement. Such marriages violated **'the covenant of our fathers'**, the covenant made between God and Israel at Mount Sinai (see Deut. 4:31). This covenant explicitly forbade intermarrying with other nations on religious grounds (Deut. 7:3-4), yet the practice was apparently widespread among the Israelites on their return from exile (see Ezra 9; Neh. 13:23-27). The motivation for these marriages may have been as much pursuit of political and economic advantage as it was sexual attraction, but the result was none the less spiritually disastrous for the people: the description of the bride as 'the daughter of a foreign god' highlights the spiritual implications of this choice. This was especially true for the children of such intermarriages, who grew up without a clear religious identity (Neh. 13:24).

This action **'profaned that which is sacred to the LORD'**. Many translations and commentaries interpret this as referring to the sanctuary, but exactly the same combination occurs also in Leviticus 19:8, where the sin involves profaning fellowship offerings by eating them after their lawful 'consume by' date. It may be that the concept of a pure seed, a holy people for God, is what is profaned by intermarriage (see 2:15). Malachi pronounces the covenant curse of 'cutting off' (*kārat*) on those who are guilty of this abomination. This verb can be used to describe the sentence of excommunication or execution. Here presumably the latter is in view, since the former sentence is implemented by human action and this request is directed to the Lord.

The phrase **'whoever he may be'** is an attempt to render an obscure idiom. It is variously explained and may mean 'the one who calls out and the one who answers', or 'witness and respondent', if we emend the text slightly. If the latter translation is accepted, it may extend culpability to include those who acted as official witnesses at such weddings.[12] This curse is applied even to the one who **'brings tribute to the LORD of hosts'** — that is, to those who try to worship the Lord and have foreign wives as well. No compromise is possible.

2:13-14. 'This is another thing you are doing: you cover the altar of the LORD with tears, weeping and groaning because he no longer responds to the offering or takes pleasure from [the offerings of] your hands.

'You say, "For what reason?"'

'It is because the LORD is testifying as a witness between you and the wife of your youth, with whom you have acted faithlessly, even though she is your marriage partner, the wife of your covenant.'

'Another thing' is literally 'this second thing' — that is, an additional offence that profanes the covenant. Covering the Lord's altar with **'tears'** while **'weeping' and groaning'** is not a mark of true repentance here; rather, this is a reference to pagan-style practices that were influencing the worship of the temple (cf. Ezek. 8:14). Many of the religions around Judah involved rituals of mourning that were intended to hasten the return of the god from the realm of the dead and thus bring about the renewal of the season of fertility.[13] Behaving in this way may have rendered the worship of the Lord more attractive to pagans from the surrounding nations, but ironically it made it less effective in the Lord's sight. The indispensable ingredient of effective worship is divine favour, which evokes a response on the Lord's part to our offerings.

The reason for the withdrawal of the Lord's favour lay in the people's abuse of the marriage relationship. The men were acting **'faithlessly'** (see 2:10), failing to live up to their covenantal commitments, by abandoning **'the wife of [their] youth'**. These marriages that had been arranged by their families within the covenant community were being forsaken, either in pursuit of romance (sex) or, more likely, politically advantageous connections with the surrounding ethnic groups, who controlled the various trade guilds. In this matter the Lord would act as a **'witness'** of the broken covenant. In antiquity, witnesses were not merely observers of the agreement; they could be called upon to enforce its terms.[14] This was especially true in the case where deities were invoked as witnesses to a covenant.

Such a situation obtained in marriages among God's people: husbands and wives had a covenantal obligation to one another. The husbands were not free simply to divorce their wives; they had a legal duty in the sight of God to **'the wife of [their] covenant'**. Yet beyond legal duty, these husbands also had a personal obligation to their **'marriage partner'**. This word is unique in the Old Testament, but a related verbal form is used in architecture for a seam or joint in a building and to describe the process of bonding or cementing something together.[15] Marriage is not merely a legal obligation; it is to be a close and intimate relationship that cannot be easily dissolved without significant damage to both parties.

2:15-16. 'Did he not make [them] one and a remnant of spirit [he gave] to them? What is the one [God] seeking? Godly seed. So guard your spirit and do not act faithlessly with the wife of your youth. If [a person] hates and divorces [his wife]' says the LORD God of Israel, 'he covers his clothing with violence,' says the LORD of hosts. 'So guard your spirits and do not act faithlessly.'

The Hebrew of the first sentence is extremely difficult and has been variously rendered in the English translations. Literally it reads, 'Not one he made,' which raises the question as to whether 'not one' is the subject or the object of the verb. Most likely, 'he' is the subject of the verb, with the antecedent being the Lord, who was the subject of the previous verb. If the subject had been 'No one', a different Hebrew form would have been used (*'ên 'āśâ*, cf. Ps. 14:1). The object of the verb, 'not one,' appears before it rather than after it in order to provide emphasis: **'Did he not make one?'** The focus would then be on the Lord's original purpose in marriage of creating one single flesh out of two individuals (Gen. 2:24). If this is correct, then the **'remnant of spirit'** would point to the fact that marriage is not merely a physical union but a spiritual one as well (for the life-imparting gift of the Spirit, cf. Ezek. 37:1-10).

'What is the one [God] seeking?' connects the goal of marriage back to the one God and Father of his people (see 2:10). The goal of this physical and

'merely' greedy and covetous (1 Cor. 6:9-11). All have sinned and fallen short of God's glory, but God's grace is gloriously sufficient for all sin.

Our hope rests in God's faithfulness, which always trumps our unfaithfulness. Israel was an unfaithful wife, who regularly strayed from her covenant commitments to her Husband, the Lord. Those who do such things deserve to be divorced, yet none the less God is faithful to his covenant promises even when we are not. He pursued his wandering bride and wooed her back to himself (see Hosea 1 – 3). God's faithfulness to his covenant commitments is thus the sure foundation for our hope of heaven. It must also be the foundation for all of our dealings with our brothers and sisters within the covenant community while here on earth (2:10). This requires us to be faithful in our own marriage relationships by guarding our hearts (spirits) in a world of great temptation and pressure. What is more, we must also invest ourselves in encouraging others to be similarly faithful to their spouses and reaching out graciously to those whose lives have been marred by the brokenness that sin brings into families in this fallen world.

Do you really want justice?
(Malachi 2:17 – 3:5)

Sometimes we struggle with the age-old problem of undeserved evil: why do bad things happen to good people? At other times, however, we struggle with exactly the opposite problem, that of undeserved good. Why do good things happen to bad people, while we ourselves continue to face trials and difficulties? In this section, the Lord addresses his people's complaint that evil men are prospering, while the faithful serve him in vain.

2:17. 'You have wearied the LORD with your words.'
   But you say, 'In what way have we wearied [him]?'
   When you say, 'Everyone who does evil is good in the eyes of the LORD and he delights in them,' or 'Where is the God of judgement?'

The people's speech was so constantly rebellious against God that the result was tiresome to him. In particular, the Lord was tired of their cynical complaints about the lack of a connection between sin and punishment. When they said, **'Everyone who does evil is good** [*tôb*] **in the eyes of the LORD,'** they were explicitly challenging the Lord's own declaration in Deuteronomy 18:12 that 'Whoever does these things is an abomination (*tō'ēbâ*) to the Lord.'[16] Because they could not see a visible connection between sin and judgement, they came to doubt that there was any such connection. In fact, according to their reading of circumstances, it appeared that the Lord actually delighted in the wicked, rather than being concerned to bring them down. They were stumbling over the same issues with which the psalmist wrestled in Psalm 73: the wicked were prospering, while the faithful seemed to be abandoned. When they asked, **'Where is the God of judgement?'** they were not questioning an abstract notion of God's justice, but rather the practical relevance of this notion. God might indeed be just and righteous in himself, but in the absence of any real and tangible acts of judgement upon the wicked, his justice appeared to have little relevance for everyday life.

3:1-2. 'Look, I am sending my messenger and he will clear the way before me, and suddenly the Master you are seeking will enter his temple, the angel of the covenant in whom you delight. Look, he comes!' says the LORD of hosts. 'But who can endure the day of his coming? Who will be able to stand when he appears? For he will be like the refiner's fire and the launderer's lye.'

The response to the people's sense of God's absence in judgement was a proclamation of his imminent[17] and terrifying presence. In antiquity, kings often sent their messengers ahead of them to **'clear the way'** before them, moving all traffic to the side of the road so that the king could have a clear passage. Here the Great King declared that he was about to send his messenger[18] to perform the same function. If the preparatory messenger was on the way, could the king himself be far behind? This preparatory messenger should not be confused with **'the angel** [or "messenger"] **of the covenant'**, who appears later in this verse. The preparatory messenger is a prophetic figure, identified as the prophet Elijah in 4:5-6, who prepares the way for the coming king. Yet even with his ministry, the coming of the Great King will be surprising, sudden, presumably because the sceptics will still be proclaiming the absence of the God of judgement. The Lord will come as their **'Master'** (see 1:6) to his *hêkal*, a word that comes from a root meaning 'big house' and can describe either a temple or a palace. In the Lord's case, the two locations are synonymous, for the Jerusalem temple is his earthly palace. Significantly, the Jerusalem palace and temple complex is where the royal thrones for judgement historically stood (Ps. 122:5). The God of justice, whose absence they have been lamenting, will soon come to dispense his judgement in their midst. **'The angel of the covenant in whom you delight'** seems to be the same person as **'the Master you are seeking'**. Just as the angel of the Lord represents the Lord personally (Exod. 14:19; Zech. 3:1-2), and in some cases is identified with him, so too the Lord's presence in the temple will be expressed in the coming of the 'messenger of the covenant'. When the Lord's personal envoy comes to enforce the terms of the covenant, it will be as if the Lord himself is there.

On that day, however, the hopeful expectations of the people will be turned on their heads. Since they are themselves sinners, as the earlier oracles of Malachi have demonstrated, they cannot endure the judgement he will bring. The Day of the Lord will not be their day of vindication, as they so fondly imagined, when they would stand up to be justified in the face of their enemies. Rather, it will be a day of purifying destruction. In the same way that the refiner uses **'fire'** to purify the dross from metal and a launderer uses a harsh alkaline **'lye'** derived from plants to cleanse away the stains that are hard to remove, so too the day of the Lord's coming will separate the righteous from the wicked in a way that reverses many of the assumptions of Malachi's hearers. They should be careful when they ask for the Lord to come in judgement lest they themselves are subjected to the judgement for which they have wished!

3:3-5. '[As] the refiner and the purifier of silver sit, he will purify the sons of Levi, and he will refine them like gold or like silver, and they shall belong to the LORD, presenting offerings in righteousness. Then the offering of Judah and Jerusalem will be pleasant to the LORD, as in days of old and as in former years.

'I will draw near to you for judgement. I will be a prompt witness against sorcerers, against adulterers, against those who swear falsely, against those who extort the wages of the hired worker, the widow and orphan and those who thrust aside the alien and do not fear me,' says the LORD of hosts.

This purifying work will specifically involve the sons of Levi, the priests who were the target of the prophet's earlier rebuke. During this period of history, **'silver'** was more precious than gold, as well as being much harder to refine. The refining process would none the less be successful, resulting in a purified priestly remnant who would **'belong to the LORD'**, and who would present acceptable offerings to him, as in the old days of Israel's faithfulness, not the defiled ones that were being offered in Malachi's day (1:7).

Where is the God of judgement whom they seek? He is drawing near to judge. Far from exonerating the wicked, he will not be slow himself to testify against evildoers of all kinds. If the Lord is both judge and witness, how will they be acquitted? In particular, the Lord describes seven specific violations of the Mosaic covenant, which between them represent the whole of the covenant code. They include a broad cross-section of ritual sins and social sins, with the focus being on the latter. The ritual sins include sorcery, where people attempted to use magical means to discern or to shape the future, and swearing falsely, lying while under oath. The social sins include adultery, which

threatened the godly seed that the Lord was seeking
(2:15), and oppressive business practices that ex-
ploited the weaker members of the community, the
'hired worker' and the **'alien'**, the **'widow'** and the
'orphan'. The seventh category of sin, **'Those who …
do not fear me'**, is a broad catch-all violation that
encompasses all kinds of breaches of proper covenant
behaviour.

Application

Why does God allow evildoers to prosper while the righteous
suffer? It would be easy to conclude that if God is truly just, he
should certainly intervene immediately and give them their just
deserts. Since he does not seem to do so, he must be either
absent from this world or irrelevant to its course. Yet the Lord
warns the people to be careful about seeking his intervention
glibly. They claim to want justice and to delight in the prospect of
the coming of the Lord's messenger. Yet when judgement comes,
they will find that they can't handle it. The Lord's messenger will
come like a refiner's fire or a launderer's lye, images that speak of
the dirt and dross that will be rejected while the object itself is
purified. God's judgement is coming against all kinds of sin, both
those against God and those against man (3:5). Who can endure
the day of his coming? Strict justice would certainly condemn us
all!

That's the bad news. The good news awaits the next section of
Malachi's message, specifically verse 6. There we learn that
because God does not change, Jacob is not destroyed. Judah
needed to learn a lesson from their ancestor's personal experience
with God. Did Jacob receive justice? He couldn't have survived
justice: he would have been swept away with the dross. What
Jacob received was God's grace because God had chosen him in
the beginning (cf. 1:1-5). And God does not change. We certainly
change; we are fickle and unfaithful; but God remains faithful
because he cannot deny himself (see 2 Tim. 2:12-13). He chose
his people before the foundation of the world and has saved them

by his grace, paying the full debt that justice demands himself at the cross. The refiner's fire purifies me because it first burned Jesus; the launderer's soap washes me clean because its painful sting was drawn by Christ.

Only when we see that truth can we truly rejoice when we see Jesus coming to take possession of his temple. We can only sing, 'Joy to the world! The Lord is come,' if we know that justice's demands in our name have been fully satisfied and there is no now more condemnation for us as individuals. It is only when we know that to be true that we can delight in the prospect of standing at the bar of God's judgement. It holds no terrors for us now because we know that the Lord does not change, and so we, his people, are not consumed.

Giving God his due
(Malachi 3:6-12)

This passage is often viewed as a proof text for tithing, but in reality it addresses the broader problem of a lack of Godward-orientation in our lives, of which our failure to give freely and generously to his service is symptomatic. Instead of grumbling in their hearts about how useless it is to serve God, Judah needed to demonstrate their faith in him by trusting his power to bless them. If they truly trusted his goodness, it would transform their outlook on money — and, indeed, on all of life.

3:6-7. 'Indeed I, the LORD, do not change, so you, the sons of Jacob, have not been destroyed. From the days of your ancestors, you have turned aside from my statutes and you have not kept [them]. Return to me and I will return to you,' says the LORD of hosts.
  But you say, 'In what way shall we return?'

Verse 6 looks both ways, concluding the preceding oracle as well as introducing this one. The Lord's faithfulness to Israel stands in stark contrast to their persistent faithlessness. This is not a new trend in Malachi's time, but a return to the pattern of **'the days of your ancestors'**. Ever since the beginning of their history, the Lord's people turned aside from his **'statutes'**, the laws given to them in the days of Moses. Yet the Lord's hands are still extended to them in forgiveness. If they return to him in repentance and faith, then they will find him more than ready to return to them.

As with all of the other affirmations in this book, this speech too generates a counter-question: **'In what way shall we return?'** It does not seem that this is a genuine question: if those who asked it had really sought to return to the Lord, there was more than enough information on how to do that in the Scriptures that they already possessed. Rather, this question is an attempt to excuse their own lack of action, which is why they receive no answer to their enquiry from the Lord.

3:8-10. 'Can a human rob God? Indeed, you are robbing me.' But you say, 'In what way have we robbed you?'

'Tithes and offerings! You are truly cursed since it is me you are robbing — the whole nation of you! Bring in the whole tithe to the storehouse so that there may be food in my house. Come on, test me in this,' says the LORD of hosts. 'I will surely open for you the floodgates of the heavens and pour out blessing for you until there is not sufficiency [of space to store it].

One key mark of their failure to return to the Lord was their refusal to fulfil their covenantal obligations in terms of **'tithes and offerings'**. These were not voluntary gifts, but specific payments that were mandated by the Sinai covenant, debts that were owed by the vassal to the Great King. Failure to bring them therefore constituted robbing God. The Lord retained the fundamental ownership of the promised land of Canaan even when he gave it to the Israelites. They were sharecroppers on land that they did not own. Because of this fact, a tithe — ten per cent of the fruits it produced (whether animal or vegetable) — belonged to him, as a mark of their vassal status. A similar motivation lay behind the year of jubilee, in which human rights over the land were radically redistributed every fifty years. This required tithe should not be confused with voluntary vows to tithe, such as that given to Melchizedek by Abraham after a victory in battle (Gen. 14), or the vow made by Jacob to tithe everything he received during his time away from home (Gen. 28). These could be made at any time and for any reason.

The compulsory tithe belongs distinctively to the period of Israel's history when the Mosaic covenant was in force, the period when Israel occupied the land of Canaan (see Num. 18; Deut. 14:22-29). It is sometimes suggested that the tithe in the Old Testament functioned rather like taxation in the present economy. This is not strictly accurate. Other taxes were levied to support the civil economy (the king, the army, state officials etc.). The tithe was intended to meet the tribute requirements of the Great King and the divine economy, rather than the needs of the earthly king and his government. Specifically, it provided for the support of those involved in full-time ministry, the priests and Levites (Num. 18:21); however, a separate tax covered the costs of the temple itself (2 Chr. 24:5). The tithe was also intended to provide for the needs of the poor in the community (Deut. 14:28-29) and to give an opportunity for regular celebration for the family of God's people in God's presence (Deut. 14:23). This family celebration of fellowship involved feasting and drinking, explicitly permitting the purchase of alcoholic beverages with the tithe money.

Because the tithe was a covenant obligation, specific blessings and curses were attached to it. Obedience to the law of the tithe would lead to fruitfulness; disobedience would lead to the land becoming barren and cursed, which was the situation in Malachi's day. The **'whole nation'** (*goy*, an ascription that normally carries negative connotations) was robbing God and therefore faced the consequences. If they were serious about returning to God, that would show itself in their meeting their covenantal obligations, of which the tithe was the most tangible example. The tithe had to be brought into the temple **'storehouse'**, from where it could be dispensed as required to the priests and Levites and to the poor of the community. If the people of Judah returned to the Lord in this concrete way, under the terms of the Mosaic covenant they could expect equally tangible agricultural blessings. These would come as the Lord opened the **'floodgates of the heavens'** — a pictorial way of saying that the Lord controlled the all-important rainfall supply by opening and closing the heavenly sluices (see Zech. 10:1). Sufficient rainfall in its due season is a key covenant blessing (Lev. 26:4). The result would be fruitfulness beyond their ability to contain it.

It is rarely advisable to **'test'** the Lord, since this is normally an expression of unbelief (see Ps. 95:9). Yet in certain circumstances, the Lord invites his people to put him to the test — that is, to step out in faith trusting his word and evaluating him on the basis of his response. To refuse such an invitation would be unbelief. Thus in Isaiah 7:11-12 the Lord offers Ahaz the opportunity to ask for a sign to bolster his faith, which Ahaz declines because he claims that he doesn't want to put the Lord to the test. Yet, given the Lord's invitation to do so, his refusal to ask for a sign is reprehensible. Likewise here, Malachi's contemporaries are invited to trust in the Lord and test his faithfulness to his own covenantal promise. As they return to him in obedience to their covenantal obligations, so they will find him returning to them in blessing.

3:11-12. 'I will cut off for you the devourer, so that he will not destroy for you the fruit of the soil and the vine in the field will not be barren for you,' says the LORD of hosts. 'All nations will call you blessed, for you will be a delightful land,' says the LORD of hosts.

In addition to providing the covenantal blessing of rain (3:10), the Lord will remove the **'devourer'**, the destructive crop pests that were also part of the covenantal curse (see Deut. 28:38-42). This term most obviously describes locusts, but also includes other agricultural hazards, and the removal of such pests would mean that the land would not be **'barren'** but fruitful. **'The fruit of the soil and the vine'** of the land were key harvests from which the tithe would be taken, so abundance in these crops would vindicate the Lord's promise. Since barrenness was another covenantal curse (see Exod. 23:26), its removal would indicate to the surrounding nations that Judah was once again experiencing the Lord's favour.

Application

Since the Old Testament tithe was an annual obligation to give ten per cent of the produce of the land, it belongs distinctively to the period of Israel's history when the Mosaic covenant was in force — that is, the time when Israel occupied the land of Canaan. This law was part of the civil law given to Israel by the Lord, like the laws of first fruits and of jubilee (Exod. 23:19; Lev. 25:11). The *Westminster Confession* argues that such laws do not bind us as Christians *except in their general equity* — that is, in the general principles of behaviour before God which can legitimately be extracted from such laws.[19] Christians are certainly obligated to give to the Lord, but that obligation to give is transformed in key ways with the coming of Christ.

For example, Christianity radicalizes the source of the tithe: for Christians, it is not simply our garden produce which is directly under the lordship of God, but the whole of life. Of course, in the Old Testament the tithe was just the beginning: freewill offerings and other taxes were added to the basic ten per cent. Christianity, however, personalizes the amount of the tithe: Christian giving should be proportional (1 Cor. 16:2), willing and generous (2 Cor. 9:7), even over-generous (2 Cor. 8:2), but a particular proportion is not specified in the New Testament. There is, however, no excuse for giving less under grace than was required of those under the law.

Significantly, Christianity affirms the purposes for which the tithe was received. The tithe had at least three objectives in the Old Testament: to provide for the support of those involved in full-time ministry, the priests and Levites (Num. 18:21); to meet the needs of the poor in the community (Deut. 14:28-29); and to supply the resources for God's people to celebrate together in God's presence (Deut. 14:23). It is therefore appropriate for Christians by their giving to provide for the regular support of the gospel ministry in the community (1 Cor. 9:14). However, an appropriate confession of God's lordship in our life also involves using our monetary gifts to the Lord not simply to pay the pastor and the building costs, but to meet the needs of the poor in our community — especially Christians (Acts 6:1; 2 Cor. 8:14; 1 Tim. 5:16) — and to practise hospitality (Rom. 12:13; 1 Peter 4:9).

The main point of the text, though, is that our giving is a window into how we view God. If we see God as the gracious giver of good gifts, then we will desire to excel in the grace of giving so that others too can become worshippers of this great God. If, on the other hand, we view him as a hard taskmaster who isn't fair and just and whose service is a great weariness to us, then this will become visible in our reluctant giving. The question is attitude, not amount.

What enables us to excel in the grace of giving is remembering the death and resurrection of Christ. In the light of that, how can we think God's service a burden, or complain that God is not fair? If we remember that, we shall never wish that we had given less to God and kept more to spend on ourselves. Though it is certainly true in the New Testament, as well as the Old Testament, that what you sow you will also reap (2 Cor. 9:6), our sowing and reaping are not merely this-worldly, but are spiritual, heavenly. Those who give generously to the Lord are not promised a large bank account and a successful business, but they are guaranteed a reward, which flows out of the gift we have already received.

Hard words for God
(Malachi 3:13 – 4:6)

There are a number of connections between this concluding section and the preceding oracles. The prosperity of those who flaunt their sin in the Lord's face was a theme in 2:17. Whereas the Lord declared that in the days to come the nations would envy Israel and assert her blessedness (3:12), God's own people still regarded the godless as those who were blessed. In the previous oracle, Judah was invited to test God and see him act in faithfulness to his promises, while here the people complained that evildoers were testing God by rebelling against him, yet they were escaping unharmed. The answer to these complaints was to remain a faithful God-fearer, maintaining faith that the Lord would in the end demonstrate the true distinction between the righteous and the wicked.

3:13-15. 'Your words have become hard against me,' says the LORD.

But you say, 'What have we said to one another[20] against you?'

'You have said, "Serving God is useless. What profit [is it] that we keep his service and that we go about dressed as mourners before the LORD of hosts? Now we call the godless blessed. Evildoers are not only built up; they even test God and escape."'

The Lord's opening charge against his people is that they have spoken **'hard'** words against him, words that revealed their underlying hard hearts. In fact, the hardness of their hearts is in evidence throughout the book of Malachi in the lack of any confession and repentance on their part. Instead of repenting, they consistently denied the statements the Lord made against them, as they do once again here. The prophet responded with additional accusations: they had asserted the futility of serving God, since the **'evil-doers'** not only survive but prosper, putting God to the test and yet still becoming established. In contrast, they claimed that those who obeyed the Lord (those who **'keep his service'**), faithfully observing the temple rituals and going about **'dressed as mourners'** (literally, in clothes that are dark — either in colour or through the application of ashes, or both), have not benefited from their obedience.

3:16-18. Then those who feared the LORD talked among themselves, each to his companion, and the LORD took notice and heard, and a book of remembrance was written before him concerning those who feared the LORD and valued his name. 'They shall be mine,' says the LORD of hosts, 'a special treasure on the day when I act. I will show compassion on them just as a man has compassion on his son who is serving him. You will again see [a difference] between righteous and wicked, between the one who serves God and the one who does not serve him.'

Not everyone shared the general attitude of cynicism, however. The phrase **'those who feared the LORD'** seems to designate a faithful subgroup distinct from the majority of the Israelites. Unlike those priests who despised the Lord's name (1:6), these people **'valued his name'**, glorying in his character. They too talked among themselves, just as the community as a whole did, presumably encouraging one another to remain true to the Lord. While the content of their speech is not recorded for us, the impact that it had on God is.

'**The LORD took notice and heard**' them, proving
that the God of judgement is not absent from his
world (see 2:17). He also caused '**a book of remembrance**' to be written before him in heaven. Just as
the Persian kings kept precise records designed to
ensure the proper rewarding of acts of faithfulness
(see Esth. 6:1), so too the Lord maintains a heavenly
record of people and events on earth for the same
purpose. The importance of this heavenly record is
that it demonstrates clearly that serving the Lord was
certainly not useless, as the majority were saying. The
Lord was attentive to what was happening on earth
and would in due time act on behalf of those who were
his.

This faithful remnant would belong to the Lord, to
be kept safe as a '**special treasure**'. This word comes
from the Akkadian *sikiltum*, which means a 'private
hoard or accumulation'. Originally it was an economic
term, but over the course of time it began also to be
used of precious personal possessions.[21] In the Old
Testament, it is applied to gold and silver twice but to
Israel six times, notably in Exodus 19:5, where it
describes their unique relationship to the Lord. In the
light of this background, to be kept as a special treasure suggests that the faithful remnant of those who
fear the Lord will constitute the new Israel on the Day
of the Lord. This coming day is described as '**the day
when I act**', because that day will decisively disprove
the sceptics' assertion that serving the Lord is useless.
The Lord's faithful ones will receive his '**compassion**',
but there will be no compassion for the wicked. The
idea of a '**son**' appropriately serving his father recalls
the Lord's complaint in 1:6 that his people were not
showing him the respect he deserved as their Father.
Those who fear the Lord, however, are serving him
properly and will therefore receive his favour and
forgiveness.

4:1-3. 'For look, the day is coming, burning like a furnace, when every godless one and everyone who does evil will be chaff; the coming day will set them ablaze,' says the LORD of hosts, 'a day that will not leave them root or branch.

'But the sun of righteousness shall rise for you who fear my name, and healing shall be in its wings and you shall go out and you shall leap like well-fed calves. You will crush the wicked — indeed, they will become ashes under your feet — on the day when I act,' says the LORD of hosts.

Not so the wicked! Those who flaunted their sin and tested God will not escape for ever. The coming day will be a day of fiery judgement in which the wicked will be like **'chaff'**, the combustible dry straw that remains after the grain has been harvested (see Ps. 1). Putting such material into a **'furnace'** would inevitably **'set'** it **'ablaze'**; it would be utterly consumed, from the bottommost **'root'** to the topmost **'branch'**, leaving nothing behind.

The Day of the Lord was often portrayed in the prophets as a fearful day of gloomy cloud and darkness (see Isa. 13:10), yet those who feared the Lord's name would experience it as a day of warm sunshine, the welcome daybreak that drives the shadows of the night away once and for all. The rising sun would be **'the sun of righteousness'** for the God-fearers, in the sense that the coming of the light would vindicate them, finally making clear the distinction between them and the wicked.[22] This rising sun would also bring **'healing ... in its wings'**. In antiquity, the sun was often depicted as a disc, with its rays represented as wings. So here, the rays of the rising sun will convey health and strength, as well as warmth, to the faithful remnant of God's people. It will invigorate them so that they act like 'calves of the stall' — that is, fattened or **'well-fed calves'**, who have excess energy to burn and so prance joyously around the field. In contrast, the charred **'ashes'** of the wicked (who were

earlier burned like chaff in the oven) will be even
further crushed under the hooves of the righteous on
that great day of the Lord's decisive intervention. On
that day there will no longer be any doubt as to the
fact that there is a distinction between the righteous
and the wicked.

4:4-6. 'Remember the law of Moses, my servant, which I
commanded him at [Mount] Horeb concerning all Israel —
[its] statutes and judgements.
   'Look, I am sending to you the prophet Elijah before the
coming of the great and wondrous day of the Lord. He will
turn the hearts of the fathers to [their] sons and the hearts of
the sons to their fathers, lest [when] I come I strike the land
with a decree of destruction.'

Having affirmed the reality of a final distinction between righteous and wicked, the prophecy closes by
pointing Malachi's hearers back to **'Moses'** and
'Elijah', representatives of the law and the prophets.
The Lord's words remind them of the **'law'** given to
Moses at Mount **'Horeb'**, also known as Mount Sinai.
This law, with its **'statutes and judgements'**, which
are all of its constituent decrees, was given to all Israel
on the day when they were constituted as a nation.
This law was what the priests had been failing to
teach to the people as a whole (2:6). Yet those who
feared the Lord were exhorted to **'remember'** the law,
which means not merely to recall it to mind, but to act
on that knowledge.
   If the role of Moses was to bring the law, the role of
the prophets was to preach the necessity and possibility of repentance. So **'Elijah'**, the archetypal prophet,
will come prior to the final Day of the Lord to preach
repentance. He will turn the hearts of **'fathers to
[their] sons'** and **'sons to their fathers'**, bringing
reconciliation not merely within families, but between
God (as Father) and his people (as errant sons, see

1:6). Should there be no repentance, however, the curses of the covenant would be unleashed in full force: the land would be placed under a decree of destruction (*herem*), the same declaration of total annihilation that the Lord placed on Sodom and Gomorrah in Genesis 19 or on the Canaanites in the days of Joshua. Failure to repent would inevitably lead to death, but the purpose of the prophetic preaching was to turn those who heard it away from that destination towards life (Deut. 30:19-20).

In Luke 1:17, John the Baptist is identified as the Elijah who would precede Jesus Christ in his first coming. Significantly, the angel's message focuses exclusively on the positive side of Malachi's prophecy, declaring that 'He will go before him in the spirit and power of Elijah, to turn the hearts of the fathers to the children, and the disobedient to the wisdom of the just, to make ready for the Lord a people prepared' (ESV). The possibility of the judgement curse is not mentioned because in his first coming Jesus came to seek and to save those who are lost. On the Mount of Transfiguration, Jesus met with both Moses and Elijah, and talked about his 'exodus' (Greek, *exodon*) from Jerusalem through which he would bring redemption to his people (Luke 9:30-31). Yet for those who refuse to accept Christ during the time of salvation, there is another coming to be reckoned with when he will return as the rider on the white horse bringing destruction on the unrepentant (Rev. 19:11-21).

Application

This oracle speaks to those whose hearts have become hardened against God. Two classes of people are being addressed: the generic 'you' of 3:13 and the 'God-fearers' of 3:16. The generic 'you' speaks to unbelievers, both ancient and modern, who genuinely believe that serving God is worthless (even though they may still go through the religious motions of attending church for all kinds of social or cultural reasons). The God-fearers represent the covenant community, who are tempted, through the difficulty of their circumstances, to believe with the unbelievers that obedience is worthless. Ultimately, the two groups are different in their attitudes to God and in God's attitude to them. The Lord hears and responds to what we say privately to one another (which is not necessarily the same as what we say publicly about God).

The answer to the concern that there is at present no distinction between these groups is that there is a *present* difference in God's attitude to them that will work itself out in an *eschatological* difference in their fate. God notes and knows the God-fearers: even now they are his treasured possession, the Israel of God (Exod. 19:6). Because the Lord knows them, their eschatological destiny is healing and joyful vindication. However, the eschatological destiny of the wicked is to be stubble for the fire, ashes that will be trampled underfoot; for them the refiner's fire will be the destroying fire, for there is no gold in them to refine. When God finally acts, this difference between the righteous and the wicked will be visible to all.

How is this ultimate difference between righteous and wicked possible if we are all sinners, though? Which of us has ever kept the law of Moses? The loud thunderings of Sinai's law surely condemn us all. By nature, we are all *ḥerem,* subject to a decree of destruction. By nature, none of us has any internal gold. Why should the refiner's fire not destroy all of us, without exception? The answer is that the Lord has already sent his prophet Elijah to announce the open door of repentance in the person of John the Baptist (Matt. 11:14). Yet he was merely the forerunner for the great day of salvation which arrived in the person of Jesus. In Christ, the door is opened for us to receive righteousness and healing through his sufferings (Matt. 17:12).[23] He was burned in the oven of God's wrath for our iniquity. He was crushed underfoot by the weight of transgressions for our healing. He is the Son on whom the Father did not show compassion, even though he served him faithfully, so that we, the unfaithful sons, might receive adoption through his blood.

The messenger of the covenant has thus come not simply to reconcile the generations to one another, by turning the hearts of fathers to their sons and vice versa. In the light of Malachi 1:6, he comes to reconcile all generations to God, and God to them. He has come so that we might be his people and he be our God. This is the goal of every page of the Scriptures, and it is this promise of fellowship with God that shows that serving God is not at all useless and vain. No one serves God and loses, just as ultimately no one tests God and escapes. Rather, they miss out on the true and eternal rest that is the inheritance of the saints. As the psalmist put it when faced with the same temptation:

> Whom have I in heaven but you?
> And there is nothing on earth that I desire besides you.
> My flesh and my heart may fail,
>   but God is the strength of my heart and my portion for
>   ever
>
> (Ps. 73:25-26, ESV).

Those who mock the gospel will go to eternal destruction, but those who fear the Lord receive what they most desire: eternal life in his presence for ever.

List of abbreviations

AB   Anchor Bible
AJSL   *American Journal of Semitic Languages*
BDB   F. Brown, S. R. Driver and C. A. Briggs, *A Hebrew and English Lexicon of the Old Testament* (1907)
CBQ   *Catholic Biblical Quarterly*
IEJ   *Israel Exploration Journal*
JAOS   *Journal of the American Oriental Society*
JSOTS   Journal for the Study of the Old Testament Supplements
NICOT   New International Commentary on the Old Testament
NIVAC   New International Version Application Commentary
SBLDS   Society of Biblical Literature Dissertation Series
SJT   *Scottish Journal of Theology*
TDOT   G. I. Botterweck and H. Ringgren, eds., *Theological Dictionary of the Old Testament* (1974–)
VT   *Vetus Testamentum*
WBC   Word Biblical Commentary

Notes

Introductory matters

1. See the Cyrus Cylinder in James B. Pritchard, *Ancient Near Eastern Texts Relating to the Old Testament* (Princeton: Princeton University Press, 1969), pp.315-16.
2. See Mark J. Boda, *Haggai, Zechariah,* NIVAC (Grand Rapids: Zondervan, 2004), pp.31-2.
3. The vision of the reclothing of Joshua lacks key terminology shared by the other visions and thus stands distinct from them. See C. L. Meyers & E. M. Meyers, *Haggai, Zechariah 1-8,* AB (Garden City, NY: Doubleday, 1987), pp.liv-lviii. The result of this structure is a central focus on chapters 3 and 4 of Zechariah.

Haggai

1. Literally, 'by the hand of'. This phrase often indicates instrumentality and may have originated in the practice of entrusting written messages into the hand of a courier whose task it was to deliver them safely to the intended recipient. Thus it emphasizes the prophet's role as faithful messenger rather than creative author.
2. Meyers & Meyers, *Haggai, Zechariah 1-8,* p.5.
3. See A. T. Olmstead, *History of the Persian Empire* (Chicago: University of Chicago Press, 1948), p.87.
4. The date on which to begin counting the seventy years is not clear in Jeremiah; nor is the ending date. 2 Chronicles 36:21-22 and Ezra 1:1 locate the ending point for the seventy years of desolation in Cyrus' decree that the Jews may return to Judah, issued in 538 BC. The seventy years would then presumably have begun in 605 BC, when Nebuchadnezzar first invaded Judah and brought Jerusalem under his control. That is perhaps a fitting date for the description of 'serving the king of Babylon', yet the land was hardly reduced to a wasteland at this point. That description better fits the date of 586 BC, when Nebuchadnezzar levelled Jerusalem and burned the temple. Since the seventy years of judgement still seem to be in progress and nearing an end in Zechariah 1:12, which dates to 520 BC, it may be that Zechariah

understood the seventy years to run from the destruction of the temple in 586 BC until its rebuilding in 515 BC. Whether the dates are 605–538 or 586–515, in either case the anticipated period of exile is close to seventy years, a period that describes the span of a normal human life in Psalm 90:10. The exile thus lasts a lifetime, we might say. See Boda, *Haggai, Zechariah*, pp.197-9.

5. For a fuller evaluation of the issue, see H. G. M. Williamson, *Ezra-Nehemiah*, WBC (Waco, TX: Word, 1985), p.17.

6. J. L. Berquist, *Judaism in Persia's Shadow* (Minneapolis: Fortress, 1995), pp.62-5.

7. P. A. Verhoef, *Haggai & Malachi*, NICOT (Grand Rapids: Eerdmans, 1987), p.52.

8. D. R. Hillers, *Treaty Curses and the Old Testament Prophets* (Rome: Pontifical Biblical Institute, 1964), pp.28-9.

9. H. W. Wolff, *Haggai: a Commentary*, trans. M. Kohl (Minneapolis: Augsburg, 1988), p.49.

10. The last clause of verse 15, **'in the second year of King Darius'**, is sometimes detached from the end of chapter 1 and identified as the beginning of chapter 2 (so already in the Septuagint and in a number of modern translations). However, in its present position the full date forms an *inclusio* with 1:1. Since the date of both oracles is clearly the second year of King Darius, it is perhaps better to see it as doing double duty, closing off chapter 1 and beginning chapter 2.

11. See note 10 above, on the text of 1:15.

12. Wolff, *Haggai*, p.76.

13. Williamson, *Ezra-Nehemiah*, p.296.

14. Meyers & Meyers, *Haggai, Zechariah 1-8*, p.72.

15. The NIV translation is similar.

16. For a thorough discussion of the translation issues involved in this verse, see C. F. Keil, *The Twelve Minor Prophets*, trans. James Martin (Eerdmans: Grand Rapids, 1988 reprint), vol. 10, part 2, pp.192-4.

17. The Hebrew word for 'place' (*māqôm*) frequently has overtones of a special religious place (see Roland de Vaux, *Ancient Israel*, London: Darton, Longman & Todd, 1961, pp.289, 291); therefore, I think that **'In this place...'** is most naturally taken as having reference to the temple in a narrow sense, rather than to Jerusalem as a city. Insofar as the reference is broader, it is to Jerusalem as the home of the temple and, therefore, the special place of God's dwelling.

18. For this illustration, see J. A. Motyer, 'Haggai' in *The Minor Prophets: An Exegetical and Expository Commentary*, ed. T. E. McComiskey (Grand Rapids: Baker, 1992), vol. 3, p.995.

19. Meyers & Meyers, *Haggai, Zechariah 1-8*, p.63.

20. The Ezekiel passage probably represents a heightening of the standards of protection of the holy in comparison with the laws of the Pentateuch. See I. M. Duguid, *Ezekiel*, NIVAC (Grand Rapids: Zondervan, 1999), pp.503-5.

21. For a full discussion of the transmission of holiness, see J. Milgrom, *Leviticus 1-16* (Anchor Bible; New York: Doubleday, 1991), pp.443-56.

22. D. L. Petersen, *Haggai and Zechariah 1-8*, Old Testament Library (Philadelphia: Westminster, 1984), p.82.

23. Emending the consonantal text slightly, in line with the Septuagint and most modern English versions.

24. Petersen, *Haggai and Zechariah 1-8*, p.88.

25. *Ibid.*, p 91.

26. J. G. Baldwin, *Haggai, Zechariah, Malachi* (Downer's Grove, IL: InterVarsity, 1972), p.52.

27. Luke's language echoes the Septuagint of Haggai 2:15.

28. The Hebrew word translated 'filthy' (*'iddîm*) actually implies 'stained with menstrual blood'. It is therefore an unclean object with the power to defile anything it touches under the ceremonial law (see Lev. 15:20-23).

29. Petersen, *Haggai and Zechariah 1-8*, p.99.

30. Gerhard von Rad, *Holy War in Ancient Israel*, trans. M. J. Dawn (Grand Rapids: Eerdmans, 1981), p.60.

31. Meyers & Meyers, *Haggai, Zechariah 1-8*, p.68.

32. Petersen, *Haggai and Zechariah 1-8*, p.105.

Zechariah

1. This is not to suggest, as many scholars do, that Zechariah chapters 9 – 14 are secondary oracles added by a different hand (or hands) at a much later date. Though the style and organizing principles of Zechariah 9 – 14 are certainly different from those of Zechariah 1 – 8, the fundamental concerns are essentially similar.

2. Haggai 2:1 could be considered to make reference to 'Darius the king' before the calendar date, since the year in Haggai 1:15 does double duty, but it is not an exact parallel with the date formula in Haggai 1:1 and Zechariah 7:1. See Meyers & Meyers, *Haggai, Zechariah 1-8*, p.381.

3. See Meyers & Meyers, *Haggai, Zechariah 1-8*, p.xlix.

4. See J. Gordon McConville, *Grace in the End: A Study in Deuteronomic Theology* (Grand Rapids: Zondervan, 1993), pp.132-9.

5. Meyers & Meyers, *Haggai, Zechariah 1-8*, p.96.

6. Petersen, *Haggai and Zechariah 1-8*, p.138.

7. Although the reclothing of Joshua is also a vision, it lacks several verbal features that link together the surrounding visions, a fact which makes it best to see this as a sequence of seven

visions plus the reclothing of Joshua (for a full argument, see Meyers & Meyers, *Haggai, Zechariah 1-8*, pp.liv-viii). The pattern of 7 + 1 recurs a number of times elsewhere in Haggai / Zechariah. For the overall structure of the visions, see the section in the introduction on 'The structure of the books'.

8. The verb *rākab* normally means riding, but here the rider is evidently stationary.

9. Petersen, *Haggai and Zechariah 1-8*, p.141.

10. The colour is a mixture of red and white. Depending on whether the colours are blended or juxtaposed, you end up with light brown or dappled, both of which are common equine features.

11. Meyers & Meyers, *Haggai, Zechariah 1-8*, p.111.

12. A. L. Oppenheim, 'The Eyes of the Lord,' *JAOS* 88 (1968): 173-80.

13. The Hebrew form m^e '*āṭ* can mean either 'a little [angry]' or '[angry] for a little while'. In view of the characterization of the Lord's wrath as 'great' in Zechariah 1:2, the latter translation is best in this instance (cf. Ezek. 11:16).

14. Compare the frequent use of *lō' 'ôd* in Ezekiel to express the complementary idea, 'never again'.

15. The Hebrew verse numbering begins chapter 2 here; consequently the Hebrew verse numbers are all four higher than in the English Bible throughout Zechariah 2.

16. One might compare the similarly symbolic use of seven in Zechariah 3:9; 4:2 (twice) and 4:10.

17. Compare Ezekiel 38:11, where Gog thinks to himself, 'I will go up against a land of unwalled villages. I will fall upon the quiet people who dwell securely, all of them dwelling without walls, having no bars or gates.'

18. There is no preposition in the Hebrew, which makes it likely that Zion is being addressed in the vocative rather than that Zion is the direction in which they should flee. It is possible that the preposition is omitted because of the poetic nature of the oracle, yet in that case it would be hard to explain the use of the feminine singular participle to identify those who were meant to flee. See McComiskey, 'Zechariah', in *The Minor Prophets: An Exegetical and Expository Commentary*, ed. T. E. McComiskey (Grand Rapids: Baker, 1992), vol. 3, p.1058.

19. **'Daughter'** followed by a place name is a standard way of collectively personifying the inhabitants of a location. See H. Haag, '*bath*', *TDOT*, vol. 2, pp.116-20.

20. For a similar combination of *šālaḥ* + '*aḥar*, see Jeremiah 49:37: 'I sent the sword in pursuit of them.'

21. The Masoretic Text has 'the pupil of his [own] eye', which is perhaps a scribal correction to avoid the anthropomorphism in this passage.

22. Baldwin, *Haggai, Zechariah, Malachi*, p.113. Compare the similar alternation between the Lord and his prophet in Zechariah 2:9,11 and Joshua 5:13 – 6:5, where the commander of the Lord's army appears before Joshua with a message that is simply introduced by the words: 'The Lord said to Joshua' (Josh. 6:2).

23. See James A. Borland, *Christ in the Old Testament: A Comprehensive Study of Old Testament Appearances of Christ in Human Form* (Chicago: Moody Bible, 1978). For a contrary view, see Robert B. Chisholm, 'Theophany' in *The New Dictionary of Biblical Theology*, eds. T. D. Alexander, B. S. Rosner (Downer's Grove, IL: InterVarsity, 2000), p.816.

24. Oppenheim, 'Eyes of the Lord', pp.173-80.

25. In Hebrew conditional clauses, it is not always clear where the protasis ends and the apodosis begins. Does the 'then' clause begin after 'if you keep my charge' (with most English translations), or after 'if you guard my courts' (with many commentators)? I have chosen the latter translation, since $w^e gam$ does not normally begin the apodosis of a conditional clause. See Petersen, *Haggai and Zechariah 1-8*, p.203; Wolter H. Rose, *Zemah and Zerubbabel — Messianic Expectations in the Early Postexilic Period* (Sheffield: Sheffield Academic Press, 2000), p.69.

26. This translation of this word is uncertain since $mahl^e k\hat{\imath}m$ is a unique form. In the singular, it means 'journey' or 'walkway', but neither of those fit here. It has been suggested that instead of being rendered as a noun meaning 'access', it should be identified as a *Piel* participle with unusual vocalization, meaning 'men who go' (see Rose, *Zemah and Zerubbabel*, pp.74-9). This is how the ancient versions translated it. The end result of this translation would still be that Joshua had unusual access to the presence of God, albeit in a more mediated form.

27. See Moshe Weinfeld, 'The Covenant of Grant in the Old Testament and in the Ancient Near East', *JAOS* 90 (1970): 186.

28. Although **'the Branch'** is the customary English translation of *ṣemaḥ*, it is not a perfect equivalent, since a branch is an offshoot of an existing tree. The Hebrew word is a more general term for vegetation, like the name 'Flora'.

29. Or 'eyes'. There may be a play on words here. The seven eyes recall the seven eyes of the Lord which roam throughout the earth in Zechariah 4:10. It is not only Joshua's attention which is directed towards the stone, but the Lord's attention also.

30. Meyers & Meyers, *Haggai, Zechariah 1-8*, p.205. It is also possible that this stone is not part of Joshua's clothing but is the

same stone that is found in Zechariah 4:7, where it is an essential part of the temple. Since priest and temple function together in the removal of sin, and since both point us forward to the work of Christ, there is not a great deal of difference in the exposition of the passage, whichever alternative is chosen.

31. For pictures, see Meyers & Meyers, *Haggai, Zechariah 1-8*, plate 12.

32. It is customary for critical scholars to treat the oracle as an insertion that deals with an entirely different issue from the vision (see Petersen, *Haggai, Zechariah 1-8*, p.224). However, on this approach it is hard to explain why this material was inserted here when it is, according to their hypothesis, so obviously intrusive.

33. The word *ḥayil* can sometimes mean 'strength', but its semantic range is broader than mere 'might'. It encompasses efficiency and wealth (see *BDB*, p.298b) — that is, the resources necessary to get a job done well. In Proverbs 12:4 and 31:10 it is a summative adjective describing the ideal wife, where it may be translated 'excellence'.

34. Meyers & Meyers, *Haggai, Zechariah 1-8*, p.248.

35. McComiskey, 'Zechariah', p.1088.

36. So also McComiskey, 'Zechariah', p.1090.

37. See R. Ellis, *Foundation Deposits in Ancient Mesopotamia* (New Haven: Yale, 1968).

38. Petersen, *Haggai and Zechariah 1-8*, p.227.

39. Meyers & Meyers, *Haggai, Zechariah 1-8*, p.258.

40. On the significance of this preposition, see Rose, *Zemah and Zerubbabel*, p.198.

41. This view was advanced already in the last century by T. T. Perowne and is persuasively argued by Rose, *Zemah and Zerubbabel*, pp.202-7.

42. Meyers & Meyers, *Haggai, Zechariah 1-8*, p.280.

43. Petersen, *Haggai and Zechariah 1-8*, p.247.

44. The word 'falsely' is implied here and is explicit in the next verse.

45. McComiskey, 'Zechariah', p.1095.

46. The Hebrew verb here (*niqqâ*) could be either *Niphal* or *Piel*. The translation given here assumes that it is a *Niphal* (so also *BDB*), and the perfect is a 'prophetic perfect' indicating future actions that are certain. Some commentators argue that it is a *Piel* definite perfect, meaning 'have been left unpunished' (Meyers & Meyers, *Haggai, Zechariah 1-8*, p.286). The difference in interpretation does not affect the meaning of the verse as a whole, since if these offenders have been left unpunished thus far, the purpose of sending out the curse is to render punishment upon them, purging them out from the midst of the people.

47. See C. Jeremias, *Die Nachtgeschichte des Sacharja. Untersuchungen zu ihrer Stellung im Zusammenhang der Visionsberichte im Alten Testament und zu ihrem Bildmaterial* (Göttingen: Vandenhoek & Ruprecht, 1977) p.193.

48. Literally, an ephah.

49. Reading *'āwônôm* with the Septuagint. If the reading of the Masoretic Text, *'ênām*, is correct, then it must mean something like 'their appearance'.

50. See William Horbury, 'Extirpation and Excommunication,' *VT* 35 (1985): 34.

51. The analogy of the genie and the lamp indicates the reason why questions of size ('How do you get a fully grown woman into a bushel measure?') are not really relevant, any more than were questions about the practicality of a flying scroll.

52. So S. Marenof, 'Note concerning the Meaning of the Word "Ephah," Zechariah 5:5-11,' *AJSL* 48 (1931-32): 266-7.

53. Petersen, *Haggai and Zechariah 1-8,* p.258.

54. Theoretically, the lead stopper could be being inserted into *her* mouth. But it seems more likely that the phrase refers to the jar.

55. See comments on 1:7-17.

56. Meyers & Meyers, *Haggai, Zechariah 1-8,* p.320.

57. The imagery of the sun god appearing on his chariot between two mountains is common in ancient Near-Eastern iconography, which may provide a background for the entrance of the Lord's chariots from between two glowing mountains. See Meyers & Meyers, *Haggai, Zechariah 1-8,* p.319.

58. The colours of the horses do not seem to have any particular significance in this vision, any more than they did in the opening one. It is perhaps worth noting, however, that when the four colours here are added to the three colours in the opening vision this produces a total of seven, symbolizing completeness.

59. The number of crowns has vexed translators and commentators alike. The reading of the Masoretic Text appears to be plural, although a similar construction in verse 14 is construed with a singular verb, and the versions consistently translate it as a singular. At least in verse 14, and plausibly also here, the Masoretic Text may reflect a version of the word with an old Phoenician singular ending (*'ṭrṭ*). On this form, see A. Petitjean, *Les Oracles du Proto-Zacharie* (Paris: Gabalda, 1969), p.281. If there is only one crown, the subsequent action is easier to follow. If there are separate crowns of gold and silver, used in different ways and imparting varying degrees of glory to their recipients, one would expect the designations 'gold' and 'silver' to be more prominent.

60. This could be translated 'he will be a priest on his throne', in which case the counsel of peace would be between the two offices

of king and priest, or between the king-priest and the Lord. The theological attractiveness of such a translation for Christian exposition is immediately apparent, but it is not the most natural reading of the Hebrew. One would expect an emphatic, 'he himself will be a priest' (*wehû' hāyâ kōhēn*), if that were the intent. Moreover, the future of the priesthood as a separate issue alongside the future of the monarchy is also in view in Jeremiah 33.

61. See A. Demsky, 'The Temple Steward Josiah ben Zephaniah', *IEJ* 31 (1981): 100-102.

62. The names and roles here are rendered differently in different translations. Did Bethel (the place) send Sarezer and Regem-Melek? (So NASB; NIV; NLT; ESV; HCSV). Did Sarezer and Regem-Melek send to the house of God (*bêt-'ēl*)? (So KJV and NKJV, following the Septuagint and Targum). Did Bethel-Sarezer, together with Regem-Melek and their men, send? (So NJPS). Grammatically speaking, a named person who is the object of the verb ought to be preceded by the direct object marker ('*et*, e.g. Gen. 46:28), which seems to rule out the first translation. Nor is there any need to emend the text, as the second proposal suggests. The third reading, which assumes two composite names (Bethel-Sarezer and Regem-Melek) for the sending agents, is the most straightforward. The objection that these names sound Babylonian rather than Hebrew seems overly subtle after seventy years of Babylonian rule. The meaning of the passage is not greatly affected by the choice of translation, however.

63. Meyers & Meyers, *Haggai, Zechariah 1-8*, p.381. The *inclusio* is strengthened by the reversal of the order from month followed by day (Hag. 1:1) to day followed by month (Zech. 7:1)

64. Meyers & Meyers, *Haggai, Zechariah 1-8*, p.388.

65. The Masoretic Text has 'he called'. The change from third person to first person within the verse is awkward, and the Syriac reads, 'I called'. However, the transition from third person to first had to be made somewhere, and would probably be difficult wherever it occurred.

66. In his generally helpful expository commentary, T. E. McComiskey identifies eleven sections in Zechariah 7 – 8, which he treats almost entirely separately from one another. The danger of such an approach is that the distinctive flow of the prophet's thought in its original context is obscured and the diverse topics are expounded as though they were a disparate collection of 'timeless truths'.

67. Meyers & Meyers, *Haggai, Zechariah 1-8*, p.420.

68. See the comprehensive discussion in Andrew Hill, *Malachi* (AB; New York: Doubleday, 1998), pp.136-40.

69. McComiskey, 'Zechariah', p.1161.

70. An exception to this is Genesis 49:10-11, where the coming king from the tribe of Judah binds his donkey to a vine and a 'colt of the she-asses' (the phrase is identical to Zech. 9:9) to a choice vine before washing his robes in the blood of grapes. In this passage, riding a donkey is connected with a strongly martial image. See Iain Duguid, 'Messianic Themes in Zechariah 9-14,' in P. E. Satterthwaite, R. S. Hess, G. J. Wenham (eds.), *The Lord's Anointed. Interpretation of Old Testament Messianic Texts* (Grand Rapids: Baker, 1995) pp.267-8.

71. There is a play on words here, since in Hebrew *ṣārôn* ('fortress') and *ṣiyyôn* ('Zion') sound alike.

72. J. G. S. S. Thomson, 'The Shepherd-Ruler Concept in the Old Testament and its Application in the New Testament,' *SJT* 8 (1955): 410.

73. The point that the Lord is the one who will provide these leaders is obscured by most translations, which take the antecedent of *mimmennû* as 'the house of Judah' (e.g. NIV) and therefore often render it as 'from them' rather than **'from him'** (so e.g. RSV, NASB). However, since the house of Judah is referred to in the plural as **'them'** in the immediately preceding clause, we should translate in the singular and identify the antecedent from whom the rulers come as the Lord of hosts (so ESV).

74. Meyers & Meyers, *Zechariah 9-14,* pp.200-201.

75. McComiskey, 'Zechariah', p.1183.

76. The roaring of lions is not a sign of distress on their part, but of impending attack (Amos 3:4; Zeph. 3:3). See Boda, *Haggai, Zechariah,* p.460.

77. Boda, *Haggai, Zechariah,* p.462.

78. Mark Boda, 'Reading Between the Lines: Zechariah 11:4-16 in its Literary Contexts,' M. Boda and M. H. Floyd (eds.), *Bringing Out the Treasure: Inner Biblical Allusion and Zechariah 9-14* (JSOTS 370; Sheffield: Sheffield Academic Press, 2003), pp.277-91.

79. See the NIV and the discussion in McComiskey, 'Zechariah', p.1194. The ESV follows the Septuagint and puts two Hebrew words together to render it: 'I became shepherd of the flock doomed to be slaughtered by the sheep traders.' The same alternatives exist also in 11:11.

80. Most English translations render the Hebrew word *ᵉvîlî* as 'foolish', but this translation loses the overtones of moral rather than mental incompetence which are central to the meaning of the Hebrew word.

81. The term 'antishepherd' comes from Steven L. Cook, 'The Metamorphosis of a Shepherd: The Tradition History of Zechariah 11:17 + 13:7-9,' *CBQ* 55 (1993): 459.

82. McComiskey, 'Zechariah', p.1207.

83. Petersen, *Zechariah 9-14 and Malachi*, p.112.
84. Boda, *Haggai, Zechariah*, p.485.
85. The Masoretic Text reads, 'and all the holy ones with you'.
86. Some translations render it 'fight against Jerusalem', since that is the normal meaning of *lhm* + *b^e* in the Old Testament. However, that doesn't fit the context, and in 14:12 *lhm* + *'al* is used to mean 'fight against'.

Malachi

1. Beth Glazier-McDonald argues in favour of the ominous understanding of *maśśâ* in *Malachi: the Divine Messenger*, SBLDS 98 (Atlanta: Scholars, 1987), pp.25-6, though her view has been criticized by Hill, *Malachi*, pp.138-40.
2. Notice the contrast, in the record of Jacob's encounter with Esau, between Jacob's ascription of his prosperity to God's grace (Gen. 33:5,11) and Esau's assertion that he has plenty, without any reference to God (Gen. 33:9).
3. Hill, *Malachi*, p.151.
4. *Ibid.,* p.181.
5. On this translation, see Milgrom, *Leviticus 1-16*, pp.196-7.
6. Bruce K. Waltke, *Genesis: A Commentary* (Grand Rapids: Zondervan, 2001), p.97.
7. The nominal clauses that make up this verse are time-neutral (P. Joüon and T. Muraoka, *A Grammar of Biblical Hebrew*, Rome: Pontifical Biblical Institute, 1993, p.153), and so the temporal reference must be supplied by the context. In Malachi's situation, it is unlikely that he is making a positive statement about the pagan worship of the contemporary nations being unknowingly directed towards the Lord, so the most plausible interpretation is that this anticipates a future spread of true worship to encompass all nations, as is the case in Psalm 113:3. On this, see Baldwin, *Haggai, Zechariah, Malachi*, pp.228-30.
8. See Claus Westermann, *Praise and Lament in the Psalms* (Louisville: Westminster John Knox, 1981), pp.64-70.
9. On this more forceful rendition of the *Piel* of *šālaḥ*, see Hill, *Malachi*, p.198.
10. Douglas Stuart, 'Malachi' in *The Minor Prophets: An Exegetical and Expository Commentary*, ed. T. E. McComiskey (Grand Rapids: Baker, 1992), vol. 3, p.1337.
11. Many English translations have translated *battôrâ* as 'by [your] teaching'. However, the Hebrew definite article on *tôrâ* suggests that a well-known entity is being referred to, namely God's law, over which the priests have made many stumble by their false instruction. See Hill, *Malachi*, p.215.

Notes

Notes 255

12. See Hill, *Malachi*, p.235.
13. D. L. Petersen, *Zechariah 9-14 and Malachi*, Old Testament Library (Philadelphia: Westminster, 1995), p.202.
14. Stuart, 'Malachi', p.1337.
15. Hill, *Malachi*, p.242.
16. Petersen, *Zechariah 9-14 and Malachi*, p.208.
17. The combination *hinneh* + participle often has the sense of immediacy. See B. K. Waltke and M. O'Connor, *An Introduction to Biblical Hebrew Syntax* (Winona Lake, IN: Eisenbrauns, 1990), 40.2.1b.
18. **'My messenger'** is literally *malā'kî*, the same word as the title of the book.
19. See *Westminster Confession of Faith*, 19:4. People sometimes appeal to the example of Abraham and Jacob, who gave tithes in Genesis, and to Jesus' words to the Pharisees in Matthew 23:23 to argue that tithing is a continuing requirement of the moral law. However, Abraham and Jacob gave tithes not as an annual obligation, but as a unique one-time commitment. Jesus, on the other hand, was in an interim position during the days of his earthly ministry: the Mosaic covenant was still in force, though about to be superseded. For that reason, he also paid the temple tax (Matt. 17:24-27), a tax which Christians are not obligated to give.
20. The *Niphal* of *dābar* often has a reflexive sense of conversation within a group of people.
21. Glazier-McDonald, *Malachi: The Divine Messenger*, p.223.
22. Stuart, 'Malachi', p.1388.
23. It would not be correct to say that Christ *is* the sun of righteousness (*pace* Wesley's 'Hark the Herald Angels Sing'). None the less, he is the one through whose coming the sunlight of God's favour and healing shines upon us, so perhaps Wesley's instincts were not too far off the mark.